OXFORD WORL

HENRY V, WAF

AND OTHER SHAKE

D0000925

JOHN SUTHERLAND is Lord Northcliffe Professor of Modern English Literature at University College London, and is the author of a number of books, including *Thackeray at Work*, *Victorian Novelists and Publishers*, and *Mrs Humphry Ward*. He has also edited *Vanity Fair*, *Pendennis*, *The Woman in White*, Trollope's *Early Short Stories*, *Late Short Stories*, and *The Way We Live Now* and has written *Is Heathcliff a Murderer?*, *Can Jane Eyre Be Happy?*, and *Who Betrays Elizabeth Bennet?* for Oxford World's Classics.

CEDRIC WATTS is Professor of English at the University of Sussex. His critical books include *A Preface to Keats*, *A Preface to Conrad*, and *A Preface to Greene*, in addition to studies of Shakespeare's *Romeo and Juliet*, *Hamlet*, and *Measure for Measure*. For Oxford World's Classics he has edited Conrad's *'Typhoon' and Other Tales* and *'Heart of Darkness' and other Tales*.

STEPHEN ORGEL is the Jackson Eli Reynolds Professor of Humanities at Stanford University. He has edited *The Tempest* and *The Winter's Tale* for The Oxford Shakespeare.

OXFORD WORLD'S CLASSICS

For almost 100 years Oxford World's Classics have brought readers closer to the world's great literature. Now with over 700 titles—from the 4,000-year-old myths of Mesopotamia to the twentieth century's greatest novels—the series makes available lesser-known as well as celebrated writing.

The pocket-sized hardbacks of the early years contained introductions by Virginia Woolf, T. S. Eliot, Graham Greene, and other literary figures which enriched the experience of reading. Today the series is recognized for its fine scholarship and reliability in texts that span world literature, drama and poetry, religion, philosophy and politics. Each edition includes perceptive commentary and essential background information to meet the changing needs of readers.

OXFORD WORLD'S CLASSICS

JOHN SUTHERLAND AND
CEDRIC WATTS

Henry V, War Criminal?
and Other Shakespeare Puzzles

Introduction by
STEPHEN ORGEL

OXFORD
UNIVERSITY PRESS

OXFORD
UNIVERSITY PRESS

Great Clarendon Street, Oxford OX2 6DP

Oxford University Press is a department of the University of Oxford.
It furthers the University's objective of excellence in research, scholarship,
and education by publishing worldwide in

Oxford New York

Athens Auckland Bangkok Bogotá Buenos Aires Calcutta
Cape Town Chennai Dar es Salaam Delhi Florence Hong Kong Istanbul
Karachi Kuala Lumpur Madrid Melbourne Mexico City Mumbai
Nairobi Paris São Paulo Singapore Taipei Tokyo Toronto Warsaw

with associated companies in Berlin Ibadan

Published in the United States
by Oxford University Press Inc., New York

First published as an Oxford World's Classics paperback 2000

British Library Cataloguing in Publication Data

Data available

Library of Congress Cataloging in Publication Data

Data available

ISBN 0–19–283879–2

1 3 5 7 9 10 8 6 4 2

Typeset in Ehrhardt
by RefineCatch Limited, Bungay, Suffolk
Printed in Great Britain by
Cox & Wyman Ltd.
Reading, Berkshire

Contents

Acknowledgements

Cedric Watts wishes to acknowledge the generous advice of various colleagues: Mario Curreli, Hugh Drake, Tony Inglis, Stephen Medcalf, Tony Nuttall, Alan Sinfield, and Norman Vance.

John Sutherland—unlike Professor Watts and Professor Orgel, no professional Shakespearian scholar—is grateful for friendly instruction from Reg Foakes, Henry Woudhuysen, Jenijoy La Belle, and René Weis.

Introduction

Shakespeare loves loose ends. At the conclusion of *Love's Labour's Lost*, when the women and men have finished their wit contests and seem on the verge of a general wedding, the women suddenly decree a year's delay and a complex penance for the men before they will even discuss the question of marriage—thus necessitating that mysterious sequel *Love's Labour's Won*, of which only the title, frustratingly, survives. At the end of *Twelfth Night*, with the twins reunited and Cesario revealed as Viola, and all the lovers paired off with appropriate partners, it is suddenly announced that Viola and Orsino cannot marry until Viola's female clothes, the costume we first saw her in, have been recovered, and that these can only be produced by the sea captain who brought her to shore, who has been imprisoned on some unexplained charge of Malvolio's, who alone can release him, but who has exited swearing revenge on the entire cast—this all materializes in the final two minutes of the play, and seems to require a sequel with Malvolio as its hero. At the end of *Measure for Measure*, the Duke offers himself in marriage to Isabella, who is given not a word in reply (and in modern productions occasionally mutely refuses him). At the end of *All's Well that Ends Well* Helena, having passed every test set for her by her beloved but disdainful Bertram, including becoming pregnant by him without his knowledge, is merely given one more test to pass: 'If she, my liege, can make me know this clearly | I'll love her . . .', and the king concludes the play not triumphantly proclaiming the final success of love, but only with the ambiguous 'All yet seems well . . .' Most striking perhaps is the end of *The Tempest*, in which the reconciliation of Prospero with his usurping younger brother Antonio, toward which the whole play has seemingly been moving, never comes: Shakespeare gives Antonio not a word of apology or contrition.

Shakespeare also loves red herrings. When Cassio is first mentioned in *Othello*, he is described as 'a fellow almost damned in a fair wife', but the wife is never mentioned again, and for the remainder of the play Cassio is clearly unmarried. Early in *The Tempest*, Ferdinand alludes to a son of Antonio's among those lost in the wreck, but thereafter Antonio has no son. In *The Comedy of Errors*,

Adriana's servant Luce appears in Act 3, scene 1; in the next scene she is named Nell. These are small examples—evidence, doubtless, that Shakespeare sometimes changed his mind during the process of composition—the most puzzling aspect of which is why they remained a permanent feature of the texts: didn't the actors playing Cassio and Antonio wonder about the missing wife and son? Didn't the boy cast as Luce/Nell demand to know, as soon as he got his part, what his name was? How did the confusion survive the first rehearsal?

Shakespeare sometimes seems to court confusion deliberately. He introduces a character named Lord Bardolph into *2 Henry IV*, a play which already includes a character named Bardolph; and into *1 Henry IV*, a character named Gadshill, which is also the name of the scene of some significant action. When Lear sends the disguised Kent with letters to 'Gloucester', only our editorial notes will reveal to us that it is the city, which is mentioned nowhere else, that he means, not the Earl of Gloucester, a major figure in the play. Unlike the red herrings, these confusions are obviously calculated, but their point seems to be merely to confuse.

A much larger structural loose end informs *The Taming of the Shrew*. The play opens with a drunken beggar named Christopher Sly, on whom a lord decides to play a joke. Dressing Sly, in his drunken stupor, in rich garments, providing him with servants and even a boy actor claiming to be his wife, the lord persuades Sly that he is an amnesiac aristocrat. The play *The Taming of the Shrew* is in fact a play within this play, a performance enacted for Sly's entertainment. For the first two scenes Sly is a willing enough spectator, though he would clearly rather go to bed with his 'wife', but by the end of Act 1, scene 2, he declares himself thoroughly bored. The play nevertheless continues, apparently with Sly a mute, and possibly sleeping, onstage audience. And he is never heard from or mentioned again; he presumably remains onstage, but Shakespeare completely ignores him—the play within the play becomes the play. What happens to Christopher Sly? In another version of the play called *The Taming of a Shrew* (which probably derives from Shakespeare's play, not the other way round), there is a concluding scene with Sly, now returned to his senses and to his own person, who heads for home declaring that he has learned from the play within the play how to tame his own wife. It is certainly possible that this was how

Shakespeare originally ended his comedy; but if so, he apparently thought better of it. The loose end was, for Shakespeare, a second thought and an improvement.

Implausibilities, and even impossibilities, abound in Shakespeare's plays. At the beginning of *Hamlet* Horatio identifies the ghost as the dead King Hamlet by his armour and his frown—

> Such was the very armour he had on
> When he th'ambitious Norway combated.
> So frowned he once when in an angry parle
> He smote the sledded Polacks on the ice . . . (1.1.60–4)

thereby implying that he was an eyewitness of these events. But in Act 5, in the scene with the gravediggers, we learn that the fight with old Fortinbras took place on the day of Prince Hamlet's birth, when his schoolmate Horatio must have been, if he was alive at all, at most in his infancy. Even more confusingly, this event turns out to have occurred about thirty years ago—Yorick's skull has been in the ground 'three and twenty years', and Hamlet recalls being 'borne . . . on his back a thousand times'. Is Hamlet still a university student at the age of 30?

At other times, however, the implausible is the essential stuff of Shakespeare's art. *Othello*, famously, does not allow enough time for the action it contains. It is a mass of temporal impossibilities. The action of the play goes very fast, and is, with one exception, uninterrupted. Act 1 covers the night of Othello's elopement with Desdemona. Othello and Cassio go to Cyprus the next morning, and Desdemona and Iago follow in however long we want to imagine it takes them to get ready and make the voyage—say ten days (Cassio says they have come unusually fast, a week earlier than they were expected; the distance is about fifteen hundred miles, and a really fast ship could do it in a week). From then on again the action is continuous, through the night of Desdemona's arrival, the next day, and that night, which is the night of the murder (the usual estimate is thirty-three hours). The action needs to be continuous, and the play keeps reminding you that it is, because the whole credibility of Iago's plot depends on speed, and Iago is continually aware of this. It is made clear a number of times that if Othello ever gets a chance to compare notes with anyone, the scheme will fall apart.

But if we take that aspect of the play seriously, the play as a whole will be nonsense. When, in this thirty-three hours, was the adultery supposed to have taken place? Othello left Venice on the wedding-night, taking Cassio with him—this is the man he believes has been cuckolding him. (When?) In order to prevent the audience from noticing this, Shakespeare uses some brilliant sleight of hand, compelling our belief in the plot through references to action that there is no time for in the time scheme of the play, action that could never have happened. For example, Othello tortures himself imagining Desdemona's stolen hours of lust (stolen when?—leaving aside the voyage to Cyprus, when no adultery could have occurred, the marriage is scarcely two days old at this point); Iago tells a story about a night that he recently spent in bed with Cassio, when Cassio in his sleep took him for Desdemona (there was no night since the marriage when Iago and Cassio were in the same place); Cassio's mistress Bianca complains that she hasn't seen Cassio for a week (Cassio has been on the island for scarcely more than a week); Cassio tells Iago about how Bianca runs after him, and fell on his neck in public 'the other day', and Othello, overhearing this, thinks he is talking about Desdemona (what other day? the only other day was yesterday, which is the day she arrived); Othello questions Emilia about whether she has seen Desdemona and Cassio together, and a long period and a number of occasions are alluded to. This dramatic strategy is astonishingly effective; and the reason it works is that we are treated just the way Othello is, persuaded parenthetically, not given time to ask any questions or compare notes. Shakespeare, not Iago, is the real villain in this play.

The play builds its picture of villainy around tricks played by Iago upon Othello, but the impossibilities I have described are tricks played by Shakespeare upon the audience. The most striking is a geographical one, and probably the least visible dramatically, though it becomes visible if we plot the play's topography. It occurs in the scene where Othello is recalled to Venice and Cassio is appointed in his place because the Turks have been defeated. The defeat took place only the day before—Othello arrives from the battle just after Desdemona and Iago have landed. Messengers are then sent to report the victory to the Venetian senate. How long does it take for the news to travel from Cyprus to Venice, and for the Venetian emissaries to travel back again with the order for Othello's return?

Travelling as fast as Desdemona and Iago had done earlier in the play, the messengers would have required two weeks or more for the round trip. We are taught by the history of theatre not to question such conventions; and this is one of the moments that make us think there is much more time in the play than there really is. The space of that voyage constitutes precisely the period of time when Desdemona and Cassio are supposed to be carrying on together; but the deception is not being practised on Othello by Iago, it is being practised on us by Shakespeare.

Some of the questions in this collection are concerned with issues like these, questions of why Shakespeare makes the choices he does; but many of the most interesting ones take a different form, asking what really happened. Did Lady Macbeth really faint when the murder of Duncan was revealed, or was she faking? How was Desdemona actually killed, so that she was able to speak after her murder? Did Othello smother her, strangle her, or stab her? How could Jaquenetta be pregnant by Armado if the ladies and men have only been together for two days? Is Lear really over 80, or when he says he is 'fourscore and upward' has he forgotten his age—how can an 80-year-old man enter the final scene of the play carrying Cordelia's corpse? Did Bottom and Titania really have sexual intercourse during their night together? Was Oberon really cuckolded? I love such questions. Here are some others: What satisfaction does Oberon get out of making his wife fall in love with another man, in effect arranging his own cuckoldry? When Othello calls Iago a demi-devil, this is presumably not to be taken literally; but in that case, is Caliban really the child of Sycorax by Satan, as Prospero claims, or is this too merely a piece of furious invective? When Rosalind enters at the conclusion of *As You Like It* accompanied by the god Hymen, is it really the marriage god, or some rustic assistant dressed up for the occasion; and why aren't we told? Helena in *All's Well that Ends Well* travels from Paris to Florence dressed as a pilgrim, explaining both to those she leaves behind and to the Florentines who welcome her that she is on her way to Compostela in Spain, in which case Florence would constitute a remarkable detour. Is this simply Shakespeare's bad geography? If there are Christian moneylenders in Venice who lend out money gratis, what are Antonio and Bassanio doing with Shylock? Why is the ghost haunting Hamlet rather than Claudius? Since fraternal twins are never identical, why does everyone in *Twelfth Night* mistake Sebastian and Viola for each other? Such questions imply a reality behind the play that the play only imperfectly represents—they imply that the inconsistent play is a version of a consistent reality, or at least of a narrative that corresponds to one.

We do in fact ask such questions of classic novels, which characteristically strive to create a coherent world. Shakespeare's world is coherent poetically and linguistically, but it is not an image of our world. 'How can you get from Cyprus to Venice and back in thirty hours?' is clearly an irrelevant question; whereas Dickens spends a good deal of energy insisting that death by spontaneous combustion is not a symbolic fiction but a possibility in the real world. To the novelist, some significant part of the artistic validity of *Bleak House* depends on the scientific validity of this claim. John Sutherland's three wonderful volumes of novelistic puzzles are therefore able to produce persuasive solutions to their puzzles, which are intriguing but also relatively straightforward. Why doesn't Daniel Deronda know he's Jewish—have we caught George Eliot out in a bit of anatomical suppression? No: as the child of an absent father and a totally assimilated mother, Deronda would have been uncircumcised. In *Mansfield Park*, does the fact that Sir Thomas Bertram's money comes from the West Indies mean that he has been a slave-owner or involved in the slave trade—are Jane Austen's politics suspect? Given the date and the context, most likely not. But Shakespearian puzzles are much less straightforward than these, and their solutions often depend not on reading the text more closely or finding some crucial bit of historical context, but on a recognition of how genuinely different Renaissance minds were from ours. Cedric Watts's answer to why Juliet says 'wherefore art thou Romeo?' instead of 'wherefore art thou Montague?' has to do not only with Juliet's psychology, and even with Shakespeare's, but also with a radical change between the sixteenth century and now in the way language refers to things. In fact, in a Renaissance index of names, we would be much more likely to find Romeo listed under 'Romeo' than under 'Montague'. For example, Halle's *Chronicle*, an essential source-book of modern English history for Shakespeare's age, indexes Anne Bulleyn under Anne, and Stephen Gardiner under Stephen. What's in a name indeed!

Often what this collection shows is the genuine imponderability of

Shakespearian puzzles. John Sutherland's analysis of the question of Juliet's age is shrewd and comprehensive, but it produces no answer to why Shakespeare makes Juliet so extraordinarily young—in his source she is 16, but in the play she marries, and loses her virginity, when she is not yet 14. This has, indeed, been a perennial stumbling block for three centuries of productions, which have consistently represented her as older. In this case, moreover, as Sutherland makes clear, historicizing is no help at all: Shakespeare is not following the customs of his age. While youthful marriages were occasionally negotiated when dynastic or financial issues were at stake, the young husband and wife were not permitted to sleep together until they were considered to have reached maturity—the age varied, but in the woman's case it was rarely less than 16, and 18 in the man's. This became a critical issue in Henry VIII's attempt to annul his marriage to Katherine of Aragon on the grounds that she had previously been married to his elder brother Prince Arthur, and the remarriage there-fore was technically incestuous. But Katherine argued that her first marriage had been invalid precisely because it had never been con-summated: husband and wife were both 15, and Arthur died before his sixteenth birthday.

To frame the questions this book poses so that they can be answered in a way that seems to us satisfactorily conclusive, it is often necessary to treat the plays as if they were novels, neatening, clarifying, and imposing consistency on them. When Lady Macbeth either does or does not faint, Sutherland says that Macduff and Banquo 'order the servants to "Look to the lady"', and that she 'is duly carried out, still insensible.' But the moment is more puzzling than this. In fact, the servants have to be told twice to 'Look to the lady', first when she says 'Help me hence, ho' and perhaps faints, but then again nine lines later—if she has fainted, she has clearly not been carried out, and the second command may well imply that she has not even fainted, but merely requires more assistance than she has received at her first request, and subsequently leaves on her own feet. There is, in any case, no exit marked for her until the general *Exeunt* twelve lines later, when everyone departs except Malcolm and Donalbain. Some interpretative strategy must certainly be applied to this moment, but, like Sutherland's explanation, it will have to involve changes or cuts (some editors deal with it by remov-ing the second 'Look to the lady', which is rather like dealing with the puzzle of Juliet's age by changing it to 16), or at least it will require the insertion of an *exit*; and Shakespeare characteristically gives us no guidance about how to proceed.

I conclude by returning to the ghostly *Love's Labour's Won*. Since, as Watts correctly observes, both the title and the ending of *Love's Labour's Lost* point to a sequel, the real puzzle is why *Love's Labour's Won* disappeared from the Shakespeare canon. The play really did exist; it is mentioned by the miscellaneous writer Francis Meres in 1598, and appears again in a bookseller's catalogue in 1603. Watts is clearly right to insist that it cannot be an alternative title to some surviving play: the issues of *Love's Labour's Lost* are left significantly unresolved; a *Love's Labour's Won* about different characters will do nothing to resolve them. But if the play existed, and was in the repertory, why did Shakespeare's first editors, Heminges and Condell, leave it out of the First Folio in 1623? Had the company's prompt book of the play simply disappeared by 1623? But in 1603, at least, there were printed copies to be had; had all of these too disappeared in the intervening twenty years? Or was there in fact no book—does the bookseller's list merely record an intention to publish the play, but not that books were actually in existence? If the book was printed, why is there no entry for it in the Stationers' Register, in which all books produced by members of the Stationers' Guild were required to be listed—though, of course, not all were? Perhaps the answer is that these speculations are as fruitless as the question of Caliban's parentage, and that Shakespeare's first editors liked loose ends as much as Shakespeare did.

S.O.

Note on Editions Used

Shakespearian quotations are often from the editions of the plays published in Oxford World's Classics. For plays not yet published in the series, quotations are usually taken from *William Shakespeare: The Complete Works*, edited by Stanley Wells and Gary Taylor (Oxford: Clarendon Press, 1986).

Cleopatra—deadbeat mum?

When the round-ups were done in the English newspapers in the last days of December 1999 one date loomed large in the annals of the twentieth century—possibly largest of all for Britons under 30: namely, Sunday, 31 August 1997. During the small hours of the morning of that day Diana, Princess of Wales, died in Paris.

The British nation was convulsed in grief unwitnessed since the death of Queen Victoria. The comparison is not quite appropriate, since the public mood was infused with a mass hysteria more recently associated with the death of showbiz queens like Marilyn Monroe. What few asked, and none publicly, in the days following Diana's death was how the circumstances of her last hours reflected on her as the mother of two young boys—one of them the direct heir to the British throne. Anyone voicing such a query outside Kensington or Buckingham Palaces in the period between Diana's death and interment at Althorp would probably have been tarred and feathered (a number of irreverent newspaper photographers were, in fact, threatened by irate mourners in London).

At this period the tabloid newspapers regularly ran exposés of so-called 'deadbeat mums', living on national assistance (typically illegally drawn), who left their children to fend for themselves while they went off on holidays to the Costa Brava or wherever. One such mother was jailed in the period immediately before Diana's death. Popular sentiment heartily approved the punishment. Princesses and queens, however, have traditionally been seen as excused the menial chores of biological motherhood.

In October 1998 there was a sumptuous revival of *Anthony and Cleopatra*, with Alan Rickman and Helen Mirren in the lead roles. There was much discussion of the performance in the press—some of it approving: some of it critical of Rickman's 'limp' interpretation of his part. It is a notoriously difficult piece to stage. But no commentator in 1998 (none ever does in my experience) indicted Cleopatra as a deadbeat mum.

The play is none the less rich in epithets for Cleopatra. She is

Egypt's queen, the enchanting queen, a lustful gypsy, Egypt's widow, a rare Egyptian, Anthony's 'Egyptian dish', the foul Egyptian, a serpent of old Nile, salt Cleopatra, a cow in June, a witch, a trull, a whore, a triple-turned whore. But, among all this hailstorm of description, she is never 'mother', or any variant of that term.

Shakespeare touches on maternal character and obligations with feather-tip lightness. And Octavia's being mother to Anthony's children, as North's *Plutarch* records, is touched on not at all. There are, however, parenthetic references to Cleopatra the mother which can be picked up—although we are not encouraged by the text to make much of them.

The first such reference, oblique enough, is found in Agrippa's gloating comments to Enobarbus:

> Royal wench!
> She made great Caesar lay his sword to bed,
> He ploughed her, and she cropped.   (2.2.234–5)

Julius Caesar, we gather (from the 'harvesting' reference), had a child by his conquered queen. What sex that child was we do not immediately know, although we deduce a little later that it must be the homonymic 'Caesarion'—a prince. (Historically, Cleopatra aged 18 bore Caesarion after Caesar—having helped her seize the throne of Egypt from her brother—had returned to Rome, in 46 BC.)

Cleopatra in the play makes only one reference to Caesarion, and chilling it is. In one of her passionate effusions of love to Anthony she says that if she should be 'cold hearted' to her lover then let her cold heart 'engender hail':

> and the first stone
> Drop in my neck: as it determines, so
> Dissolve my life; the next Caesarion smite,
> Till by degrees the memory of my womb,
> Together with my brave Egyptians all,
> By the discandying of this pelleted storm,
> Lie graveless, till the flies and gnats of Nile
> Have buried them for prey.   (3.13.161–8)

There are distant evocations of the plagues of Egypt and the destruction of the country's firstborn (knowledge of which Cleopatra has presumably inherited through Ptolemaic royal family history). The sentiment embodied in 'next Caesarion smite' is, in the highest degree, unmaternal. Anthony, who is not her husband, means more to her than her child. And, although the point is not entirely clear, there would seem to be at this stage other 'memories of her womb' than the eponymous Caesarion. She has 'cropped' for Anthony as well. The lady is, after all, as fertile as Nile mud. (Historically, Cleopatra bore Anthony a twin son and daughter after they became lovers in 41 BC, when she was in her late twenties; she later bore him another child, a son, during their eight-year long love affair.)

Cleopatra's nameless and un-noted children flit across the screen of our consciousness in such a barely glimpsed way that their threatened extinction worries us little. They are evoked again, at second hand, in the middle of the action (Act 3, scene 6). Anthony has at this point returned to the soft beds i' the East deserting Octavia (the lawful mother of his children). Her brother, Octavius, has heard ill report of his in-law.

> CAESAR Contemning Rome, he has done all this and more
> In Alexandria. Here's the manner of 't;
> I'th'market-place on a tribunal silver'd,
> Cleopatra and himself in chairs of gold
> Were publicly enthroned; at the feet sat
> Caesarion, whom they call my father's son,
> And all the unlawful issue that their lust
> Since then hath made between them   (3.6.1–8)

(The historical reference seems to be to the so-called 'Donations of Alexandria' of 34 BC in which Cleopatra and Anthony effectively set up themselves and their dynasty in opposition to Rome.) Through the euphemism which Caesar employs ('unlawful issue') we apprehend that the couple were accompanied on their dais by Julius Caesar's (reputed) offspring and sundry other children of Cleopatra's by Anthony. How many, and what sex, we are left to guess at as our imaginations fill in the detail of the scene Octavius paints (as the adopted son of Julius Caesar (his great-uncle), Octavius is—as he disgustedly realizes—a kind of half-brother of Caesarion). As far as the audience of Shakespeare's play is concerned the children (three or four of them) are merely distantly viewed décor—of no more importance than a barge, a fan, a crocodile, or a diadem. But they are there.

Later on, after the débâcle at Actium (ten years later, historically), a furious Anthony upbraids Cleopatra, hurling as much wounding insult at her as he can rake up for her treachery in the face of the enemy:

> You were half blasted ere I knew you. Ha!
> Have I my pillow left unpressed in Rome,
> Forborne the getting of a lawful race,
> And by a gem of women, to be abused
> By one that looks on feeders?   (3.13.105–9)

What he implies by this is that although (as he historically did) he has gone through a form of divorce from Octavia and a form of marriage with Cleopatra the world (specifically Rome) does not regard the arrangements as legal. The 'race' he has engendered on the queen is not 'lawful' (he may also mean that he has not sired a son by Octavia, only daughters). There is here, one may deduce, a back-handed acknowledgement to the 'unlawful' race he has begotten on Cleopatra. If so it is Anthony's sole reflection on parenthood and his three Egyptian children. If Cleopatra is a neglectful mother, he seems a totally uncaring father, a deadbeat dad.

After Anthony's death, through the pliant Proculeius, Cleopatra pleads that Caesar 'give me conquered Egypt for my son'. She means, presumably, Caesarion. It is not clear whether she means that she will abdicate in his favour (and manipulate the little fellow). A little later as she and Octavius make the treaty which she, secretly but resolutely, intends to break, he threatens

> if you seek
> To lay on me a cruelty by taking
> Anthony's course, you shall bereave yourself
> Of my good purposes, and put your children
> To that destruction which I'll guard them from,
> If thereon you rely.
>
> (5.2.128–33)

This is the only occasion in the play that 'children' is used in direct apposition to Cleopatra. As A. C. Bradley notes, 'She is a mother; but the threat of Octavius to destroy her children if she takes her own life passes her like the wind (a point where Shakespeare contradicts Plutarch)'.[1] In her famous last invocation, 'Husband, I come', we should hear not the declaration of a daring bigamist (Octavia is still alive), but the subtext 'Children, I leave you.' But these four offspring do not merit even a passing word in her otherwise expansive and leisurely last speeches. She is 39 at this stage of the action (Diana was three years younger when she died).

The conclusion of the play, a cursory wrap-up while the audience turns its thoughts towards leaving, as often with Shakespeare, does not indicate whether Caesar carries out his threat of exterminating Cleopatra's children if she kills herself. The majority of the audience who have not studied North's Plutarch will, of course, assume that he does. Octavius is a man of his word and not sentimental about judicial killing to preserve good order and discipline. In historical fact only the luckless Caesarion was 'smitten'. Anthony's three children by Cleopatra were, apparently, spared. According to Plutarch they were looked after (including the daughter, provocatively named 'Cleopatra') by the long-suffering Octavia, as good a mother as Cleopatra is bad.

How should we take Cleopatra's indifference to the fate of her children? One could argue as some commentators do that four centuries ago parents did not bond in the same way with their infants: childhood was such a perilous and fatal stage of life.[2] So many died in infancy that it was best not to get too fond of little strangers. On the other hand Lear seems to love his daughter Cordelia. And even Lady Macbeth's enigmatic remark:

> I have given suck, and know
> How tender 'tis to love the babe that milks me . . .[3]

would argue that Shakespeare, whatever differences in parental emotion, had observed that mothers—even aristocratic and queenly mothers—felt tenderly towards their offspring. How should we read the echoing protestation of Cleopatra's:

> Dost thou not see my baby at my breast,
> That sucks the nurse asleep?
>
> (5.2.308–9)

She is, of course, referring not to any of her actual babes, but the asp. What one seems to have here is the automatic presumption which was so apparent with Diana, that the ordinary canons of conduct were suspended. A kind of Antoinettish exclusivity applies: as for motherhood—our servants can do it for us. F. Scott Fitzgerald was right: the rich (or at least the rich and royal) *are* different.

J.S.

The watch on the centurion's wrist

In early 1999 the recurrent controversy about the authorship of Shakespeare's plays flared up in the columns of the *Spectator*. The Oxfordians, the most aggressive of the 'Shakespeare is not Shakespeare' factions, mounted one of their letter-writing campaigns to the magazine, asserting their conviction that an unlettered, untravelled grammar-school boy from Warwickshire could never have written the most distinguished works of literature in the English language. The aristocratic Edward de Vere, 17th Earl of Oxford, was the true bard. He used the hack-actor William Shakespeare as his frontman—it being beneath the dignity of an earl to write for the theatre.[1]

The Oxfordians are very pertinacious and they can play dirty. One of my colleagues who dared to mock their (eminently mockable) theories in an article was summoned to the office of the President of her university. There she was informed that 'complaints of a serious nature' had been received, via the Trustees, about her conduct. The over-riding sanctity of the 'Endowment', that most sacred of academic cows, was invoked. These advocates of the top-people's Shakespeare knew how to use top-people's muscle to advance their cause.

There is, it should be noted, no academic Shakespearian of any standing who goes along with the Oxfordian theory. Apart from anything else, Oxford died in 1604. The theory requires, therefore, that the play-writing nobleman left a stack of unpublished masterpieces for serviceable Will to churn out, until he'd accumulated enough by the masquerade to retire in 1611 to Stratford on his ill-gotten gains. Alternatively, you can believe that the Oxfordian thesis is tosh.

Whatever else its faults, the *Spectator* is not susceptible to bullying (at least from literary-critical sects) and the correspondence was firmly terminated by a no-nonsense letter (23 Jan. 1999) from one of the paper's lead-critics, Philip Hensher. 'Please, no more of this Lord Oxford nonsense,' Hensher began:

There is absolutely nothing in Shakespeare's plays which displays any kind of exceptional learning; they show much what one would expect, a mind of enthusiastic but patchy reading. He was obviously fond, like many of his contemporaries, of Ovid, though not learned enough, say, to know that there were no clocks in classical Rome . . . It is rubbish to say that the author of Shakespeare's plays must have travelled widely in Europe; a play may be set in Venice or Verona, but there is never any local colour, and it is hard to believe that a seasoned traveller would fail to remember that Bohemia didn't have a coastline . . . The whole Oxford claim rests on ignorance, a deplorable and unpleasant snobbery, and a ridiculous assumption that the limitless genius displayed in the works of Shakespeare must have had an expensive education and the right sort of friends.

(With regard to Shakespeare's giving landlocked Bohemia a coastline in *The Winter's Tale*, how many of us—for all its headlines in our newspapers—could say, without looking at an updated map, whether modern Slovenia has a seaport or not?)

Hensher's aside about 'clocks in classical Rome' alludes, clearly enough, to *Julius Caesar*, where there are at least four 'anachronistic chronometers'. The historical solecism recalls a (probably) apocryphal Hollywood legend. The shooting of a vastly expensive crowd-scene in one of Cecil B. de Mille's biblical epics was (supposedly) ruined when it was seen during the 'rushes' that one of the bare-armed centurions was still wearing his wristwatch.

For the modern audience, the clocks in *Julius Caesar*—'Shakespeare's most notorious boner', as they have been called—are all the more jarring since Shakespeare alludes to the precise time of day so frequently in that play (more often than in any other, I suspect).[2] So persistent are these 'clock references' that if one were a certain kind of nineteenth-century critic (Frank Harris, say) one might hazard that the Shakespeare family (enriched by the success of the 'Henry' plays) had recently (around 1600) become the proud possessors of a timepiece. Or, possibly, some church had just put up a clock alongside the Globe theatre and the chiming bells were constantly interrupting matinée performances.

The second act of *Julius Caesar* opens with Brutus 'in his orchard' (as the directions tell us), debating with himself whether to join Cassius's conspiracy. As is usual with Shakespeare, the audience (who would have been watching by daylight) are given a *mise en scène* dropped into the dialogue, informing them that this is a night setting. He cannot, Brutus says, 'by the progress of the stars', give guess to how near to day it is. It is a portentously wild night. As Brutus later says, 'The exhalations whizzing in the air | Give so much light that I may read by them' (a line with which, I am convinced—as with 'moon' in *Pyramus and Thisbe*—Shakespeare intended to raise an irreverent laugh).

Brutus asks the young servant attending him, Lucius, about the date: 'Is not tomorrow, boy, the first of March?' He then instructs the lad to run inside and check 'in the calendar' (Elizabethans pinned 'almanacs'—calendars encrusted with miscellaneous information— on their kitchen walls). Romans are, we infer from Brutus's comments, particular about dates and time. (Although, oddly, in the First Folio Brutus is a full fortnight out in his guess: the next day is the fifteenth, the 'ides' of March.)

At this point 'Enter the conspirators'. They, too, are not sure what time it is and whether day is near or still some hours off. There ensues some rather distracted discussion on the subject. Other matters are, we assume, weighing on their minds—matters which they are all nervous about bringing up. Brutus finally elects to throw in his lot with these desperate men. Then, as the stage direction records, a 'clock strikes'—off-stage, of course.

BRUTUS Peace! Count the clock.
CASSIUS   The clock hath stricken three.
TREBONIUS 'Tis time to part.

                                                    (2.1.193–4)

Before the conspirators break up there is some discussion as to whether the superstitious Caesar can be lured to the Capitol (where they intend to assassinate him) next morning. There have been so many portents in the heavens and in the Roman streets that night. The conspirators resolve that they will foregather *en masse* at Caesar's house, to cajole and fetch him to the Capitol. 'By the eighth hour. Is that the uttermost?' Brutus inquires. They so agree. Eight o'clock it is. If this were a commando raid, they would then all synchronize their watches, as in the movie *Where Eagles Dare*. But since they are ancient Romans, they merely salute each other ('Vale!'), throw their togas around themselves (it is a stormy night), and go to their *lares et penates* for a few hours' rest before changing the history of the world.

The next morning at Caesar's house the conspirators wait on their victim at his house, as agreed. The time reference is hammered home:

> CAESAR   Welcome, Publius.
>   What, Brutus, are you stirred so early too?
>   Good morrow, Casca. Caius Ligarius,
>   Caesar was ne'er so much your enemy
>   As that same ague which hath made you lean.
>   What is't o'clock?
> BRUTUS   Caesar, 'tis strucken eight.   (2.2.109–14)

Ha, ha! thinks the audience. Zero-hour.

In the next scene, Rome's Big Ben is heard chiming yet again during an ominous exchange between Portia and the soothsayer:

> PORTIA Come hither, fellow. Which way hast thou been?
> SOOTHSAYER At mine own house, good lady.
> PORTIA What is't o'clock?
> SOOTHSAYER   About the ninth hour, lady.   (2.4.21–3)

The soothsayer evidently hasn't noticed any recent tolling of the clock, but possibly heard the 8 a.m. peal some time ago.

On the face of it, one might well see these clock references as jarring anachronisms of the 'watch on the wrist of the centurion' kind and sigh condescendingly with Philip Hensher about the quality of Elizabethan grammar-school education. But, if one were to enquire further as to how, exactly, the Romans of the first century BC *did* tell the time, brows (even modern, university-educated brows) might well furrow.

As must have been clear to Shakespeare from his reading in North's Plutarch, the Roman Empire surely needed some way of accurately measuring the units of the day. Big organizations—and none were bigger than Rome during Caesar's era—have to be precise in their operations. The business in the Capitol, not to say the complicated logistics of moving large, modern armies, could not be done by such rough-and-ready reckoning as 'sunrise', cock-crow, 'noon', 'dusk', 'when the cows come home', or whatever.

Bare-legged Macbeth, up there in primeval Scotland, can mark the time for his assassinations with the thickening of the light and the crow making to the rooky wood (whatever a 'rooky wood' is), and the porter can measure his debaucheries by recalling that he was drinking till the second cock (whatever the second cock is). But Rome has to be punctual: 'Is it eight o'clock already? I must dash for my nine o'clock meeting at the Temple of Jupiter—the sibyls, you know. Very tedious. I'll be back at the usual time, Calpurnia, six o'clock on the dot. Remember we're dining with Mark Antony at seven.'

As Shakespeare knew from Plutarch, the Romans demonstrably had calendars in which, literally, the 'Kalends' and the 'Ides of March' were marked as high-days. But with what devices did they tell the hours of the day? Films of the Cecil B. De Mille kind routinely show the Roman sets with huge egg-timers lying around in the background and the Roman equivalent of E. M. Forster's punkah-wallahs to turn them over. If we credit Hollywood, the Roman empire ran not on the tick-tock of clockwork but the silent slither of dry silicon through narrowed glass. Shakespeare might well have concurred. Hence Gower's metaphor in *Pericles* (5.2):

> GOWER Now our sands are almost run;
> More a little, and then dumb.[3]

'Sands' and 'time' are proverbially connected by this primitive time-keeping machinery.

With this in mind we may return to *Julius Caesar*. In the play Shakespeare nowhere has a character actually pointing to a clock 'reading' the time from the hands on a clock-face. Brutus, the conspirators, Caesar, and Portia 'tell' the time from the heard tolling of a chiming bell—out of their and the audience's sight. The characters in *Julius Caesar* 'hear' what o'clock it is, they do not 'see' it. It might be conceivable, in the night scenes at least, that what they hear is not a striking clock, but a 'bellman' (the 'fatal bellman', as he is called in *Macbeth*) going through the streets of Rome (as bellmen went through the streets of London), tolling the hours at strategic places—such as rich men's houses. These bellmen were also called 'watchmen' and the abbreviation 'watch' was, originally, not a miniaturized timepiece compact enough to be strapped on one's wrist, but a 'clock'. Thus when Richard III withdraws to his tent on the eve

of Bosworth battle and commands 'give me a watch' what he means
(as David S. Landes points out[+]) is 'give me a clock with a dial so that
I can read the time and get up early to arm myself.' In my experience, he is never shown at this point being given an alarm clock,
although it would not have seemed strange to Elizabethan audiences,
I imagine.

It is significant that all the 'clock' references in *Julius Caesar* per-
tain to night, or the period before the sun has fully risen (as in
Portia's inquiry of the sooth-sayer). Shakespeare would have been
familiar with that most common article of Elizabethan garden furniture, the sundial. He would have associated these 'natural clocks'
with the Romans, since they typically carried Latin inscriptions of
the 'Dum spiro, spero' kind. Sundials, like straight roads, were visible
relics of the Roman occupation. Shakespeare may not have known
that, for night-time or clouded days, the Romans had the *clepsydra*,
or water clock (these are not much use in cold northern climes, like
England, because of temperature fluctuations). Water clocks, however, do not generate enough force for striking mechanisms. You
cannot use them to operate chimes.

It would be sophistical to argue that there is no anachronism
in Shakespeare's use of the term and idea of 'the striking clock'
in *Julius Caesar*. But we need, I think, to read the contexts carefully. And the main thing to note is that the Romans, like the
Elizabethans, *read* the time by day (either by sundial or public clock
face) and *heard* the time by night: either through the watchman's
cries ('Four o'clock and all's well!'); or through the tolling of the
bellman on the hour; or through the chiming of some public (or
domestic) clock. It is very likely that there would be a sundial in
Brutus's orchard—wholly useless, of course, even with all those
exhalations whizzing in the air. Brutus could read his letter, but not
his 'clock'.

Having said that it would be sophistical to argue that in *Julius
Caesar* there is no anachronism in references to 'clocks' I will, briefly,
allow myself the luxury of sophistry. English, of Shakespeare's time,
had a choice of foreign words to adapt for mechanical timepieces
(largely a foreign invention). The language could, for example, have
Anglicized the Latin *horologia* (French *horloge*, Spanish *reloj*).
Instead, it took its word 'clock' from the Dutch 'klokke', a word
linked to the German 'Glocke' ('bell') and French 'cloche' (bell).

'What is a clock but a bell?' David S. Landes asks.[5] What indeed. When, therefore, Brutus says 'Count the clock,' and Caesar says 'what is't o'clock?' they could mean, 'how many times has the bell (carried, or rope-pulled by the Roman bellman) clanged out?' We do not, that is, have to visualize a glaringly anachronistic Roman Timex or Westclox, if we don't want to.

J.S.

'Too much i' the sun': is it summer in Elsinore?

This is a very minor puzzle, but I have not seen it discussed. It relates to the *mise en scène* in *Hamlet*. The play has a powerfully realized location (the 1948 Olivier film does a kind of real-estate video of the castle's interior by way of prelude). *Hamlet* opens vividly on the night-time battlements at Elsinore. The sentries are jumpy, prone to fire on sight (are they expecting an invasion?). Challenges and passwords are in strict operation. The point is forcefully made that it is freezing cold:

> BARNARDO Who's there?
> FRANCISCO Nay, answer me. Stand and unfold yourself.
> BARNARDO Long live the King!
> FRANCISCO Barnardo?
> BARNARDO He.
> FRANCISCO You come most carefully upon your hour.
> BARNARDO 'Tis now struck twelve. Get thee to bed, Francisco.
> FRANCISCO For this relief much thanks. 'Tis bitter cold,
> And I am sick at heart.
>
> (1.1.1–9)

The sentries are muffled up in cold-weather gear ('unfold thyself') and it is, as Francisco mutters, freezing cold. The temperature is again alluded to in the next midnight scene on the castle battlements:

> HAMLET The air bites shrewdly, it is very cold.
> HORATIO It is a nipping and an eager air.
> HAMLET What hour now?
> HORATIO   I think it lacks of twelve.
> MARCELLUS No, it is struck.   (1.4.1–4)

In these scenes one glimpses the fires of the armourers in their forges, working day and night, the flare of the king's torches as he keeps wassail (and beyond that, the searing flames of purgatory) glimmering in the rimy cold. A deep winter scene, in a word. Kenneth Branagh's 1990s film version builds on the deduction to set the opening scenes in thick snow.[1]

In folklore the temperature drops sharply just before ghosts appear. But this, surely, is seasonal chill rather than supernatural premonition. As we encounter Elsinore it does not seem to be one of those 'smiling' summer Scandinavian nights beloved by Ingmar Bergman in his (infrequent) comic moods. As Shakespeare would have known, Scandinavia is a northern region. For most of the year Denmark is a cold part of the world, on the edge of a still colder 'climature', where its king does battle with the sledded Polack on the ice. But even Scandinavia has a few warm months.

One of the reiterated points in the play is that the action takes place in the interval between the second month and the sixth month after the death of Old Hamlet. In his first soliloquy Hamlet is precise on the haste with which his mother has finished mourning her first husband and married her second:

> frailty, thy name is woman—
> A little month, or ere those shoes were old
> With which she followed my poor father's body,
> Like Niobe, all tears, why she, even she—
> O God, a beast that wants discourse of reason
> Would have mourn'd longer—married with my uncle,
> My father's brother, but no more like my father
> Than I to Hercules; within a month,
> Ere yet the salt of most unrighteous tears
> Had left the flushing in her gallèd eyes,
> She married. O most wicked speed . . .
>
> (1.2.146–56)

In the play scene, putting on his antic disposition, Hamlet observes to Ophelia 'look you how cheerfully my mother looks, and my father died within's two hours.' 'Nay, 'tis twice two months, my lord,' she pedantically (and reliably) corrects. At best we can calculate another month or two will encompass the kidnap by pirates, Ophelia's drowning, and Laertes' vengeful return. Adding everything up, the play's passage of time should comprise six months. This constitutes a long 'delay' on Hamlet's part but not implausibly long.

But what six months of the Danish year are we dealing with? As the ghost tells Hamlet he was poisoned

> Sleeping within my orchard,
> My custom always in the afternoon . . .   (1.5.59–60)

Despite 'always' it must—one assumes—be summer, unless Old Hamlet is very hardy. Taking a nap in the frost would seem unwise for an elderly monarch with a 'grizzled' beard. But, if it is summer, how can it be arctic winter on the battlements a brief two months later? The hawk-eyed Kenneth Branagh seems to have picked up this anomaly. In his dumb-show vignette of the king being poisoned in the 1990s film, he shows a glowing brazier alongside the couch. Olivier's parallel vignette, in the 1948 film, has the king in a leafy *locus amoenus*. The icy steppes over the castle walls are another world.

There is a linked anomaly. Before drowning herself, Ophelia enters to distribute her meaningful posy of wild flowers. I am no botanist, but they seem to indicate blooming—not to say late— summer.[2] This is confirmed by the queen's report of her death:

> There is a willow grows aslant a brook
> That shows his hoar leaves in the glassy stream.
> There with fantastic garlands did she come
> Of crow-feathers, nettles, daisies, and long purples
> That liberal shepherds give a grosser name . . .
>
> (4.7.141–5)

If one assumes, for logic's sake, that Old Hamlet went to sleep in his orchard in late autumn, one could just about credit the wintry temperature, two months later, on the battlements. But one could not— without elasticating the action unreasonably—fit in the August/ September scene of Ophelia's drowning.

The simple explanation is that Shakespeare, like Prospero, can make whatever climatic condition suits him at any moment. It is whatever weather that, for dramatic purposes, he wants it to be. In *King Lear*, for example, the wintry storm in which poor Tom's a-cold and not a bush is standing for miles around changes in the twinkling of an eye to the balmy summer in which Lear can also enter fantastically garlanded with wild flowers.

In *Hamlet*, however, the effect is not one of artistic arbitrariness. The jumbled seasons contribute, albeit subliminally, to the disturbing sense that the time is out of joint. There is something, if not rotten, strange in the state of Denmark.

J.S.

Where is the Ghost from? Is he stupid? and: Is Hamlet really Hamleth?

———

First, the good news. In 1999 Monsignor Corrado Balducci, the Vatican's chief exorcist, reported that of every thousand people who sought the services of an exorcist, only 'five or six' were in reality possessed by evil spirits. Thirty cases in a thousand qualified as victims of 'demonic obsession, infestation or disturbance'. The rest were 'in need of psychiatric help'.[1] Perhaps Monsignor Balducci should have been available to lend a hand at Elsinore. Whether or not he gave consideration to Horatio's belief that psychiatric disorder may be the result of Satanic agency, the Monsignor gave new relevance to an old conundrum in *Hamlet*: what is the Ghost and where is he from?

The dominant critical opinion is that the Ghost is who he says he is: the spirit of Hamlet's father. Now, the bad (if old) news: a minority opinion is that he is the Devil (or a devil) in disguise. The mystery of the Ghost's provenance is vigorously established at the outset of the play and then, as the action proceeds, is not so much solved as dispelled, and not so much dispelled as merely outdistanced and superseded by other and more engrossing matters. This is typical of *Hamlet*, which delights in setting up puzzles which lack solutions in the play. Hence the critical industry around it: commentators seek to offer solutions, fill the gaps, smooth what is rough, help Shakespeare out.

When the Ghost appears to Hamlet, the possibility that he may be diabolic is clearly expressed by both Hamlet and Horatio. Thus Hamlet:

> Angels and ministers of grace defend us!
> Be thou a spirit of health or goblin damned,
> Bring with thee airs from heaven or blasts from hell,
> Be thy intents wicked or charitable,
> Thou com'st in such a questionable shape
> That I will speak to thee.

(1.4.18–23)

Thus Horatio:

> What if it tempt you toward the flood, my lord,
> Or to the dreadful summit of the cliff
> That beetles o'er his base into the sea,
> And there assume some other horrible form
> Which might deprive your sovereignty of reason,
> And draw you into madness? Think of it.
>
> (1.4.48–53)

And draw Hamlet into madness it does, if we credit Hamlet's later words about himself, 'His madness is poor Hamlet's enemy'. On hearing the apparition's story, however, Hamlet appears to be convinced by it; and subsequently he tells Horatio that 'It is an honest ghost'. But his suspicions return:

> The spirit that I have seen
> May be the devil, and the devil hath power
> T'assume a pleasing shape; yea, and perhaps
> Out of my weakness and my melancholy,
> As he is very potent with such spirits,
> Abuses me to damn me.
>
> (2.2.587–92)

The purpose of staging *The Murder of Gonzago* (also known as *The Mousetrap*) is to test simultaneously Claudius and the apparition. Claudius evinces guilt, and the Prince, elated, says, 'I'll take the ghost's word for a thousand pound'. A safe bet, however, is not the same as sound knowledge; and even a veracious ghost could still be diabolic, since the Devil can tell the truth to suit his purposes. As Banquo says in *Macbeth*:

> . . . oftentimes, to win us to our harm,
> The instruments of darkness tell us truths,
> Win us with honest trifles, to betray's
> In deepest consequence.[2]

Nevertheless, on seeing Claudius's dismay and on hearing Claudius's troubled prayer, many spectators are likely to assume that the Ghost's provenance has now been established and will concentrate on other matters. The apparition returns when Hamlet is berating his mother. Spectators who believe that it is 'honest' will note that its uxorious concern for Gertrude tallies with what it had said previously ('nor let thy soul contrive | Against thy mother aught') and with the sense that this spirit is still 'human, all too human' in its character.

The 'diabolonian' interpreters (led by Eleanor Prosser[3]) notice rightly that in Act 1 the Ghost not only appears 'offended' and 'stalks away' when Horatio invokes heaven but also retreats guiltily when the cock (associated with Christ) crows: 'it started like a guilty thing | Upon a fearful summons.' Furthermore, the apparition urges a bloody course upon a prince made susceptible by melancholy; and, at its final appearance, its main concern is to whet Hamlet's 'almost blunted purpose' of revenge. To many Roman Catholics, though it was a probability that ghosts were devils, it remained a possibility that a ghost might indeed be the spirit of a sufferer in Purgatory. At the Reformation, of course, Protestants had tidied up the afterlife by declaring the non-existence of Purgatory; so the orthodox Protestant explanation of ghosts was that they were devils in disguise, busily spreading evil. Sir Thomas Browne, in *Religio Medici*, reflected this position:

I believe . . . that those apparitions and ghosts of departed persons are not the wandering souls of men but the unquiet walks of devils, prompting and suggesting us unto mischief, blood and villainy, instilling and stealing into our hearts that the blessed spirits are not at rest in their graves, but wander solicitous of the affairs of the world.[4]

In Act 4 of *Hamlet*, when Claudius asks where Polonius is, the Prince replies: 'In heaven. . . . If your messenger find him not there, seek him i'th'other place yourself.' Only Heaven or Hell then, in the Prince's view; no Purgatory for Polonius.

The Ghost could hardly be more specific about his daily abode:

> My hour is almost come
> When I to sulph'rous and tormenting flames
> Must render up myself . . .
> I am thy father's spirit,
> Doomed for a certain term to walk the night,
> And for the day confined to fast in fires,
> Till the foul crimes done in my days of nature
> Are burnt and purged away.
>
> (1.5.2–4, 9–13)

So, because he was poisoned, he was cut off even in the blossoms of his sin, 'Unhouseled, dis-appointed, unaneled' (unshriven by a

priest, denied Extreme Unction) and has therefore been consigned
to Purgatory. It might appear, then, that for devoutly Protestant
members of the early audience, this can mean only that the Ghost is
lying: he must be a devil from Hell, ascending to tempt the susceptible. It might also appear that for Catholics in the early audience,
there's a tricky problem. The Ghost may be genuine, or he may not.
If genuine, he's an ideologically subversive figure in a Protestant
Denmark (and in an English theatrical milieu censored by Protestant
authorities). If not, then suspense is increased: will the susceptible
Prince recognize the snares of Satan? But the relationship between a
spectator's beliefs and the religious matters presented in a play can
be as variable as Hamlet's cloud that resembled a camel, a weasel,
and a whale. In Kyd's *The Spanish Tragedy*, one of the sources of
Hamlet, Andrea has been slain in a modern battle between Roman
Catholics of Spain and Portugal; but his ghost ascends from the
classical underworld where Pluto and Proserpine have taken a sympathetic interest in his plight. What matters in *Hamlet* is that the
play itself raises very specific questions about the Ghost's origin and
nature.

Various other plays by Shakespeare maintain the usual dramatic
convention that ghosts are who they purport to be. It's generally
accepted that Banquo's ghost is the ghost of Banquo, Caesar's is the
ghost of Caesar, and the nocturnal apparitions conducting psychological warfare on Richard III are indeed Prince Edward and sundry
other victims of Richard. The Ghost in *Hamlet* does sound reasonably convincing (its tones are not sinister or sardonic but are plausibly those of a doubly betrayed—self-righteous—warrior-king).
Then the allegation of Claudius's guilt is fully confirmed by the
malefactor; and when Hamlet does fulfil the Ghost's behest by slay-
ing Claudius, the action is fully condoned by Laertes (who remarks
'He is justly served' of his late employer) as well as Horatio, and can
even be regarded as fulfilment of the will of divine providence.
'There's a special providence in the fall of a sparrow', declares the
Prince on the way to the duel; and, when Hamlet dies, Horatio
invokes 'flights of angels' to sing him to his rest.

But if we accept the orthodox view that the apparition is indeed
the spirit of King Hamlet, we find that the Ghost is morally and
theologically contradictory. He confirms the existence of Purgatory
and, thereby, of Heaven, Hell, and the God of Roman Catholic

Christianity; yet he commands Hamlet to carry out a patently anti-Christian task: bloody revenge. 'Thou shalt not kill'; 'Vengeance is mine; I will repay', had declared the God of both the Old Testament and the New;[5] and Elizabethan spokesmen had often emphasized that God forbids revenge. Clarence in *Richard III* sums up the position:

> If God will be avengèd for the deed,
> O know you yet, he doth it publicly.
> Take not the quarrel from his pow'rful arm;
> He needs no indirect or lawless course
> To cut off those that have offended him.[6]

One complication is that, as Belleforest pointed out when recounting the story of 'Hamblet', biblical warrant could be found for private vengeance: Numbers 35: 19 says 'The revenger of blood himself shall slay the murderer'; another is that Elizabethan politicians (notably in the Bond of Association, 1584) advocated 'uttermost revenge' against would-be usurpers of the throne. For these and other reasons, the theatrical convention that the fulfilled avenger must himself perish was sometimes breached—usually when, as in the case of Malcolm's 'great revenge' against Macbeth, the victim's crimes had been particularly heinous and the avenger could be seen as the saviour of traditional moral and political order.

What, in *Hamlet*, tends to make the Ghost's injunction of revenge seem morally and theologically questionable is the intermittent moral and theological sophistication of the context. A Hamlet who can recall that 'the Everlasting' has 'fixed | His canon 'gainst self-slaughter' is fully capable of recalling that the Everlasting has also fixed his canon 'gainst revenge and murder. There is a soliloquy which the Prince never utters but which is easily within his range of character and reflection. It goes like this:

> 'Thou shalt not kill', th'Almighty's words declare;
> 'Hamlet, revenge', enjoins my father's voice,
> An embassage from death. Each way I'm snared.
> O limèd soul, that struggling to be free
> Art more engaged! If God will Claudius slay,
> Why, God may do't, without my stir; for me,
> Though with such high wrongs I am struck to th'quick,
> Yet with my nobler reason 'gainst my fury
> Do I take part: the rarer action is
> In virtue than in vengeance.

This pastiche borrows some words from Claudius, to suggest that Claudius's plight is not totally different from Hamlet's (for both men register the sense of being ensnared); a few words from Macbeth; and some famous lines from Prospero, as a reminder that Shakespeare's plays frequently and tellingly commend mercy instead of revenge. Hamlet cannot utter such a soliloquy, for that would expose as self-contradictory the very premisses of the plot. (The Prince's dilemma would vanish, and several lives would be saved; not least the Prince's.) But reflections of this kind are evoked by some of Hamlet's suspicions of the Ghost as well as by his procrastinations. Furthermore, the eventual death of Claudius occurs not as a result of any Machiavellian murder-plot by the Prince but very soon after Hamlet has shrugged off Horatio's warnings about the impending duel by making a strongly fatalistic utterance: 'If it be now, 'tis not to come. If it be not to come, it will be now. If it be not now, yet it will come.' In the theatre, one of the functions of *The Murder of Gonzago* may be to persuade the audience that the problem of the Ghost is solved if the Ghost is proven to be truthful, when actually the members of the audience have thereby been deflected from focusing their misgivings on the far greater problem—the theological oddity of a divinely sanctioned injunction to revenge. In any case, if the Ghost seems an 'honest ghost' in his apparent wish to safeguard Gertrude, he may seem less honest in his willingness to imperil young Hamlet. As Samuel Johnson drily observed long ago: 'The apparition left the regions of the dead to little purpose; the revenge which he demands is not obtained but by the death of him that was required to take it . . .'[7] The Ghost, to put it mildly, is destructively illogical. If he is not a devil in disguise, the eventual body-count suggests he might as well have been. Two families have been destroyed.

He is also peculiarly anachronistic. According to editors' readings of the stereoscopic crux in the first scene, 'smot the sledded pollax on the yce', the king represented by this Ghost either (during 'an angry parle') smote the sledded Polacks on the ice or smote his leaded pole-axe on the ice. Either way, he seems a warrior-king of ancient times who anachronistically intrudes into a civilized modern world of duels by rapier, of fashionable boy-actors in the city, of foppish courtiers; a world in which a prince is the advocate, not quite of Method acting, but at least of a realism that improves on the old bombastic style fashionable around 1590; and it is a world in which sceptical reflection is current. The Ghost is hot (perhaps literally) from Purgatory, if his claims are true; but he enters a Protestant Denmark whose sons are educated at that citadel of Protestantism, Luther's Wittenberg University. What's more, it's a Denmark in which Hamlet, even after a confrontation with a peripatetic ghost, can speak of death as 'The undiscovered country, from whose bourn | No traveller returns', and can be sufficiently agnostic to say that 'there is nothing either good or bad, but thinking makes it so'.

When Hamlet enjoins Horatio and Marcellus to swear secrecy, the Ghost moves around beneath and receives jocular treatment from the Prince. He is 'boy', 'truepenny', 'old mole', 'worthy pioneer' and even 'this fellow in the cellarage'. Some commentators seek to redeem this jocularity as psychological realism. Coleridge says:

[L]aughter is equally the expression of extreme anguish and horror as of joy: as there are tears of sorrow and tears of joy, so is there a laugh of terror and a laugh of merriment. These complex causes will naturally have produced in Hamlet the disposition to escape from his own feelings of the overwhelming and supernatural by a wild transition to the ludicrous,—a sort of cunning bravado, bordering on the flights of delirium.[8]

Alternatively, a modern spectator, feeling that the reference to 'this fellow in the cellarage' suggests not a Ghost drifting intangibly beneath the battlements of the castle but an actor scuttling about in the dusty area beneath the planks of the stage, might hail this as a Brechtian alienation-effect which briefly dispels theatrical illusion. There are many intermediate responses. Like Cleopatra's reference to the 'squeaking' boy-actor who might mimic her, the reference to the man in the cellarage may imply confidence that disbelief is being suspended. In the same scene, Hamlet addresses the Ghost as the 'perturbèd spirit' who should now rest. (Eleanor Prosser takes the literally shifty conduct of the subterranean Ghost as further evidence of his hellish provenance.)

As a consequence of the train of action initiated by the Ghost, Claudius is killed; so in that respect the Ghost's declared aim was achieved. But the same train of action entailed the death of Gertrude too, an event which the Ghost purportedly sought to prevent. And the son, Hamlet himself, dies. If the Ghost is genuine, then Hamlet's father, after being killed by Claudius, had been vouchsafed knowledge of covert past events; it's a pity he wasn't given information about possible future events; if so, he might have saved himself the trouble of repeated journeys. If the Ghost was still in process of having his sins purged away, his injunctions may well have been tainted and unreliable; perhaps he didn't have the intelligence to see that he was, as yet, all too fallible an emissary. The Player King's advice to his queen would have been good advice for the Ghost too:

> Our will and fates do so contrary run
> That our devices still are overthrown;
> Our thoughts are ours, their ends none of our own.
>
> (3.2.199–201)

Whether devil or not, a ghost is always subject to God's will; and devils may tempt, but cannot compel.

One answer to the question, 'Where does the Ghost come from?', is: 'Kyd's *Hamlet*'. Not much is known about that lost Hamlet play; but in 1596 Thomas Lodge (in *Wits Miserie*) referred scornfully to its pallid ghost 'which cried so miserally at the Theator like an oister wife, *Hamlet, reuenge*'.[9] So that early play contained a ghost, and one which could seem ludicrous. In *'Hamlet': A Study in Critical Method*, A. J. A. Waldock has suggested that Shakespeare's play is diversely problematic because it's a kind of hybrid.[10] A hybrid is the offspring of parents of different species: thus, a mule is the offspring of an ass and a horse, particularly a male ass and a mare. In this case, the mare is the source-stuff and the ass is Shakespeare's endeavour to modernize it and give it realism. Sophisticated Shakespeare is coupled with relatively primitive materials. The original story of Amlothi or Amleth probably developed in pre-Christian times; it was transmitted to Shakespeare via Saxo Grammaticus's *Historiae Danicae*, written around AD 1200, and via the *Histoires tragiques* of Belleforest and that lost play by Kyd. Shakespeare did what he could to modernize the legend and make it more subtle, sensitive, and realistic. But, alas (we may argue), too much of the old barbaric plot and of the old crude Amleth remain; and the result is inconsistency. Hamlet himself is a hybrid because he's half a modern philosopher and half a primitive avenger. His motivation is largely inherited and literary: he does certain things because they're what the legendary Prince traditionally did. Why does Shakespeare's Hamlet feign madness, even though that obviously attracts suspicion instead of averting it? Because that's what Amleth did. Why did Hamlet kill

poor Polonius and so callously dispose of the body? Because Amleth
had found a spy (concealed in the *straw* of the royal bed—that's how
ancient the legend was) and chopped him up and fed him to pigs.
Why does Hamlet agree to go to England, even though that contradicts his resolve to kill Claudius promptly? Because that's what
Amleth did. Why does Hamlet so ruthlessly consign Rosencrantz
and Guildenstern to their deaths by changing the letter? Because
Amleth had done the same to his two escorts. Why does Hamlet
distrust Ophelia? Because Amleth knew that a beautiful young
woman was being used as a decoy to trick him. Why are the swords
exchanged in the duel scene? Because Amleth switched swords
before killing Feng, Claudius's counterpart. Why are Hamlet's stockings fouled when he visits Ophelia? Because Amleth had wallowed in
filth. Our Hamlet swings between brutal, callous action and sensitive
introspection or civilized humanity; and the reason for the swings is
that the likeable modern character is repeatedly serving the old plot
and is forced to mimic the nastiness of his predecessor. (He even says
'Now could I drink hot blood', trying very hard to sound like the
primitive avenger from the Dark Ages.) Even when Hamlet's feigned
madness modulates into something like manic depression, there's
precedent in Amleth, whose feigned idiocy veers between melancholy and real dementia. As if to illustrate the adage 'You have to
be crazy to act crazy', Amleth, during conversation, crows like a
cockerel and flaps his arms like wings.

What about the hoary puzzle of Hamlet's delay? Well, Old
Hieronymo in Kyd's *Spanish Tragedy* reproaches himself for delay in
revenge, and is, like Hamlet, inclined to distrust evidence put before
him; so this matter wasn't entirely new. What *The Spanish Tragedy*
lacks, though, is all that interesting, but apparently digressive, dis-
cursive stuff that we find in *Hamlet*. Waldock suggests that those
passages in which Hamlet broods on the delay are 'bridge passages':
a way of saying 'The play has been digressing, but now it must be
pulled back to its original course'. To reflect, 'I've been forgetting
the task of revenge; what a procrastinator I am!', is Shakespeare's
expedient to bring the waywardly realistic course of the new material
back into line with the relatively brutal course of the old plot.
In short, if we extend Waldock's reasoning, all the main problems of
the play—including those of the Ghost and Hamlet himself—are
problems of disunity; and these problems have not a solution but

merely an explanation. (Was the re-marriage of Gertrude incestuous? The Ghost and Hamlet say so, but nobody else seems to have
noticed anything incestuous about it, and the re-marriage was public.
The play doesn't provide the information for a decision. Then
there's Horatio, who seems both a visitor to Denmark and a resident.
Another floating puzzle.[11]) The play *Hamlet*, like the Prince and the
Ghost, is historically a hybrid; its origins show through; you can see
the joins. In the light of this theory, we may conclude that the play
(and its Prince) should be called not *Hamlet* but *Hamleth*: a name
which couples the philosopher-prince Hamlet with the barbaric
killer Amleth.

On the other hand, comparison with the source-stuff emphasizes
some brilliant feats of co-ordination. To take just one example, it's in
Shakespeare's version and not the sources that you find not *one* son
seeking revenge for a slain father but *four*. Fortinbras initially leads
his so-called 'lawless resolutes' to regain lands lost by his father, who
was slain by King Hamlet: so there is an ironic note of tardy recognition when, at the end of the play, the dying Hamlet ensures Fortinbras's succession to the Danish throne—'He has my dying voice'.
Hamlet kills Laertes' father, and the outcome is Laertes' attempt to
take vengeance on Hamlet. As the Prince himself remarks, 'by the
image of my cause I see | The portraiture of his'. And the fourth
avenger is Pyrrhus. In Act 2, scene 2, the First Player is asked to
recite a speech which the Prince particularly loves: a description
of the slaughter of old Priam by Pyrrhus, the Greek warrior who
was seeking to avenge his slain father, Achilles. From his stained
armour ('o'er-sizèd with coagulate gore') to his 'eyes like carbuncles',
Pyrrhus is transformed from the human to the monstrous, and the
emphasis on the age and feebleness of the 'reverend Priam' accentuates the morally disgusting nature of the deed. And this is the
passage that Hamlet 'chiefly loved' and likes to have recalled; a
passage which speaks, as loudly as any passage could, against ruthless revenge. So, although there is no speech in which Hamlet
renounces such 'wild justice', the comparative network formed by
Shakespeare's multiplication of vengeful sons ensures that the ethics
of revenge receive very full consideration; and it makes more sense
of Hamlet's veering conduct.

Then there's the matter of the players who arrive at court. The
plot requires them to perform *The Murder of Gonzago* (and Kyd

made much of his 'play within the play' in *The Spamsh Tragedy*); but Hamlet's discussions with them may at first look wayward. But they come to court because young players have usurped their popularity (the theme of usurpation is thus amplified), and, when Hamlet discusses acting with them, we realize that much of the play is co-ordinated by the theme of 'actors, acting and action'. 'To act' may mean 'to go into action, to undertake a deed'; or it can mean merely 'to play-act', 'to feign an action'; so it relates to Hamlet's indecision as well as his histrionics ('I'll rant as well as thou'). Claudius is a usurper acting the part of a rightful king. Hamlet reflects that the Ghost may be a devil assuming a role. At various times, Polonius, Ophelia, Rosencrantz, Guildenstern, and Osric play-act to deceive Hamlet. Polonius had performed the role of Julius Caesar: having been stabbed to death in a play, he will be stabbed to death in reality. One court entertainment is designed to ambush Claudius; another is designed to ambush the Prince. The fatal duel is prompted by a visitor called Lamord, a name which sounds remarkably like 'La Mort'—Death himself in disguise. The Player-King, from within his theatrical make-up and trudging verse, seems to be commenting sardonically on both Claudius and Hamlet. Hamlet himself plays the fool, feigning madness; yet, in his harsh and hysterical moments, we may think that the feigned madness has been the disguise of a real derangement. And, when central figures are acting out roles, the theme of spying, eavesdropping and testing is entailed: people spy on each other to seek the truth behind the masks.

In 1958, when I was a petrol-pump attendant at the East End Service Station, in came an odd-looking car. The ingenious owner had welded together parts of three different old vehicles, spray-painted the whole thing to conceal the welds, and thus created a new car. (He called it 'The Asp', not in honour of Cleopatra's serpent but because it was 'all spare parts': a. s. p.) Modern editors of *Hamlet* do much the same. The three earliest printed texts of the play (First Quarto, 1603; Second Quarto, 1604–5; First Folio, 1623) differ remarkably from each other; so the editors usually try to make one coherent new text out of those diverse old texts. (Modern conventions of presentation serve as the spray-painting.) But Shakespeare had been doing something similar, too: attempting to modernize and combine diverse source-materials and diverse interests in his play. So you get *Hamlet the Asp*. If you look at a standard current edition, you find evidence, within *much* of the modern text, of a high level of intelligent co-ordination (that matter of the four avengers, for instance). There's also evidence, in *parts* of the text, of an *absence* of intelligent co-ordination, possibly even signs of confusion (for instance, Hamlet *twice* originates the idea of using a play to test Claudius). Then there's plenty of ambiguous material which prompts commentators to wrangle about whether it's evidence of intelligent co-ordination or not. Just as scholars long strove to establish an ideal text which was a conglomerate of matter selected from the early printings, so critics long sought to discover an ideal, co-ordinated *Hamlet* (and Hamlet) within the heterogeneous materials. Often they generated a story that was clearer than the plot-stuff they were looking at, and they described a Prince more coherent than the character we encounter. A. C. Bradley gave a persuasive account of a play dominated by a Hamlet who is sensitive but afflicted with pathological melancholy; but Waldock then pointed to the obvious failing of this account: 'Bradley's *Hamlet* is better than Shakespeare's: it is better in the sense that it has a firmer consistency, that it hangs together with a more irresistible logic.'[12] In other words, it was too coherent to be true; too consistent to match the puzzling original.

Hamlet, however, is more than 'Hamleth', for he is explicitly depicted as enigmatic, even to himself; and he thereby gains greater unity than the postulated hybrid. 'You would play upon me, you would seem to know my stops, you would pluck out the heart of my mystery . . . Call me what instrument you will, though you can fret me, you cannot play upon me.' One way for an author to conceal or vindicate inconsistency in a literary character is to let that character say: 'I'm a mystery, am I not?' In the play as a whole, Shakespeare has made puzzles into a theme. Whether it concerns Hamlet, the Ghost, Gertrude, or Ophelia, whether it concerns death and immortality or the morality of revenge, questioning characterizes the play. Characteristically, the opening words are: 'Who's there?' 'Nay, answer me. Stand and unfold yourself.'

Although the First Quarto of *Hamlet* is relatively short, the Second Quarto and First Folio texts are very long: exceptionally long by Shakespearian standards. The Second Quarto version is almost twice as long as *Macbeth*. A staging of the full text of *Hamlet* can last more than four hours (different from the 'two hours' traffic of our stage' promised in *Romeo and Juliet*): in 1992, the Royal Shakespeare

Company's *Hamlet*, directed by Adrian Noble, ran for four and a half. It looks as though that sequence of early texts represents not so much *The Tragedy of Hamlet, Prince of Denmark*, as *The Hamlet-Stuff for the Use of Players*. Accordingly, the *Hamlet* material is generally used selectively. Largely as a result of the textual mixture of order and disorder, this tragedy has been, and remains, astonishingly successful in the theatre. What is misery for the scholar—the inconsistency and unreliability of the early texts, the gaps and inconsistencies in the edited play—can be joy for directors, actors, and their audiences. There's so much to be done with the stuff: new ways to be found of filling the gaps, trimming awkward bits, giving tonal consistency, trying to provide a religious, political, psychological, or moral rationale for the whole thing. Hamlet himself is both actor and director: he's a virtuoso soliciting virtuosi: he tests the full range of voice and physique; yet at the same time he has his mysteries, his reticences; so there's always something new to be tried. Players of the Prince have included not only great actors but also great actresses: Sarah Siddons, Charlotte Cushman, Millicent Bandemann-Palmer, Sarah Bernhardt, Eva le Gallienne, Asta Nielsen, and numerous others: fair enough, since Gertrude and Ophelia were originally played by boys. I've even seen the Prince (like a split hybrid) played by a pair of actors simultaneously: Anthony and David Meyer. And naturally the play has been durably influenced by Stoppard's *Rosencrantz and Guildenstern are Dead*, which delights anyone who sympathizes with real or theatrical underdogs, and which, interlocking with *Hamlet*, spirals through and between the Elizabethan age and Postmodernism.

If the early texts are so diverse and standard modern texts are so lengthy, it's no disgrace if directors use them as material for shaping and re-shaping by means of cuts, compressions, and rearrangements. The play was evolving in Shakespeare's time, and it has continued to evolve as it progresses through the centuries to the present. Of course, Shakespeare (who took such liberties with his sources) would have approved of directorial pruning and even directorial additions to the text. Hamlet adds lines to *The Murder of Gonzago* to give it topical relevance, and when Polonius objects that the recitation about Pyrrhus is too long, Hamlet replies: 'It shall to the barber's, with your beard.'

Numerous potential *Hamlets* are created by Shakespeare's

endeavour to combine old and new material and by the early texts' mixtures of disorder and co-ordination. These potentials are repeatedly being realized: in the imaginations of readers and spectators, on television and cinema screens, and in theatres round the world. That's where the main puzzles of *Hamlet* are solved: not finally, but locally, temporarily, and, often enough, admirably.

C.W.

Desdemona's posthumous speeches

The bedroom scene in Othello is replete with problems which not only vex interpreters, but focus on what was—for nineteenth-century 'Anglo-Saxon' critics—the main issue of Shakespearian scholarship. Were the bard's plays universally 'true', or did they depend, at crucial junctures, on the low devices of 'fiction'? Should one read the tragedies as gospel, or as entertaining narratives, shamelessly marred where necessary with the contrivances of a bad sensation novel?

In the powerful climax of *Othello*'s action the Moor comes on stage with a terrible declaration. Desdemona is already in her bed—the polluted marital couch, as the husband thinks. (The article of furniture has been physically transported to Cyprus from Venice in the army baggage train if we credit Iago's instruction 'Strangle her in her bed, even the bed she hath contaminated.') 'It is the cause' Othello mutters. What he means by 'cause' is obscure. But his intended action is chillingly clear: 'she must die'. Yet, he avers, 'I'll not shed her blood'. This picks up the horrible advice about strangling given earlier by Iago. It is 'fitting', as Othello immediately perceives, because the act combines a parodic marital embrace with the orgasmic climax of revenge.

Shakespeare is here keeping moderately faithful to his primary source, Cinthio, where Iago suggests that in order not to 'shed her blood' (and thus give themselves away):

'I propose we take a stocking, filled with sand, and beat Disdemona with it till she dies; thus will her body bear no signs of violence. When she is dead we can pull down a portion of the ceiling, and thus make it seem as if a rafter falling on her head had killed the lady. Suspicion cannot rest on you, since all men will impute her death to accident.'[1]

This, as it transpires, is exactly what Cinthio's Othello and Iago go on to do. One of the thornier issues in the play's murder scene is whether Shakespeare wholly decontaminates *his* Othello from the horrible criminal small-mindedness of Cinthio's two low-life, blackjack-wielding crooks.

It is clear from subsequent events in the scene that Othello (a warrior skilled in hand-to-hand killing) has weapons about him—a sword and a (secreted) dagger, we suppose. The sword is taken from him by the soldiers who arrest him after Desdemona's murder. The smaller weapon remains with him (exactly where he hides it is not clear) and enables him to kill himself (he has earlier been prevented from picking up a pair of scissors, one deduces, from Desdemona's dressing table—whether this is a *ruse de guerre* designed to lull his captors into a sense of false security is similarly not clear).

Conventionally Othello is shown entering the bedroom with a taper like any other husband turning in for the night. Hence his subsequent instruction to himself, 'Put out the light'. It has, of course, a double meaning (as in Macbeth's 'out, out brief candle'). He will be snuffing out a life as well as a light. After a poignant exchange with Desdemona, who sleepily wakes up, Othello is conventionally represented on stage smothering her. While he is finishing her off, Emilia knocks at the door:

> OTHELLO What noise is this? Not dead? Not yet quite dead?
>   I that am cruel, am yet merciful.
>   I would not have thee linger in thy pain.
>   So, so.[2]   (5.2.95–8)

The clearest sense of this is that he leans down harder on his victim—possibly strangling her with his hands round her neck rather than stifling her with a pillow, so as to get it over with quickly. There is, in the exhalation 'So, so', the post-coital suggestion of ejaculation and sexual climax. But a number of interpreters, critical and theatrical, have interpreted 'So, so' as indicating that Othello stabs Desdemona—possibly with the same dagger that he has secreted about his person with which later he kills himself (this too would be 'fitting'; although he would somehow have to wipe off the blade before returning it to its hiding place on his person).

The stabbing hypothesis is given plausibility by the fact that a little later, regarding his wife's corpse, Othello observes her face to be as 'Pale as thy smock'. As is generally known, stifling and strangulation both produce a congestion of blood in the face and a purplish tinge. Desdemona's features (if asphyxiated) would partake of the beetroot rather than the pallid corpse Othello describes. In an age of public hanging, there would have been little misapprehension about what throttled facial features looked like. Some, perhaps most, members of Shakespeare's audience would have witnessed public executions.

Stabbing would also make more plausible a perplexing feature later in the scene. After Emilia has come in and had words with Othello, Desdemona revives sufficiently to utter three speeches. It takes a little time for shock and internal bleeding to kill a stabbing victim. Conventionally in Elizabethan and Jacobean drama, stabbed victims could be allowed quite long speeches after receiving their fatal wound and catching, as Flamineo puts it, 'an everlasting cold.' In real life there are many cases of stabbed people staggering some distance, talking, then dying from loss of blood, shock, or organic collapse (Stephen Lawrence, for example, managed to speak after receiving the stab wound that killed him).

On the other hand, if Desdemona were stabbed (through the heart, presumably) would her smock still be virgin 'white', as Othello says it is? The face might be pale but her nightdress would surely be smeared and bloody. As with hanging, Elizabethan audiences (who would have seen innumerable animals killed in the local shambles) would find the idea of bloodless stabbing very peculiar. (Lady Macbeth, who has never, presumably, had to do the slaughtering for her banquets, is astonished at how much mess is produced by knife-wounds: 'who would have thought the old man to have had so much blood in him', she asks.) Perhaps, if one wants to be ingenious, Othello might be portrayed with one of those very fine-pointed daggers, made out of bicycle spokes, such as the *Tsotsis* of Soweto have, which plunge in and out of flesh as seamlessly as hypodermic syringes. But, as Bradley would say, 'this becomes absurd.'

Horace Howard Furness, the wonderfully pedantic editor of the Variorum edition (whom no absurdity deters), was much worried by the pathology of Desdemona's death and consulted a number of leading medical men on the question. Dr S. Weir Mitchell made a gallant attempt to reconcile the issue. Shakespeare, Mitchell suggested, meant us to understand 'that Othello choked Desdemona insufficiently, and finished her with a dirk'. Her face 'would have been paling from blood-loss, and as to the smock, *all* wounds do not bleed externally.' And if they did, 'a little blood on the smock would not have made less for Othello its *general* whiteness.'[3] One thinks, however, of the Persil advertisements. The tiniest smudge (as every proud mother knows) makes white garments look soiled.

Mitchell's ingenuity is further contradicted by Othello's subsequent insistence that he did not, as he promised, *spill her blood*. He later declares that his 'hands' have 'newly stopped' her 'breath'. Smothering seems clearly indicated (although strangulation is not entirely excluded). Some other figure of speech than 'stopped her breath' would have been chosen, surely, if the lady were knifed. And 'one hand', not 'hands' would have been indicted for killing her, if it had been done with Mitchell's 'dirk'.

These issues are further complicated by Desdemona's unexpected resuscitation, thirty lines after she has been 'smothered', 'strangled', or 'dirked'. When she bursts into the bedchamber, Emilia does not initially see her mistress's corpse—for the good reason that it is night and Othello has put out the candle. Emilia, of course, is too much in a hurry to have brought light with her. She excitedly informs Othello that a 'foul murder,' has been committed—that of Roderigo. 'What of Cassio?' Othello asks. Iago has assured him that he will be revenged on his cuckolder. Cassio is wounded but not killed, Emilia replies. This intelligence is devastating for Othello:

> OTHELLO Not Cassio killed? Then murder's out of tune,
>   And sweet revenge grows harsh.
> DESDEMONA O, falsely, falsely murdered!
> EMILIA O Lord, what cry is that?
> OTHELLO That? What?
> EMILIA Out and alas, that was my lady's voice!
>   Help, help, ho, help! Oh lady, speak again!
>   Sweet Desdemona, O sweet Mistress, speak!
> DESDEMONA A guiltless death I die.
> EMILIA   O, who hath done this deed?
> DESDEMONA Nobody, I myself. Farewell.
>   Commend me to my kind lord. O, farewell!
> OTHELLO Why, how should she be murdered?
> EMILIA   Alas, who knows?
> OTHELLO You heard her say herself, it was not I.

EMILIA She said so, I must needs report the truth.
OTHELLO She's like a liar gone to burning hell.
    'Twas I that killed her.
EMILIA Oh the more angel she, and you the blacker devil!
OTHELLO She turned to folly, and she was a whore. (5.2.124–41)

There is a glaring physiological problem here. How can Desdemona come back from the dead to utter three grammatical and lucid speeches? And not only has Desdemona been able to speak, she can think and is quick-witted enough to put together what must have happened and to furnish Othello with an alibi. Sentimentally inclined commentators seize on her speaking as evidence that she has not in fact been murdered, merely rendered unconscious, and that she revives only to die of a 'broken heart'. In this line of interpretation, she *is* self-destroyed and the noble Moor is, at least technically, innocent. It is a case *se offendendo*, as with Ophelia. Hence Desdemona's otherwise grotesque final words of exoneration: 'Nobody, I myself. Farewell' and her deathbed description of her lord as 'kind'. He is 'kind', in this reading of his character, because he could not, at the last minute, bring himself to kill her. Othello is no more directly responsible for Desdemona's death than Hamlet is directly responsible for Ophelia's. Barry Scheck (O. J. Simpson's and Louise Woodward's attorney) could make a defence argument out of it and possibly convince a jury packed with African Americans, with the right medical experts. Modern theatre audiences are less likely to be swayed by the 'broken heart' theory.

One may note in passing that Emilia apprehends her mistress is murdered not from the sight of bloodstains on her smock (which even in the gloom of the bedchamber would have been visible— particularly to a maid-servant's trained eye), but as a suggestive echo from Desdemona's exclamation: 'O, falsely, falsely murdered', which itself echoes Othello's 'murder's out of tune'.

Were Emilia not so quick off the mark it would be nice to think that Desdemona's voice, like Banquo's spectral appearance at the feasts and the third appearance of Old Hamlet, is visionary—heard by Othello alone. It is his conscience, not her corpse, which is speaking. But clearly Desdemona *does* speak. She is audible to others than Othello. And once she hears her, Emilia does her best to revive her 'murdered' mistress (we may imagine her chafing Desdemona's wrists).

How can Desdemona speak in this way, after Othello has apparently 'murdered' her? Of the physicians consulted by Furness, the
most ingenious was Dr William Hunt. 'Her end is no pathological
puzzle to me,' this medical expert opined. 'Desdemona died of frac-
ture of cricoid cartilage of the larynx. Shakespeare is entirely consistent, and must have had, as in everything else, an intuitive, if not
practical, knowledge of the subject.' The ability to come out with a
few terminal words in this condition is quite 'normal', Hunt goes on
to explain, although the broken larynx means death is inevitable a
few moments later. 'Tracheotomy was the only thing that might have
saved her . . . There never was a clearer case. Is not Shakespeare's
universality wonderful?'[4]

Not everyone will be convinced by Hunt's 'broken larynx' theory.
But it is very convenient. There are, however, other and less easily
dispersed difficulties in the passage. What does Othello mean, when
he first asks Emilia, 'how should she be murdered?' (who knows
'how' better than her murderer himself?). What does he mean when
he seizes on Desdemona's final words to insist to Emilia—his wife's
servant—'You heard her say herself, it was not I'? (Deathbed confes-
sions have status of sworn testimony, Emilia's having heard this
statement of Desdemona's could stand Othello in good stead in any
subsequent inquest.)

What, to add to the perplexity, do we make of the fact that when
Emilia none the less states her intention to proclaim the 'murder'
(not 'suicide' or 'mysterious death') to the world, despite her employer's suggestion they keep it to themselves, Othello suddenly
changes his tune. He now says that he *did* after all 'kill' (not
'murder') Desdemona, but explains that it was a *crime passionel*—
the righteous act of a wronged husband: 'she was a whore.' Such
executions, especially among Italians, are licensed, and no 'murder',
but lawful killing. Honour, you know.

It seems clear as day that Othello's first intention was to create
what modern generals and politicians would call 'deniability', a 'fall-
back position', and 'legal defence in depth'. In the first instance he
smothered Desdemona, not just to avoid mutilating her body, but to
mislead the world into thinking that she died of natural causes (a
complication to do with childbirth is what would be assumed). Or,
perhaps, it might be thought that she accidentally took an overdose
of mandragora or poppy.

When this line of defence collapsed, Othello's next intention was to pass the buck, claim that someone else must have done the dreadful deed ('You heard her say herself it was not I'). When Emilia, who is no fool, declines to swallow that improbability he falls back on his third and last line of defence, 'she was a whore, and deserved to die. It's what any dishonoured husband would do.' This is a *faute de mieux*. The defence may well get him off the legal hook, but will not help his advancement in the military service (which is, we assume, why he did not come out with it first).

There is no doubt at this stage—but not for much longer—that Othello *did* think Desdemona was a 'whore'. Why not then shout the fact to the skies? Three reasons. The first is natural embarrassment. No man wants other men (particularly men over whom he is in command) to know that he is a cuckold. Mockery will fatally undermine his 'authority'. Secondly, killing your employers' daughters, even where 'honour' is at stake, is not a good career move. Thirdly, Othello realizes (and Emilia's blank disbelief will have confirmed it) that—to outside eyes—the evidence on which he impugns Desdemona is alarmingly slim. All that business about the handkerchief is very flimsy. 'The cause' will not look overwhelming to the world.

The main point, of course, is that a variety of low-minded and furtive thoughts are scampering through Othello's mind, and that he is preoccupied, above all, with saving his skin. It is ignoble. And it puts Bradley—who loves his 'noble Moor'—in a terrible dilemma, which he can get out of only by a kind of pained floundering:

This is a strange passage. what did Shakespeare mean us to feel? . . . Here alone, I think, in the scene sympathy with Othello quite disappears. Did Shakespeare mean us to feel thus, and to realise how completely confused and perverted Othello's mind has become? I suppose so: and yet Othello's words continue to strike me as very strange, and also as not *like* Othello.[5]

Bradley cannot bring himself actually to articulate what he takes Othello's 'strange' words to mean. His only escape from the conclusion that, after all, Othello is rather a low fellow is to argue that this is some 'other Othello' speaking. An artefact of Iago's presumably.

Pulling against Bradley's sentimentality one can rationalize the meanness of Othello's thinking at this point. Iago, we may surmise, has degraded him to his own subhuman level. If one takes this line it is hard, a few moments later; to be entirely convinced by the 'Othello music' of the hero's majestic valedictory monologue:

> Then must you speak
> Of one that loved not wisely but too well,
> Of one not easily jealous but, being wrought,
> Perplexed in the extreme; of one whose hand,
> Like the base Indian, threw a pearl away
> Richer than all his tribe . . .

> (5.2.352–7)

Of one, that is, who killed his wife and tried to make it look like an accident, so that his glorious military career might not be terminated prematurely?

J.S.

'Great thing of us forgot!': Albany's amnesia or Shakespeare's?

═══

If you look at videos of, say, *On the Waterfront* or *The Godfather*, you'll notice the following curious and fascinating characteristic of Marlon Brando's acting. During dialogues his eyes would seldom rest on the other person but would roam to the sides, above, below, beyond, around, and back. This introduced novel realism. What occasioned this intriguing innovation? According to his biographers, Brando's memory needed considerable assistance, so his lines were written down and discreetly arranged about the set for him to read.

Brando's cheat sheets and cue cards again found their way onto the set, turning up pasted on cameras, to desks, and even on fruit in a bowl . . .
  'He had his lines written all over the place,' Willis [a cinematographer] recalled with a laugh. 'Sometimes he even wrote them on his hands or on his sleeves. Sometimes I think that's where all that famous Brando style came from—the dramatic pauses, looking around before he spoke.'[1]

Marlon Brando would probably have received short shrift from Shakespeare's company of players. Then, an excellent memory was an essential part of an actor's talents. There would certainly be little tolerance of the 'unperfect actor', mentioned in Sonnet 23, who 'with his fear is put besides his part'. Dependence on a prompter is one sign of the comically untalented amateur, as Costard playing Pompey demonstrates.

Shakespeare was also interested in the failure of memory as old age looms, and in the related tendency of elderly folk to ramble from the point. Polonius shows the comic potential of this. So do Shallow and Silence in *2 Heniy IV*, rambling on about death and transience, the price of bullocks at Stamford Fair, and youthful escapades which may not have taken place. In the relatively young, a lapse of memory may be a tell-tale sign of political incompetence. In *1 Henry IV*, Hotspur says: 'In Richard's time—what do you call the place? | A plague upon it, it is in Gloucestershire'; 'A plague upon it, I have forgot the map': typical of his spluttering impatience with detail and with calculation. In contrast, Hal's apparent forgetfulness in *2 Henry IV*, Act 4, scene 5, seems calculated and diplomatic. He tells his dying father that he had taken up the crown to quarrel with it 'as with an enemy'. This does not tally with his proud address to the crown when he had thought his father dead; but Hal is showing, yet again, his skill in using shrewd tact and rhetorical fluency to prevail in a tricky situation. Sometimes a lapse of memory seems natural to a speaker who is not only ageing but also has a great deal on his mind: so, in *The Tempest*, when Prospero breaks off his dialogue with Ferdinand to say, 'I had forgot that foul conspiracy | Of the beast Caliban and his confederates', this seems to be natural and in character, rather than an instance of Shakespeare suddenly recalling a loose end of the plot. Anxiety about remembering is one of Prospero's characteristics: 'Canst thou remember . . .?', he asks Miranda; 'Dost thou forget . . .?', 'Hast thou forgot?', he demands of Ariel. But something rather different seems to be happening in the final scene of *King Lear* when Albany, no dotard or old mage but a middle-aged war-leader, becomes suddenly aware of forgetfulness.

Discussions of *King Lear* often bear on the problem of theodicy. That's the problem of reconciling belief in divine justice with evidence of injustice here on earth. It's an ancient and continuing issue for religious believers, and it's the central issue in the tradition of literary tragedies. If divine justice exists, why does it permit the existence of apparent injustice all around us? Why is it that good people often suffer, while bad people often prosper? *King Lear* seems determined to express this problem in particularly vivid, searching, and harsh ways. Repeatedly in the play, characters invoke or refer to a variety of deities and metaphysical forces: God, Jove, Juno, Hecate, Apollo, 'Nature', the sun and moon, 'the gods', the 'ever gentle gods', 'you justicers', 'the heavens'. Repeatedly there's a questioning of the forces that may govern our lives (are they kind, blind, or cruel?); and also, insistently, the play gives instances of the very kinds of suffering and cruelty that make people seek some consolatory pattern in events. The suffering of Lear is painful enough; but the blinding of Gloucester is notoriously horrifying ('Out, vile jelly!'—in the theatre, it can still make audiences flinch and look away); and the death of Cordelia seems to set the problem of theodicy in the most explicit of ways. Lear, referring to Cordelia as his 'poor fool' (which editors usually regard here as a term of endearment), cries out in his misery:

> And my poor fool is hang'd! No, no, no life!
> Why should a dog, a horse, a rat, have life,
> And thou no breath at all?[2]   (5.3.304-6)

It's a question which commentators often try to answer. Samuel Johnson, of course, found the death of Cordelia so painful that he could scarcely bring himself to read again the ending of the play until his editorial duties obliged him to do so. He contemplated sadly this text in which 'the wicked prosper, and the virtuous miscarry'; sometimes, alas, Shakespeare 'seems to write without any moral purpose'.[3] Other critics have seen the play as an affirmation of Christianity. G. I. Duthie, for example, in his introduction to a Cambridge edition of *King Lear*, says:

God overthrows the absolutely evil—he destroys the Cornwalls, the Gonerils, the Regans: he is just. God chastens those who err but who can be regenerated—the Lears, the Gloucesters—and in mercy he redeems them: he is just, and merciful. But again, God moves in a mysterious way—he deals strangely with the Cordelias of this world. His methods are inscrutable. Shakespeare presents the whole picture . . . This, however, can mean 'pessimistic' drama only to those who cannot agree that the play is a Christian play.[4]

When the commentators disagree, one way of trying to clarify our sense of Shakespeare's intentions and meanings is to look at his use of the source-materials. In the case of *King Lear*, a big paradox emerges. It can be summed up by saying that Shakespeare's adaptations seem designed both to *confirm* and to *subvert* the sense of divine ordinance of events.

The material about Gloucester and his two sons derives from the story of the King of Paphlagonia in Sir Philip Sidney's *Arcadia*. Sidney's King (like Gloucester) has two sons, one legitimate, one illegitimate; and he is tricked by the illegitimate son, Plexirtus, into disowning the legitimate son, Leonatus. Subsequently Plexirtus blinds his aged father and casts him out. Leonatus serves as his guide in the wilderness, deflecting the old man from suicide, and with friends defeats Plexirtus and his men. The King dies after being fully reconciled to Leonatus, who inherits the throne. It all sounds familiar. Shakespeare, scholars believe, was the first writer to combine the Lear material with the Paphlagonian material. As we have just seen, there are numerous parallels between the two stories: rivalry between siblings; a parent who, deceived, trusts the bad and rejects the good offspring; suffering in the wilderness; and the eventual reconciliation of the erring father with the loving child. In Shakespeare's play, Lear and Gloucester, during their separate wanderings, even gain remarkably similar moral insights into the value of being charitable to the needy. The parallelisms create the impression that the sufferings of the two men may be *ordained* sufferings: perhaps divine powers have acted to punish but also to enlighten these erring figures. The addition of the Paphlagonian material to the Lear material provides duplications of events, and thus evident patterning; and evident patterning implies a pattern-maker: some destinal force at work. Obvious. That's the first half of the paradox.

The second half is famous. If we look at Shakespeare's other changes to the traditional Lear material, we find that his intentions now seem to be quite different. The story of King Lear (or Leir) had been told by a variety of writers: among others, by Geoffrey of Monmouth, by Higgins in his *Mirror for Magistrates*, by Holinshed in his *Chronicles*, by Spenser in *The Faerie Queene*, and by the author of the anonymous play entitled *The True Chronicle History of King Leir*. And in all these versions, the story of the King ends relatively happily. After his reconciliation with the virtuous daughter, he is restored to the throne, and seems set to live happily ever after. Certainly, in some versions, the daughter then dies by suicide in prison after having been defeated in a rebellion by her nephews; but that happens a long time after the reconciliation. Only in Shakespeare's text does that daughter die *before* her father; only in Shakespeare's version do we have the hideous sense that a poignant reconciliation has been cruelly blighted by the sudden murder of the young woman; only in Shakespeare's version does the King have happiness so abruptly snatched from his grasp, and receive the mortal shock of seeing the beloved child die. There was no precedent for the harrowing bleakness, the ruthless ironies and the harsh *accidentality* of the conclusion.

In Act 5, scene 3, the concluding scene, the reunited Lear and Cordelia are sent off to prison. There, Lear says, they will enjoy many years in each other's company, blessed by benign gods.

Edmund, however, has previously resolved that they must both die, and he now gives the Captain written orders to kill the captives and to report to him immediately the deed is done. There then follows much complicated and dramatic stage business. Albany demands the prisoners but is denied them by Edmund. The sexual rivalry between Goneril and Regan becomes shockingly overt. Edgar lengthily challenges Edmund and the duel takes place; Edmund is mortally wounded. Edgar now recapitulates and extends the story of his journey with Gloucester. It seems that when Edgar eventually cast off all disguise and revealed himself to his father, Gloucester's flawed heart 'burst smilingly'. At this point, Edmund says:

> This speech of yours hath moved me,
> And shall perchance do good.

> (lines 191–2)

His words remind us of the perilous plight of Lear and Cordelia, and briefly raise the possibility of their rescue. There is suspense: will Edmund die before revealing their peril? At least this detail makes clear that if anyone is forgetful of the captives, it is not Shakespeare. Whether musingly or craftily, Edmund now continues:

> But speak you on—
> You look as you had something more to say.
> (lines 192–3)

And Edgar does have something more to say, this time on the subject of Kent, who, on seeing Edgar and the dead Gloucester, had had some kind of fit or stroke ('the strings of life | Began to crack . . . I left him tranc'd').[5] In another dramatic development, it is announced that Goneril has murdered Regan by poison and stabbed herself to death. Albany, with remarkable composure, says:

> This judgement of the heavens, that makes us tremble,
> Touches us not with pity.

> (lines 206–7)

Within a few moments of this reference to the 'judgement of the heavens', Kent enters to say farewell to Lear: 'Is he not here?'. It's then that Albany exclaims:

> Great thing of us forgot!—
> Speak, Edmund; where's the King, and where's Cordelia?
> (lines 211–12)

Now, at long last, Edmund reveals that he has given instructions for both Lear and Cordelia to be slain. There's a flurried rush to send rescue. 'The gods defend her!', cries Albany. Then, as if in sardonic answer to his plea for divine defence:

> Enter King Lear with Queen Cordelia in his arms . . .

It's a stark *Pietà* in reverse: here the male holds the dead female. So much for the 'judgement of the heavens' and the gods' guardianship.

   In short, while some of the changes to the source-materials have *increased* the sense of the possibly providential ordering of events, other changes *subvert* that sense and emphasize an *absence* of providential order. The exclamation 'Great thing of us forgot!' (rather than, say, 'Great thing to be resolved!') forms part of that subversion: accidentality and cruel ironies come to the fore. And amnesia continues to accentuate the ironies. Kent kneels before Lear, crying: 'O, my good master!' Instead of recognition, the response from the King is the uncomprehending 'Prithee, away.' Edgar intervenes, trying to jog Lear's memory: ''Tis noble Kent, your friend.' The appalling reply is: 'A plague upon you, murderers, traitors all.' Lear is not only amnesiac; he sounds for a moment every bit as wrathful and unjust as the Lear of the play's first scene, long before his suffering and reconciliation. Next, briefly, Lear veers into recognition of Kent, but promptly veers away from lucidity again. As Albany observes, 'He knows not what he says; and vain is it | That we present us to him.' Nevertheless, Albany tries to make moral sense of the outcome:

> All friends shall taste
> The wages of their virtue, and all foes
> The cup of their deservings.   (lines 278–80)

Yet it is then that Lear exclaims:

> And my poor fool is hanged!   (line 281)

—as if to say, 'Where are the wages of *her* virtue? How can Cordelia's death possibly fit any pattern of moral justice?'

   The many struggles of *King Lear* include a struggle of remembrance against amnesia. 'I will forget my nature', says Lear as madness impends. Lear and Gloucester, during their sufferings, both come to realize that when they held power they were forgetful of the poor and abject. Cordelia's 'Sir, do you know me?' reverberates. Lear's eventual failure to remember those who strove for him has appalling realism (as readers with senile and Alzheimer's-stricken relatives will know). Albany's brief forgetfulness lets cruel accidentality invade a tragic world in which, conventionally, audiences expect consolatory evidence of 'inevitability'.

King Lear is sub-tragic, in the sense that it finally inflicts so rawly on us the messy stuff of human suffering that tragedies traditionally reduce to order. It is also preter-tragic (beyond it), in the sense that the play depicts human endeavours to impose patterns of moral significance on events which ultimately prove to be a recalcitrant muddle. Amnesia accentuates that muddle while offering a grim refuge; but perhaps, if willed, it offers a hint of grace: in Lear's words, 'Forget and forgive.'

C.W.

Poor Tom's a yokel?

As A. C. Bradley rather wearily points out, 'The improbabilities in *King Lear* surely far surpass those of the other great tragedies in number and in grossness.' Much as he normally relishes such blemishes, the critic is obliged to deal with them *en masse*, so numerous are they in this play. He is particularly scathing about the improbabilities in what he calls the 'secondary', or Gloucester plot:

For example, no sort of reason is given why Edgar, who lives in the same house with Edmund, should write a letter to him instead of speaking . . . Is it in character that Edgar should be persuaded without the slightest demur to avoid his father instead of confronting him and asking him the cause of his anger? Why in the world should Gloster, when expelled from his castle, wander painfully all the way to Dover simply to destroy himself? And is it not extraordinary that, after Gloster's attempted suicide, Edgar should first talk to him in the language of a gentleman, then to Oswald in his presence in broad peasant dialect, then again to Gloster in gentle language, and yet that Gloster should not manifest the least surprise?[1]

Bradley's habitual common sense supplies the explanation that the play was probably shortened at short notice and that Shakespeare was more than usually careless about details in consequence. The killing of Oswald episode, however, seems—if anything—rather carefully worked out and up to.

Edgar's 'counterfeiting' to his father is, as Bradley points out, consistently impenetrable as to motive. Gloucester initially encounters his disguised son as Poor Tom on the heath and does not recognize him, although the old man at this point has his sight and a torch for illumination (he actually asks 'Poor Tom' his name and, taking pity on the 'poor fellow', tells him to get in the hovel and 'keep thee warm').

Gloucester later encounters Edgar–Tom in the farmhouse where he has temporarily accommodated the King. Edgar (on Gloucester's instructions, apparently) is left behind when arrangements are made to take the prostrate Lear by litter to Dover, accompanied by some thirty-five or thirty-six 'of his knights' (they seem to be the fairest of fair-weather friends and are nowhere to be seen when Lear eventually arrives at the coast). On his part, Edgar resolves to 'lurk, lurk'— hang around to see what turns up. He elects to remain undressed, presumably to sustain his disguise.

Gloucester is blinded and turned out of his own castle. It is now morning. On the heath (which lies, apparently, just beyond the castle gate), Tom–Edgar meets his father, led by an 80-year-old former tenant. ''Tis poor mad Tom,' the old man explains. Edgar, who has been speaking lucidly and *in propria persona* to himself, falls into the lunatic's part. Gloucester gives him money to be conducted to Dover. Tom–Edgar carries on ranting, not very convincingly ('I cannot daub it [dissemble] further', he mutters to himself; but daub he does).

In his subsequent pilgrimage to Dover with his father, Edgar veers between 'gentle' and common dialects. Even Gloucester, who is preoccupied with his own woes and obsessed with ideas of suicide observes, musingly, just before his jump from Dover Cliff: 'Methinks you're better spoken.' Of course, Edgar *must* speak well at this point if he is to lull Gloucester's growing suspicions ('Methinks the ground is even') that he may not be standing on a sheer cliff-face. Edgar creates a wonderful word picture to persuade his father that they are teetering on an awful brink:

> How fearful
> And dizzy 'tis to cast one's eyes so low!
> The crows and choughs that wing the midway air
> Show scarce so gross as beetles. Halfway down
> Hangs one that gathers samphire, dreadful trade!
> Methinks he seems no bigger than his head.[2]
>
> (4.5.11–16)

This is cogent verse and impossible to conceive issuing from Tom's lunatic mouth.

After the leap Tom–Edgar becomes yet another person—a passer-by who happened to be walking on the beach beneath the chalk cliffs and saw Gloucester's body come floating down like thistledown. The 'poor unfortunate beggar' that Gloucester thought was his companion was, this third incarnation of Edgar explains, 'some fiend' (with 'a thousand noses'). One would think that Gloucester, having spent so much time with this companion, would notice that there were similarities between the three assumed voices (and even some similarities with his son). When asked who he is, Edgar in his latest edition declares himself 'a most poor man, made tame to fortune's blows'.

But he is well spoken and a gentleman, we apprehend. At this point, enter Oswald. Regan has decided Gloucester must die, as he is raising sympathy against them 'where he arrives he moves | All hearts against us'. She has issued an edict the old man be killed on sight and promised a reward to whoever does the deed.

On seeing Gloucester, Oswald exults, 'A proclaimed prize.' He is a made man; the reward is his. Edgar, however, interposes between Oswald's sword and Gloucester's willing breast. Oswald apprehends that his opponent is a 'bold peasant'. Edgar, we know not how, has earlier contrived to cover his nakedness—evidently with humble attire. He assumes a correspondingly 'Mummersetshire' dialect (descending from verse into prose, as he did when he was Poor Tom):

Good gentleman, go your gait, and let poor volk pass. And 'chud ha' bin zwagger'd out of my life, 'twould not ha' bin zo long as 'tis by a vortnight. Nay, come not near th'old man; keep out, che vor' ye, or ise try whither your costard or my ballow be the harder. Chill be plain with you.

A 'ballow' is a cudgel.[3] The two men fight, and Edgar kills Oswald, getting from him in the process the letters that reveal the full extent of Edmund's treachery. He now reverts not merely to his normal speech, but is—evidently—Edgar again. He twice calls Gloucester 'father', and the scene ends with the filial instruction:

> Give me your hand.
> Far off methinks I hear the beaten drum.
> Come, father, I'll bestow you with a friend.   (4.5.284–6)

(Who is the friend? Cordelia?)

Why does Edgar go through the yokel pantomime? It's funny, as rural dialect conventionally is to metropolitan theatre audiences. But comedy seems out of place at this juncture. Thematically the imposture can be made to fit. In this play the lower classes have kinder instincts than their betters (and certainly more sympathy than the schoolboy-like gods who kill men for their sport). We never, for example, know the name of the servant who earns our admiration by killing Cornwall, at the expense of his own life. Nor do we know the name of the generous old tenant who, at the risk of *his* life, takes care of the newly blinded Gloucester. If there is hope in this play, it resides, as in *1984*, in the anonymous proles—or the 'bold peasants'.

Tactically, the imposture takes Oswald off guard. As a 'peasant', Edgar doesn't have a sword. His cudgel is no match for a trained courtier with steel unless, that is, he can trick his opponent into thinking that he is a harmless clown. One does not know the combat which Shakespeare had in mind, but conceivably Tom–Edgar might shamble and trip over his feet, to lull Oswald into a sense of false security—the better to fetch him a shattering blow across the pate.[4]

Edgar's Mummersetshire routine may also have been inspired by the fact that, as he says of the dead Oswald, 'I know thee well.' This would mean that Oswald probably knows Edgar just as well. If Oswald should suddenly realize that he is confronted not by some 'dunghill' of a peasant but the formidable (and by now implacably vengeful) son of Gloucester he may well call for help. Edgar does not know if Oswald is alone, or whether there are accomplices nearby.

Finally, there is poetic justice in Oswald's dying in the belief that he has been disgraced by a 'slave.' It recalls his gross insult to Kent by causing him to be put in the stocks, a punishment traditionally reserved for the lower orders. As Oswald sowed, so has he reaped.

Oswald's last request (servile to the end) that Edgar should deliver his letters raises another problem. How did Edgar deliver the death blow? If with his 'ballow' (or Gloucester's staff) it would have meant a mighty battering of the head, which would preclude any dying words, other than a terminal grunt or two. As stage business, a director might contrive an exchange in which Edgar comes by Oswald's sword, or Edgar's having a secreted dagger.

None of this fully answers Bradley's principal objection that Gloucester seems strangely insouciant about his companion's wildly different voices. One might plausibly assume that Gloucester is in such a state of shock that he does not register the fact that he has, apparently, five companions on the way to Dover (Tom, two anonymous 'gentlemen'—one of them a 'fiend' in disguise—a yokel, and—most mysteriously—his son Edgar). Kenneth Muir defends the plausibility of the Edgar-the-yokel scene along similar lines, claiming—in contradiction to Bradley—that there is no need for Gloucester to express surprise when Edgar begins to speak in dialect: 'Either he could appear surprised without words, or he could assume that his other senses had become imperfect with the loss of his sight.[5] It's a feeble hypothesis and impossible to justify by reference to the text. But probably as satisfactory an explanation to the puzzle as one can come up with.

J.S.

How ancient is Lear? How youthful is Juliet?

As with Hamlet and the gravedigger, Shakespeare is fond of intruding unexpected age markers into his drama. 'Spanners thrown wilfully in the chronological works', we may call them. Two other awkward examples come to mind.

Lear is explicitly said to be 80 years and more. He himself announces his retirement in the first scene and his intention to 'shake all cares and business from our age [and] Unburdened crawl towards death.'[1] His exact years are divulged late in the action when he awakes suddenly sane and finds himself reunited with Cordelia. It is in other ways a strange scene. The deposed King is initially carried on (insensible) in a chair recalling a mock throne. The tableau evokes Tamburlaine being 'drawn in his chariot by the Kings of Trebizon and Sofia, with bits in their mouths, reins in his left hand, and in his right hand a whip with which he scourgeth them.' Lear, however, is no longer in any mood to scourge. 'Pray, do not mock me,' he implores Cordelia as he regains consciousness, thinking her a tormenting wraith:

> I am a very foolish, fond old man,
> Fourscore and upward,
> Not an hour more nor less; and to deal plainly,
> I fear I am not in my perfect mind.   (4.6.53–6)

Unless this is meant to be a Rip Van Winkle delusion, eighty-plus is a huge age. Among British monarchs only Victoria (1819–1901) and George III (1738–1820) can rival Lear's span. The age is remarkable. Even more remarkable is this senior royal's phenomenal vigour. If we care to calculate, he must have been engendering offspring well into his sixties (hoping always for a son, presumably). Lear's three daughters are eligibly young and the youngest—Cordelia—is conventionally played as scarcely more than a teenager. His queen (who must have been fifty years younger to be sufficiently fertile) was obviously less durable than her indefatigable mate.

In his brief retirement King Lear hunts (the boar, presumably) and 'debauches' himself with his retinue of an evening. It is when he is just returned from the hunt that an exasperated Goneril resolves to bring matters to a head. He is, she complains, treating her house like 'a riotous inn . . . more like a tavern or a brothel | Than a graced palace.' Act your 'age' she tells him. And make less noise. Were Goneril a less nasty piece of work, we might well have some sympathy. Lear must be the royal guest from hell. If the King and his 'disordered rabble' had been less impossible, would his daughter have allowed him to crawl unburdened towards death, as he initially proposed?

Even at his advanced age and debilitated by exposure on the heath, Lear can still rouse himself to strangle the 'slave' who was hanging Cordelia (hangmen are traditionally burly customers). And then, to cap it all, Shakespeare lays on Lear the heaviest (literally) burden of any tragic hero. It forms a central strand in Ronald Harwood's 1980 play *The Dresser* in which the Donald Wolfit character is forever looking for a leading lady anorexic enough for him to carry in his arms at the end of the play.

The problem revolves around the dread stage instruction: '*Enter King Lear with Queen Cordelia in his arms*'. What this entails (the ability to bench-press 150 pounds of, literally, dead weight) has put off any number of actors, in their late maturity, from playing the part. To posterity's gain, after his late-life prostate operation, Olivier (aged 76) found it more convenient to do *King Lear* on film, in 1983. It was, as the actor reported, the right time of life ('When you get to my age, you *are* Lear in every nerve of your body').[2] But a stage performance of the part was beyond him.

The age Shakespeare ascribes to Lear is very strange. As strange, that is, as if Queen Elizabeth II were to hold her throne until 2015 (long, incidentally, may she reign!), then were to abdicate in order to spend more time on the hunting field and at London cocktail parties, keeping King Charles III and Lady Camilla awake all hours by roistering late a' nights with her equerries and ladies-in-waiting.

According to Holinshed 'Leir the sonne of Baldud was admitted ruler over the Britaines in the yeare of the world 3105, at what time Joas reigned in Juda.' By the chronicler's strange almanac, this means about 100 BC. It may therefore be that the play is set so long ago, if not in the giant age before the flood, that Methuselan laws operate. This is perhaps the intended implication in Edgar's last words:

> The oldest hath borne most: We that are young
> Shall never see so much, nor live so long.   (5.3.301–2)

Holinshed has 'Leir' reach 'great yeres' before giving over the succession of the kingdom. But, as Kenneth Muir notes, neither this Leir nor the anonymous author of 'The True Chronicle History of King Leir' makes their king as remarkably old as Shakespeare's hero; 'nor is he [so old] in any of Shakespeare's sources.'[3] Without that awkward line in the fourth act about 'Fourscore and upward' most audiences would, I think, picture Lear as a conventional 65-year-old retiree, receiving the royal equivalent of a gold watch before going off to enjoy his golden years.

It is possible to rationalize away Lear's eighty-plus years, but only by jumping to a conclusion that Shakespeare does not sanction. We may surmise that Lear's wits are so disordered when he wakes to find himself bound on his wheel of fire that he forgets how old he is. Feeling incredibly ancient he comes up with the age he feels himself to be. 'My God, I feel a hundred years old' one sometimes mutters on waking with a bad hangover or the flu. So too Lear may add a score or two of winters to his proper count. But if this were the case one would expect some such correction as Ophelia gives 'mad' Hamlet in the play scene when he says his father has only been a month dead. 'No, my Lord, not so old by many a year,' Cordelia might tenderly object, 'you are scarce three-score and may, God willing, see half as many again.'

An opposite problem arises with Juliet. In the source—Brooke's *Romeus and Juliet*—the heroine is 16. This seems about right for the quality of Juliet's mind and utterance as Shakespeare conceives them. She has some womanly speeches to deliver and yet there remains something of the 'green girl' about her. None the less, Shakespeare not only made his Juliet 13, going on 14, he insisted that the audience should be uncomfortably aware of the fact. Her pubescent juvenility is stressed, early on in the play's action, in Act 1, scene 3 ('Lammas Eve' is 31 July):

CAPULET'S WIFE This is the matter—Nurse, give leave a while.
  We must talk in secret.—Nurse, come back again.

I have remembered me, thou's hear our counsel.
Thou knowest my daughter's of a pretty age.
NURSE Faith, I can tell her age unto an hour.
CAPULET'S WIFE She's not fourteen.
NURSE I'll lay fourteen of my teeth—and yet, to my teen be it spoken, I
  have but four,—she's not fourteen. How long is it now to Lammastide?
CAPULET'S WIFE A fortnight and odd days.
NURSE Even or odd, of all days in the year
  Come Lammas Eve at night shall she be fourteen.

(1.3.8–19)

For good measure we are informed that the Nurse lost *her* maidenhead at the age of 12. Her daughter Susan died and she became
Juliet's wet-nurse. This makes her 26. Juliet's Nurse is, of course,
invariably played as middle-aged. Not least because her gums are as
toothless as those of her luckless little Susan (one notes, in passing,
that Juliet has only been weaned eleven years, by the nurse's reckoning of the earthquake; this means that Juliet must have been nursed
for two to three years—extraordinarily long by modern standards of
childrearing).

There are other problems arising from Juliet's being 13. Her
mother, Lady Capulet, is made to say:

> By my count
> I was your mother much upon these years
> That you are now a maid.   (1.3.73–5)

What this means, we must deduce, is that she bore Juliet when she
too was 13 which means that she was impregnated as early as 12
years. Juliet is, apparently, Lady Capulet's only child. She must be
25 years old or so—younger, that is, than many actresses who play
Juliet.[4] Her husband, who has (as one of his kinsmen confirms),
given up masking 'By'r Lady, thirty years', must be, as Furness
hazards, 'at least threescore'.[5] A much-loved nineteenth-century
study of Shakespeare, by Mary Cowden Clarke, speculated fancifully
about 'The Girlhood of Shakespeare's Heroines' (1852). What girlhood, one wonders, can the girls of Verona have had; brides, widows,
and corpses before their fourteenth birthday?[6] Some three decades
after Cowden Clarke wrote her book, in 1885, the journalist W. T.
Stead 'purchased' a 13-year-old girl from her mother for what
he pretended were sexual purposes. He was imprisoned for his

pains. But Stead's crusading publicity led to the Criminal Law Amendment Act and the raising of the age of consent from 13 to 16.

It complicates one's reactions that Juliet is one of the few heroines ('maids') that Shakespeare shows us in a patently post-coital state. And very happy she is during the dawn scene after her marriage night:

> Wilt thou be gone? It is not yet near day.
> It was the nightingale, and not the lark,
> That pierced the fear-full hollow of thine ear.   (3.5.1–3)

It is not just ears that have been pierced, we may deduce. Juliet, we may calculate, has lost her maidenhead at Lolita's age—and with much of Ms Dolores Haze's zest. She is that goodly thing, as Margaret archly puts it in *Much Ado about Nothing*, 'a maid and stuffed'. A child and abused, by modern law. If, as appears from his skills with the sword, Romeo is in his late teens (and old enough to be banished) he is less lover than child molester. In a contemporary court of law he would receive a longer sentence for what he does to Juliet than for what he does to Tybalt.

But, of course, Juliet is never presented as a 13-year-old (in our conception of what that age means) in stage productions. Ironically *Romeo and Juliet* is a favourite text with schools—often schools elsewhere heavily exercised to discourage teen sex and the socioeducational problems that come with it. Franco Zeffirelli, when he filmed the play in 1968, whipped up some useful publicity by casting a 15-year-old, Olivia Hussey, as Juliet. But even he, at the height of the swinging decade, did not dare make her 13. In the 1997 Leonardo Di Caprio-starring film *Shakespeare's Romeo + Juliet*, the heroine Claire Danes (born in 1979) is, to the eye, around 18. The script drops all precise references to Juliet's years, merely letting the audience know she is 'a pretty age'. In the 1961 film of *West Side Story*, a busty Natalie Wood looks her age, 24.

It is clear that by making Juliet so young and reminding us so precisely of the fact, Shakespeare is aiming at an effect here. But what effect and why? Why not follow the source and make her fifteen-plus, like Miranda (who will, we expect, be 16 by the time of her marriage to Ferdinand), or 16 like Perdita? It is feebly speculative to suggest (as some ingenious commentators have) that the boy who played Juliet at the Globe was unusually young. It remains a mote to trouble the audience's eye, and Shakespeare clearly intended it to do so.

Juliet's uncomfortable childishness has typically forced those responsible for staging Shakespeare into Orwellian doublethink, as with Harley Granville-Barker:

The first thing to mark about Juliet, for everything else depends on it, is that she is, to our thinking [in 1930], a child. Whether she is Shakespeare's fourteen or Brooke's sixteen makes little difference; she is meant to be just about as young as she can be ... A Juliet must have both the look and the spirit of a girl of from fourteen to sixteen, and any further sophistication—or, worse, a mature assumption of innocence—will be the part's ruin. One must not compare her, either, to the modern girl approaching independence, knowing enough to think she knows more, ready to disbelieve half she is told. Life to Juliet, as she glimpsed it around her, was half jungle in its savagery, half fairy tale; and its rarer gifts were fever to the blood. A most precocious young woman from our point of view, no doubt; but the narrower and intenser life of her time ripened emotion early.[7]

Perversely, Granville-Barker insists, against the textual fact, that Shakespeare makes Juliet by the calendar 14, and in the play's action 16. She is, however, as he simply cannot bring himself to say, 13 when she goes to her bridal bed. The action of the play climaxes some two weeks before her birthday. On the Wednesday morning (some three days after the play's start), when she is to marry Paris, she is—instead—found dead. Should she have gone through with the charade and bigamously married her official fiancé, he would doubtless have killed the little baggage himself when he discovered her hymen broken. In Verona, as Shakespeare's audience would have thought, the bloodstained sheets would have had to be outside the bedchamber window after the bridal night. And, if not one kind of blood, it would have to be another. One does not know what the postmortem investigations were, but it is safe to assume there will be no virgin crants for Juliet Capulet / Montague.

Granville-Barker's nervousness is understandable, given the fact that he was writing in the 1930s. The most popular guidebook of the time, Norman Haire's *Encyclopaedia of Sexual Knowledge*, notes that 'Normally, menstruation occurs regularly throughout the period during which a woman is sexually mature, that is usually from about the fourteenth to the forty-ninth year'.[8] It may be that Juliet (or that Italian girls generally) are 'unusual' in this respect. But that is a thicket in which Granville-Barker most certainly does not want to get entangled (does she have breasts yet? Pubic hair?). The girl *must* be nudged forward a year to her decent fourteenth year.

J.S.

What's in a name? Why does Juliet confuse 'Montague' with 'Romeo'?

—

The most famous line in *Romeo and Juliet* is also, it appears, the play's most illogical line. In Act 2, scene 2, Juliet, on her balcony, says: 'O Romeo, Romeo, wherefore art thou Romeo?' Her question is hallowed by long usage; it is familiar to many people who have never read the play; it has even been declaimed by Frank Bruno, the former boxing champion, wearing drag in a parody shown on British television screens. Scholarly editors generally regard the line as unexceptionable, accepting it without emendation. (Typically, Brian Gibbons' Arden edition of 1980 renders it without comment.) Yet it seems obviously wrong. Juliet is saying, in effect, 'O, why do you have to bear the name "Romeo"?' Her anguish, however, is evidently caused not by the fact that his Christian name is Romeo but by the fact that his surname is Montague (or Mountague, as the earliest texts have it): for that surname declares that he belongs to the very family with which her own family, the Capulets, has long been at feud. What she should say is, manifestly, 'O Romeo Montague, wherefore art thou "Montague"?'

This reading is supported not only by the broad context of the play but by the immediate context. In the lines which follow immediately, she says:

> Deny thy father and refuse thy name,
> Or if thou wilt not, be but sworn my love,
> And I'll no longer be a Capulet . . .
> 'Tis but thy name that is my enemy.
> Thou art thyself, though not a Montague.
> What's Montague? It is nor hand, nor foot,
> Nor arm, nor face, nor any other part
> Belonging to a man. O, be some other name!
>
> (2.1.76–8, 80–4)

Given that it is the name 'Montague' rather than the name 'Romeo' that is the cause of concern, one might suspect that there is some textual corruption in Juliet's original question; but the early texts scarcely waver in their rendering of the now-famous line. The First Quarto gives 'Ah *Romeo, Romeo*, wherefore art thou *Romeo?*'; the Folio gives 'O *Romeo, Romeo*, wherefore art thou *Romeo?*' So there is no textual warrant for editors to make the line logical, and the usage has become cemented by tradition.[1]

We might explain the matter by imputing immense subtlety to Shakespeare's characterization of Juliet at that point. We could postulate that she has been accorded a proleptic error, that is to say, an error psychologically justified by the fact that she finds the name 'Romeo' particularly fascinating and is anticipating—being subconsciously preoccupied by—the larger matter that will emerge a few lines on:

> What's in a name? That which we call a rose
> By any other word would smell as sweet.
> So Romeo would, were he not Romeo called,
> Retain that dear perfection which he owes
> Without that title. Romeo, doff thy name,
> And for thy name—which is no part of thee—
> Take all myself.
>
> (lines 85–91)

The larger matter is not the feud; it is the ancient philosophical problem of the relationship between words and their referents.

You can see how important this problem might seem. In the twentieth century various literary theorists seized with enthusiasm on a finding that they attributed to Ferdinand de Saussure's *Course in General Linguistics*:[2] the arbitrary nature of the linguistic sign. To theorists with left-wing sympathies, this notion seemed to have quite revolutionary implications. If the relationship between language and referents were arbitrary, and if it is through language that we apprehend reality, then changes in language could change the world. Catherine Belsey, in *Critical Practice*, said that 'the sign is in an important sense arbitrary'; 'ideology is inscribed in ordinary language'; 'it is in language that the ideology inscribed in language can be changed'.[3] Terence Hawkes, too, claimed (in *Structuralism and Semiotics*) that the arbitrariness of language could mean 'that reality remains genuinely ours to make and remake as we please'.[4] Jacques Lacan even declared: 'It is the world of words that creates the world

of things.'[5] It became fashionable to speak not of the linguistic con-
struing of aspects of reality but of the linguistic 'construction'
of them (as in 'constructions of identity', 'constructions of
masculinity'). Well, the *Course in General Linguistics* which bears the
name of Ferdinand de Saussure proves, on close examination, to
have been written not by Saussure at all, but by a team of students
(pooling old lecture-notes) and two editors. In an appropriate irony,
Ferdinand de Saussure became famous for a work which he never
saw and which, according to those editors, he 'probably would not
have authorised'.[6] Saussure's enthusiastic followers neglected the
fact that the book was repeating an ancient and rather obvious
finding: Aristotle's *Organon* had recognized the conventionality of
language; so had St Thomas Aquinas; so had Rabelais's Gargantua,
who declares: 'Utterances are meaningful not by their nature, but by
choice.'[7] The theorists who saw revolutionary possibilities in the
Course in General Linguistics had not read it carefully, for that book
offered the conservative doctrine that, though language is conventional, those conventions become fixed once they have been
accepted by a linguistic community: then 'the sign is unchangeable'.

In any case, as we have seen, the ancient notion of the apparent
arbitrariness of the relationship between words and referents was
vividly rendered by Shakespeare's Juliet. Furthermore, any belief
that language has primacy over objects is sensibly challenged by her
reflections.[8] What matters to her is the distinctive individual; the
name that the individual bears is surely irrelevant, she reflects. And
this larger matter, at the stage when it was impending but not yet
explicitly formulated, has apparently inflected in advance her
phrasing of the problem of love for a member of the rival family. In
the manner of a Freudian slip, the linguistic problem has been
anticipated in the illogical formulation of the political problem.
Hence, 'wherefore art thou Romeo?'

To the sceptic who doubts Shakespeare's ability to incorporate
subconscious thought-processes into a characterization, there are
various responses. One might cite, for example, various speeches by
Hamlet. The soliloquy beginning 'How all occasions do inform
against me' (in Act 4, scene 4)[9] is particularly replete for this purpose. In that soliloquy he is reproaching himself for not being as
prompt to act as are Fortinbras and his warriors, who are going to
fight the Poles. Ostensibly, Hamlet is reflecting, 'I must hasten to

action (to kill Claudius), instead of meditating and procrastinating';
but repeatedly his imagery, phrasing, and very grammar imply a
subconscious sense that Fortinbras and his men are rather stupid
and that the way of reflection may be wiser. Here are just two of
numerous apposite details:

> Rightly to be great
> Is not to stir without great argument,
> But greatly to find quarrel in a straw
> When honour's at the stake.

Ostensibly, what he is saying is: 'To be truly great, one should not
need a grand justification for action, but should be able, when honour is at stake, to find a pretext for a great quarrel in a mere straw (as
these warriors do).' But if you look closely at the grammar, you find
there's a missing 'not'. To support the intended meaning, he should
utter the words 'Is *not* not to stir without great argument'. His
grammatical lapse lets through the covert thought—that it may be
greater to require a grand justification after all. Later in those quoted
lines, the reference to the mere 'straw' might again imply inner
misgivings about such men of martial 'honour' as Fortinbras. Consider the related imagery when Hamlet purports to praise Fortinbras
for risking everything 'Even for an egg-shell'. Fortinbras's soldiers
are prepared to fight and die for a plot of land 'Which is not tomb
enough and continent | To hide the slain'—not large enough to
provide a burial-ground for the fallen.

Nevertheless, satisfactory though the evidence may be for postu-
lating a Shakespeare who could invest Juliet with a subconscious
mind, there is an alternative and more comprehensive explanation of
her initial invocation of the name Romeo rather than Montague. The
prolepsis, the curious anticipation, may well be Shakespeare's rather
than hers; or, rather, what the character's words express is a preoccupation of the author's with the oddity of the relationship
between names and objects, the preoccupation which emerges so
strongly at 'What's in a name?' In *Romeo and Juliet* as a whole, we
see Shakespeare's fascination with the following problem: are names
arbitrary, or are they informative about an individual, perhaps
expressive of an individual, even shaping the character; even, perhaps, integral with the character? Juliet's name is arbitrary in the
sense that she could have been given a different one, but it is apt and

informative because (as we learn from the Nurse) she was born in July, and has been given a name which commemorates that month. As for Romeo, he bears an Italian name which, in the late Middle Ages, meant specifically 'pilgrim (or palmer) going to Rome', and later was applied to any pilgrim going to the Holy Land.[10] John Florio's Italian–English dictionary of 1598 defines the word thus: '*a roamer, a wanderer, a palmer*'.[11] When Romeo first meets Juliet, their exchange of dialogue, in a justly famed example of symbolic form, constitutes a perfect love-sonnet: fourteen lines of iambic pentameter with an intricate rhyme-scheme. Their words chime in the concluding rhyming couplet which is the cue for their first kiss. The lovers then embark on a second sonnet, but this one is interrupted by the Nurse—an interruption which perhaps, if Shakespeare is being particularly clever, portends the rapid termination of their love-relationship. Juliet does not know Romeo's name, but he is revealing it in coded form, probably through his costume (while his upper face is concealed by a half-mask, his visor,[12] he may be wearing the palmer's gown and bearing the pilgrim's palm-branch), and certainly through his imagery, which she deftly adopts. He begins:

> If I profane with my unworthiest hand
>   This holy shrine, the gentler sin is this:
> My lips, two blushing pilgrims, ready stand
>   To smooth that rough touch with a tender kiss.

She responds:

> Good pilgrim, you do wrong your hand too much,
>   Which mannerly devotion shows in this.
> For saints have hands that pilgrims' hand do touch,
>   And palm to palm is holy palmers' kiss.

>   (1.5.92–9)

Pilgrims, pilgrim, pilgrims, palmers ... This wittily flirtatious exchange embodies a repeated subtle play on Romeo's name—even though Juliet may not yet have decoded it. Furthermore, its imagery is part of the exaltation of sexuality: the long romantic revolution in which Shakespeare participated. When courtly lovers such as Romeo addressed their ladies as saints or even goddesses, and when heroines such as Juliet addressed their wooers as pilgrims or deities (Romeo is 'the god of [her] idolatry'); when the goal of aspiration became not an infinity of otherworldly bliss in the heaven promised by theologians but the infinity of love which mortal lovers promised each other here on earth ('Heaven is here | Where Juliet lies'); then a slow revolution was taking place. The language of religion was being captured and redirected to express a newly exalted conception of human individuality and sexual mutuality. Of course, it's typical of the paradoxes of *Romeo and Juliet* that alongside the enhancive definition of sexual love, that definition implicit in the rapturous speech of the lovers themselves, there runs, in sardonic counterpoint, a reductive definition (sexual love is basically a matter of carnal lust) which is implicit in the bawdry of the Nurse, Mercutio, Sampson, and Gregory. Again, on a large scale, the question is asked: do names represent or misrepresent? Is the language of romantic love a falsification of the carnal, or is the language of bawdry a debasement of what, potentially, is tantamount to a religious experience? And when we reflect on the names of individuals, do they falsify, shape, or proclaim the characters of those who bear them? Is Benvolio benevolent because he is living up to his name? Is Tybalt cat-like because he bears the name of the Prince of Cats? (In the Baz Luhrmann film, he hissed furiously on emerging, irate, from his car.) And, centuries later, did Maurice Micklewhite, having changed his name to Michael Caine (which, apart from being conveniently brief, recalls a sword-wielding saint and a fratricidal sinner), prove the arbitrariness of nomenclature or its power to influence readings of, and expressions of, character? Or, more seriously, when Joseph Vissarionovich Dzhugashvili became Joseph Stalin ('Man of Steel'), did that falsify his character, or express his inner nature, or help to shape him into the ruthless dictator that he became?

In *1 Henry IV*, the impetuous Harry Percy, who gains the apt nickname Hotspur, lives and dies for honour. In the same play, it is the cynical Falstaff who remarks: 'What is honour? A word. What is in that word honour? . . . Air.' Hotspur is a valiant warrior; Falstaff is a cowardly rogue. This might seem to imply Shakespeare's verdict on Falstaff's cynical nominalism. Falstaff, of course, would point out that Hotspur dies, while Falstaff lives. In *Romeo and Juliet*, the name 'Montague' is lethal, for the feud between Montagues and Capulets (a feud 'born of an airy word') brings about the tragic dénouement;

but lethal too, in a sense, is the name 'Romeo', for it is love as 'devout religion', desire regarded as a pilgrimage to a saint, romantic love given sacrificially religious force, which also brings Romeo to his death. Perhaps that is another reason why editors have left inviolate the echoing name in the line 'O Romeo, Romeo, wherefore art thou Romeo?' Politically, Juliet may have been illogical; but, symbolically, her logic was impeccable.

C.W.

Lady Macbeth: feint or faint?

———

One of the more interesting, if piddling, of Bradley's notes is entitled: 'Did Lady Macbeth Really Faint?' It relates to the aftermath of Duncan's death in Macbeth's castle. The sequence of events is intricate and tumultuous. Having negotiated the castle's defective porterage, Macduff arrives to wait on his monarch at 'timely' dawn, as he has been summoned to do.[1] They intend to make an early start on their progress south. He goes to the royal chamber as arranged and discovers—'horror, horror, horror'—that the King has been murdered.

Following the uproar of Macduff's shouting, Macbeth is apprised of the terrible news and—as master of the castle—goes with 'young' Lennox (a character dubiously in and out of the know) to the blood-spattered bedchamber. In the meanwhile a night-gowned Lady Macbeth, who has been brought in by the hubbub, utters her thoughtless ejaculation, 'What, in our house?', only to be rebuked by a suddenly suspicious Banquo with his 'Too cruel, anywhere'.

Macbeth returns with Lennox and, with uncharacteristic circumlocution, confesses that the grooms (Duncan's personal bodyguard) whom they found 'all badged with blood' have been slaughtered. 'O yet I do repent me of my fury,' Macbeth says, 'that *I* did kill them.' The pronoun is significant, indicating that Lennox did not participate but (presumably) watched as his master went round the room, serially cutting the throats of the sleeping men, not shriving time allowed.

'Wherefore did you so?' Macduff sharply asks. It is a pertinent question. Time enough to kill the murderers after they have confessed (the execution—on penalty of treason—will be much less swift and merciful than quietus by Macbeth's bodkin). In response to Macduff's awkward question Macbeth launches on a long and rhetorically overblown speech:

> Who can be wise, amazed, temperate and furious,
> Loyal and neutral, in a moment? No man . . .
>
> (2.3.110–11)

'Here lay Duncan,' he says—pointing at an imaginary corpse and thus avoiding eye-contact with his interlocutors, who may be supposed at this stage to be looking at him very closely. There follows an extravagant conceit about Duncan's 'silver skin laced with his golden blood'. It is the feeblest description of the bodily fluid in this famously sanguinary play.[2] The longer Macbeth talks, the hollower his explanations ring. Interrupting this burbling flow of over-protestation—which, we may suppose, is going down badly—Lady Macbeth suddenly cries out: 'Help me hence, ho!' and faints.

Macbeth studiously ignores his collapsed wife, although both Macduff and Banquo are alarmed. They order the servants to 'Look to the lady.' That is now where everybody is looking. The lady is duly carried out, still insensible. After this disturbance Macduff does not continue his line of suspicious cross-examination. Macbeth is off the hook.

'Did Lady Macbeth really faint, or does she pretend?' Bradley asks.[3] Interpretation of the words on the page can be angled either way. Lady Macbeth is still at this stage the ferociously unsexed woman who should 'bring forth men-children only' (how many daughters does she have?). It was she, we recall, who drugged the grooms' possets and took the daggers ('infirm of purpose'). She it was who gilded their faces, daggers, and their bedclothes with Duncan's blood—setting up the cover story.

It might well be worryingly evident to her that Macbeth's wordy apology for his summary execution of the sleeping grooms is going down badly. One guesses that the pair have been wrong-footed. They may not have anticipated that Macduff would be the first person in the King's bedchamber. They cannot be absolutely certain that he has not had some talk with one of the drowsy grooms.

Even if all is going to plan, some diversionary action is called for before her husband draws too much attention to what is the weakest link in their plot. Why, that is, should the grooms kill Duncan, then hang around so conveniently at the scene of their crime? 'Drunkenness' is not a satisfactory explanation. Scotsmen do terrible things when drunk, as any Saturday night in Sauchiehall Street or Leith Walk witnesses. But rarely do they lie down in the city thoroughfares to enjoy a good night's sleep alongside the luckless victims of their battery. The alternative suggestion, immediately put out by the

Macbeths, that the grooms have been 'suborned' by Malcolm and Donalbain is, if anything, even less convincing. One would hardly recruit contract killers known to have a weakness for the bottle and a tendency—literally—to go to sleep on the job.

Macduff's probing at the weak places in the Macbeths' plot is dangerous and could quickly become calamitous. As in *Lucky Jim* (where the hero, Jim Dixon, arranges to have a friend faint in the audience to get him off the lecture-stand if things should begin to look sticky), Lady Macbeth's swoon could be a pre-arranged ruse by the guilty pair. Or it could be a happy improvisation on her part.

On the other hand, one could argue that a vein of sensitivity in Lady (soon to be Queen) Macbeth is opening up and this is the first physical sign of it. An unexpected queasiness emerged with the confession, that she could have performed the murder herself, 'Had he not resembled my father as he slept' (one pictures her going, knife in hand, into the chamber, hesitating, then turning back—or perhaps even fainting as she saw the paternal resemblance).

Lady Macbeth is already, we may suspect, showing early signs of the phobia about blood which will climax in the horrible line 'Here's the smell of the blood still'. The public faint reminds us that she is not just a schemer, but a woman. This, we may think, is the crucial moment of interchange at which she becomes ever more conscience-ridden and the previously tender Macbeth ever more ruthless.

If we follow this line, there is a telling prolepsis in her husband's reaction. Macbeth, as has been said, wholly ignores her faint. Assuming he did not know it was coming, his indifference (more so given Macduff's and Banquo's gentlemanly concern) is strangely callous. It prefigures in little his grotesquely unfeeling response to the news of his wife's death, years later (as we may assume). There is a cry within. Seyton enters to tell Macbeth 'The Queen, my lord, is dead'. Instead of going to her, Macbeth merely notes 'She should have died hereafter' (which cynics might read as, 'we all have to go sometime'). He does not even go inside to look at her body. It seems that he never knows *how* she died, nor apparently does he care—he does not even inquire of Seyton on the matter (did he, horrible thought, arrange to have her done away with himself?).

How *does* Queen Macbeth die? By her own hand, we have to suppose. In his final speech Malcolm refers in passing to the 'fiend-like Queen | Who, as 'tis thought, by self and violent hands | Took

off her life.' The fact that 'tis thought, not known, invites speculation. Attended by her women did she, like Portia, 'swallow fire'?
Did she clasp a Scottish adder to her bosom like Cleopatra? Did she
throw herself into some convenient muddy burn, under a willow, like
Ophelia? Did she poison herself like Gertrude? Did she starve herself to death, anorexic with guilt? Was she perhaps murdered by
command of Macduff, in revenge for his wife's killing? There are, as
Banquo's fate indicates, killers for hire in Scotland. Macbeth neither
knows nor cares. Instead of paying final respects to his partner, he
delivers himself of a supremely world-weary soliloquy and goes out
to his own dusty death, his harness on his back. This indifference
was anticipated, one may conjecture, by Macbeth's ignoring his wife
when she faints after Duncan's murder. Then strangers were left to
take care of her unconscious body. Strangers, again, will dispose of
that dead body.

As Bradley points out, it would strain the actress to project
genuineness or falsity in Lady Macbeth's faint, without melodramatic
exaggeration. Some mute business or an eye-signal could be
arranged, but it would not be sanctioned by anything in the text.
One has to weigh psychological probabilities. What, that is, seems
right, as one understands the characters of the principals. Judgements
will be necessarily subjective but, on balance, Lady Macbeth's swoon
seems more likely genuine than feigned to me.

                                                            J.S.

Hamlet's knock-knees

There are other enigmatic moments in Shakespearian tragedy in which we can invoke Bradley's 'pretend or real?' query. Hamlet, for example, as he is described by an 'affrighted' Ophelia to her father. The Prince, she reports, has come to her chamber where she was sewing:

> with his doublet all unbraced,
> No hat upon his head, his stockings fouled,
> Ungartered and down-gyvèd to his ankle,
> Pale as his shirt, his knees knocking each other . . .
> (2.1.79–82)

The dutiful Ophelia goes on to describe how Hamlet took her by the wrist, with his hand over his brow, and 'falls to such perusal of my face | As he would draw it'. It's a beautifully evocative vignette. Then, as she reports, he wordlessly left her chamber.

It's a long speech and more memorable than most of what Ophelia says, at least while she has her wits about her. Vivid as it is, this episode bears strikingly little relation to the Hamlet we know, in the immediately preceding or succeeding scenes—the 'knocking knees' are particularly hard to integrate.

It has been supposed by some scholars that this apparition (together with the abysmally artificial lover's letter 'to the celestial, and my soul's idol, the most beautified Ophelia') is a calculated ruse on Hamlet's part. It is a strategically florid display of his 'antic disposition' which will, he knows, get back to Polonius, who will jump to the conclusion, 'mad for thy love', thus throwing up a useful smokescreen.

On the other hand, it may be asked (and Polonius would certainly get round to asking) what is the libidinous young rascal doing in Ophelia's chamber in the first place? She is, it would seem, unattended. Laertes' fears about her laying open her 'chaste trea-sure' to the young prince's 'unmastered importunity' would seem to be well founded. A less candid daughter than Ophelia might well be prudently reticent about her gentleman callers. More so a maiden with a father as strict on such matters (and as dirty-minded) as Polonius.

Harold Jenkins, in his edition of the play, notes tetchily that this scene has provoked 'much perplexity and groundless inferences.'[1] Some of these inferences return interpretation to the play's primitive sources in which the Ur-Hamlet (Amleth—which apparently means 'witless' in some Gothic tongue) is given to clownish antics of a knee-knocking kind.[2] In this analysis the scene is of archaeological interest only, a fragment of undigested source gristle.

On his part, Jenkins sees the episode romantically as 'Hamlet's despairing farewell to Ophelia, and emblematically to his hopes of love and marriage'. Philip Edwards similarly sees the scene as 'a silent ritual of divorce'.[3] This is how it was played by Olivier in the 1948 film in an inset dumbshow, and by Mel Gibson in the Zeffirelli movie in 1991. Actors (screen idols, to boot) of this calibre are unwilling to come on like George Formby, the greatest knee-knocker the screen has ever known (Buster Keaton is runner up, I think).

But if Jenkins's interpretation is right, another letter to Ophelia, stating the matter plainly ('Ophelia, farewell, forgive me, Hamlet') would have been kinder and more effective. Or why not tell the lady to her face that their relationship is over? There is no continuity in Hamlet's manner between this scene and his later treatment of her, which is politely cool and callously dismissive by turns.

And what, if one accepts the 'romantic' Jenkins/Olivier/Gibson–Zeffirelli interpretation, has made a farewell necessary? When, that is, did Hamlet actually pay court to Ophelia? Surely not during the period of his mourning for his father's recent death (the lover's letter, with its fantastic conceits, would have been horribly inappropriate at that juncture).

If, on the other hand, the courtship dates from the period before the King's murder and Gertrude's remarriage another crop of difficulties springs up. Notably the problem which looms large for Bradley: 'Where was Hamlet at the Time of his Father's Death?' If we assume that the Prince has had a long enough relationship with Ophelia to warrant the kind of portentous 'farewell' that Jenkins envisages, he must have been at Elsinore when Old Hamlet died (a short two months ago) and for some time before.

As Bradley notes, we are twice told that Hamlet has 'of late' been seeking the society of Ophelia. And yet, Claudius's remarks about his wanting to return *back* to Wittenberg would argue against his having been at Elsinore for longer than a normal vacation. He has, it is usually assumed, broken off his studies to come back for his father's funeral.

Not to get lost in that thicket of antecedent events, from which it is impossible to emerge in any orderly state, we may close the issue by reconsidering those knees. It is impossible, I think, to imagine Hamlet as we know him having his knees knock. Hatless, yes; muddy socks round the ankles, yes; pallor, yes; knocking knees, no. A man who can face down a ghost, commit murder, and not have his pulse-rate go up a single beat will not turn to jelly for love. In their discussion of this scene, romantically inclined critics simply ignore this uncomfortable detail (although whole articles have been written about his holding Ophelia at arm's length, as if he would draw her). The knocking knees are too embarrassingly clownish. If we do weigh it with the other evidence, the conclusion is, I think, inescapable. Hamlet's performance is deliberately over the top. He is 'feigning', putting on an act.

J.S.

Does Cleopatra really care about her 'petty things'?

━━━━

Our third 'real or pretend?' conundrum is taken from *Anthony and Cleopatra*. After Anthony dies, by his own hand, Cleopatra becomes Caesar's captive. She has already been informed by the mysteriously infatuated Dolabella that her imperious captor is not to be trusted. Despite his honeyed words, he intends to take her back to Rome, to augment his triumph, by leading her in chains behind his chariot. There 'Some squeaking Cleopatra' will 'boy my greatness | I'th'posture of a whore'—a fate not to be thought of (an in-joke since, as scholars remind us, Cleopatra was played by a boy on the Jacobean stage).[1]

Cleopatra and Octavius have a stilted meeting in which he (unconvincingly) reassures her as to his *bona fides*, backing up his kind words with the brutal threat that he will 'put your children | To . . . destruction' if she follows 'Anthony's course' with a Roman death.[2] As Caesar makes to leave, Cleopatra quite gratuitously hands him a scroll (some stage directions describe it as a 'paper'). It is, she explains, a 'brief of money, plate, and jewels' that she is possessed of—'not petty things admitted' ('just the valuables,' that is; some editions emend to 'omitted', which would mean 'everything, down to the last ear-ring'). The Queen then calls in Seleucus (a eunuch, we gather), whom we have not encountered earlier. The scene is set in the 'Monument'—a logical place for the treasure and its keepers to be in time of invasion.

Seleucus is, it transpires, the royal treasurer. Cleopatra (again without any prompting or urging) tells Caesar:

> Let him speak, my lord,
> Upon his peril, that I have reserved
> To myself nothing. Speak the truth, Seleucus.
> (5.2.142–4)

Seleucus, in some embarrassment apparently, takes his mistress at her word. He tells Caesar that Cleopatra has kept back, 'Enough to purchase what [she has] made known.' Fury erupts when Cleopatra hears this 'treachery'.

On his part, Caesar is amused and—man of the world that he is—'approves' his prisoner's shrewdness. 'Caesar's no merchant', he reassures her. The amount of treasure she has reserved—whether 'petty' or gross—means nothing to a Roman emperor. Cleopatra meanwhile, as she did earlier with the luckless messenger who informed her of Anthony's marriage to Octavia, flies at Seleucus's face with her nails. It's a very impressive display of wrath.

When she finally recovers her equanimity, Cleopatra reflects much along the same lines as did Anthony, when authority melted from him: 'Must I be unfolded | With one that I have bred?' Who, that is, can trust servants, fair-weather friends that such underlings are? But why, it may be asked, does Cleopatra care about her 'immoment toys'? She has by now apprehended her fate and the choice that faces her. She is not fooled by Caesar's reassurances ('He words me, girls'). Either she will be paraded in triumph through Rome, with all the 'boying' humiliation that she graphically describes to Charmian, or she must choose one of her 'easy ways to die'. With this second option in mind she has already arranged for the asp to be delivered by the clown in the basket of figs. Whatever happens, treasure can be of no use to her whatsoever. Nor to her children, since Caesar has promised that they will follow her into the grave.

In a marginal note to his translation of Plutarch's *Lives* (Shakespeare's primary source), North comments 'Cleopatra finely deceiveth Caesar as though she desired to live.' J. Dover Wilson, in his 1950 Cambridge edition, is the editor who has invested most heavily in this clue. 'Shakespeare never neglects anything in North he can turn to dramatic use,' Dover Wilson observes, and the dramatist would never 'overlook a first-rate hint like this'.[3] The Seleucus episode is manifestly 'a put-up job', or, to echo North, 'a fine deceit'—that is, a smokescreen behind which Cleopatra can stage her last act undisturbed. She goes through this charade, that is, to induce Caesar to lower his guard—or, more precisely, to take away his guards (which he has prudently posted on what modern prisons call 'a suicide watch').

This, though logical, seems rather too pat. What Cleopatra,

through Seleucus, offers Caesar is 'her books', as they are called in modern business establishments. She has, of course, a second set of books, in which her true transactions and properties are recorded. Cooking the books, so as to deceive the accountants which Caesar will surely have brought in his train, is not something that can be quickly done.

Egypt and its queen are fabulously wealthy—they rival Rome itself. Inventories of national wealth take time to put together. Nor has Cleopatra had much time, what with naval defeats and the death of Anthony (even if she were a conscientious monarch, which—as Shakespeare portrays her—she is not). She is a wealthy queen of a fabulously wealthy country. The 'brief' of her belongings will not be a simple document, nor all that brief. One assumes, therefore, that she and Seleucus had this schedule made up for some time, for just such a deception (Dover Wilson goes so far as to suggest 'that, like a good strategist, she did a little rehearsing with Seleucus'[4]). Like the proprietor of a crooked firm, she has a second set of books for the auditors. She may even have toyed with the idea of using these cooked books to deceive Anthony, should the need arise.

What we may assume is that in producing the 'brief' Cleopatra was, as North astutely notes, intending to deceive Caesar; 'feigning' a desire to survive at any cost. She had seduced other Caesars, and may well have thought that she had at least a long-shot chance of winning over even this cold-blooded fish of a Roman. (To this end, as we may think, Shakespeare ignores Plutarch's record that she was a physical wreck, and less than her usual seductive self, at this stage of her career. In Act 5, as the play presents her, Cleopatra is every inch a queen.)

We may also assume, however, that the treachery of Seleucus is unexpected and provokes an uncontrollable and wholly irrational bout of rage, as did the messenger's earlier news about Anthony's marriage, which it parallels. Even on the brink of eternity, Cleopatra is Cleopatra. That is to say, this scene shows the two, irreconcilable, sides of Cleopatra's 'infinite variety'. Her deep cunning and love of deceits; and her passionate high temper, which she cannot control, even in this extremity of her life.

If, then, Lady Macbeth's faint is 'real', and Hamlet's knee-knocking madness in Ophelia's chamber 'pretend', Cleopatra's little performance for Caesar is a mixture of the two. She pretends that she wants to live, and really loses her temper with Seleucus. The secondary point arises, can the actress—however skilful—project these ambiguous motivations of Cleopatra's?

J.S.

Othello's magical handkerchief

The handkerchief, of course, is crucial to the plot of *Othello*. In Act 3, scene 3, there's a point at which matters are going badly for Iago. He seemed to be succeeding in persuading Othello of Desdemona's infidelity, but then the Moor has shrewd doubts.

> Villain, be sure thou prove my love a whore.
> Be sure of it. Give me the ocular proof,
> Or, by the worth of mine eternal soul,
> Thou hadst been better have been born a dog,
> Than answer my waked wrath.[1]   (3.3.364–7)

All hinges on 'ocular proof'; and that will be the handkerchief, that fine silk handkerchief embroidered with strawberries which was Desdemona's first love-token from the Moor. In the next scene, Othello proceeds to ask Desdemona for it, and she, of course, can't find it, since Emilia (at Iago's behest) has already stolen the thing and passed it to Iago. Othello then explains to Desdemona why losing that item is such a big mistake (in the event, a fatal mistake):

> That's a fault. That handkerchief
> Did an Egyptian to my mother give.
> She was a charmer, and could almost read
> The thoughts of people. She told her, while she kept it
> 'Twould make her amiable, and subdue my father
> Entirely to her love; but if she lost it,
> Or made a gift of it, my father's eye
> Should hold her loathèd, and his spirits should hunt
> After new fancies. She, dying, gave it me,
> And bid me, when my fate would have me wived,
> To give it her. I did so, and take heed on't.
> Make it a darling, like your precious eye.
> To lose't or give't away were such perdition
> As nothing else could match.

DESDEMONA   Is't possible?
OTHELLO 'Tis true. There's magic in the web of it.
    A sibyl that had numbered in the world
    The sun to course two hundred compasses
    In her prophetic fury sewed the work.
    The worms were hallowed that did breed the silk,
    And it was dyed in mummy, which the skilful
    Conserved of maidens' hearts.
DESDEMONA   I'faith, is't true?   (3.4.55–75)

'Is't true?', indeed. As early as 1673 the indispensably irreverent Thomas Rymer, who is to political correctness as Hugh Hefner is to feminism, had summed up 'the Moral . . . of this Fable':

First, This may be a caution to all Maidens of Quality how, without their Parents consent, they run away with Blackamoors . . .
Secondly, This may be a warning to all good Wives, that they look well to their Linnen.
Thirdly, This may be a lesson to Husbands, that before their Jealousie be Tragical, the proofs may be Mathematical.

Regarding the 'ocular proof', the handkerchief, Rymer was gleefully indignant:

So much ado, so much stress, so much passion and repetition about an Handkerchief! Why was not this call'd the *Tragedy of the Handkerchief*? . . . Had it been *Desdemona*'s Garter, the Sagacious Moor might have smelt a Rat: but the Handkerchief is so remote a trifle, no Booby, on this side *Mauritania*, cou'd make any consequence from it . . .[2]

But the whole point of Othello's account of the handkerchief's history is that this is no trifle at all, but a magical and symbolic object of immense significance. His account of it is harmonious with the accounts that Othello has previously given of his career: a nobleman born, who has travelled much of the world, has been sold into slavery, has escaped, has fought in numerous battles and seen strange sights: indeed, he has travelled on the frontiers between history and legend, the factual and the mythical, encountering, for instance,

    The Anthropophagi, and men whose heads
    Do grow beneath their shoulders. These things to hear
    Would Desdemona seriously incline . . .

                                        (1.3.143–5)

That phrase 'seriously incline' bears consideration. Perhaps he means merely that she was an attentive listener, inclining towards him so as not to miss a word. Perhaps he means that the sympathetic Desdemona believed his true story, as others might not have done. Or is he saying to other mature men of the Venetian Council, 'She was not only charmingly sympathetic, she also took seriously my yarns, which, as you may guess, sometimes laid on the exotic colour with a trowel'?

That the story of the handkerchief is harmonious with Othello's projected image of Othello the exotic warrior does not guarantee its truth. If it is true, it is very odd. The 'Egyptian charmer' or enchantress who gave it to Othello's mother said (we are informed) that it works by subduing Othello's father entirely to her love; but if the handkerchief were lost or given away, the father would loathe his wife and seek 'new fancies'. If Othello believes this, then his marriage to Desdemona is based on appalling premisses: the belief that magic has to be invoked to maintain the bond of love, and that if such an easily losable item as an embroidered handkerchief goes astray, the result will be hatred from the husband and multiple acts of adultery by him. Never did a marriage have so flimsy yet so coercive a foundation. This marriage, it now appears, is based not on mutual attraction but on supernatural compulsion. What we learn here contrasts dramatically with the poignant, if worryingly egoistic, account that Othello gave the Council:

> She loved me for the dangers I had passed,
> And I loved her that she did pity them.
> This only is the witchcraft I have used.
>
> (1.3.166–8)

Well, if he's right about the handkerchief, he's wrong about not using witchcraft. (The handkerchief was his first love-token for Desdemona, so she would have received it prior to the wedding which preceded Othello's appearance before the Venetian Council. Of course he told her 'she should ever keep it'.) There's something else that's troublesome about Othello's description. It sounds like a huckster's preposterously hyperbolic account of his wares. No ordinary seamstress made this item. A 200-year-old Sibyl, no less, sewed it; and she did it in a 'prophetic fury': in a mystical zeal of prophetic inspiration. Traditionally, the Sibyl sat on a tripod over a hole in the earth and, in an intoxicating cloud of smoke, uttered in a trance the Delphic words inspired by Apollo. (William Golding's *The Double Tongue* provides a vivid re-enactment; the Sibyl suffers a paroxysm of coughing and swoons.) The point here is that a sibyl in a prophetic fury would be about as capable of the delicate embroidery of those strawberries on the handkerchief as a stoned heroin addict would be of completing the *Times* crossword puzzle. And Othello doesn't stop there. The very worms that provided the silk were 'hallowed': sanctified, holy. And then it was dyed 'in mummy', in a necromantic liquor or mystic goo, which 'the skilful', fore-runners of today's genetic engineers, have manufactured from the hearts of dead virgins.

He's protesting too much. Take away the iambic pentameters, the lyrical eloquence and the exotic vistas, and the basis of his account is familiar. Any parent who has thrown into the dustbin a child's battered toy, any wife who has given her husband's old anorak to Oxfam, will recognize that basis. The child will soon say something like: 'Throw it *out*? What *for*? You're *gross*! It was *special*! It was *magic*!' And the husband may well say something like: 'Why *that* one? There were years of life left in it; very comfortable it was. That was the anorak I wore to the Cup Final; my *lucky* anorak!' And as for Othello's rhetoric: it might bring to mind Barabas in Marlowe's *Jew of Malta* as he poisons the nuns' rice pudding, invoking

> the blood of Hydra, Lerna's bane,
> The juice of hebon, and Cocytus' breath,
> And all the poison of the Stygian pool

—a hyperbolic flight on which his henchman, Ithamore, aptly comments, 'Was ever pot of rice-porridge so sauced?' Or we might recall Volpone as mountebank, vending

the powder that made Venus a goddess (given her by Apollo), that kept her perpetually young, cleared her wrinkles, firmed her gums, filled her skin, coloured her hair.

Then there's that later mountebank and pioneering homoeopathist, Physician Vilbert in *Jude the Obscure*, who sells Arabella 'a love-philtre, such as was used by the Ancients with great effect', which is 'a distillation of the juices of doves' hearts' ('It took nearly a hundred hearts to produce that small bottle full').

In short, as Desdemona's vacillating response begins to confirm

Othello's belief in Iago's slander, Othello accentuates the value of the missing handkerchief. He literally provides a mystifying myth of it, and, in characteristic style, it's an exotically Othello-aggrandizing myth which invokes far-off places and times. But if we seek proof that, like many another myth, it's a power-seeker's lie, Othello himself provides it. How did Emilia have an opportunity to steal the handkerchief? Because Desdemona, seeking rather optimistically to heal Othello's supposed headache with it, had let it fall.

> OTHELLO   Your napkin is too little.
> *He puts the napkin from him. It drops.*
> Let it alone. Come, I'll go in with you.   (3.3.291-2)

Here, after she has vainly held the too-small handkerchief to his head, he sees that it falls; and, instead of saying, 'That handkerchief's the mainstay of our love! | Quick, take it up!', or some such pentametrical speech recognizing its importance, his response is merely 'Let it alone', much as if one should say, 'Don't bother with it; there's plenty more where that came from.'[3] And in the final scene, there's further proof that Othello lied about it. He says:

> It was a handkerchief, an antique token
> My father gave my mother   (5.2.223-4)

—a flat contradiction of the claim that originally it was given to his mother by the Egyptian enchantress.

The matter has further implications. A bit of semiotics is useful here. Semiotics is the study of signs or signifying systems. Umberto Eco, a leading semiotician (and author of *The Name of the Rose*), has helpfully explained that 'Semiotics is in principle the discipline studying anything that can be used in order to lie'.[4] Perhaps Eco was prompted by the Caliban who said: 'You taught me language, and my profit on't | Is I know how to curse'. Possibly recalling Polonius's 'By indirections find directions out', another expert, Michael Riffaterre in *The Semiotics of Poetry*, adds: 'Poetry expresses concepts and things by indirection. To put it simply, a poem says one thing and means another.'[5] A particular poem might at first seem to be about a desert landscape (that's the 'heuristic' reading, in this theorist's jargon); but as we read on we find details that don't fit; there are tell-tale anomalies. Therefore we re-read, seeking a comprehensive explanation, and find that the poem is really about the plight of a lonely poet who feels that he is not communicating, so he imagines he is in a wilderness or desert. That is the 'hermeneutic' reading. Many poems, this argument suggests, make us perform what Riffaterre calls 'the praxis of the transformation': we move from the superficial 'meaning' to the more comprehensive and contrasting 'significance'. You can see how this semiotic stuff applies to *Othello*.

The play *Othello* is replete with lying, ironic, or reversed signs. The famous example is Iago: he's called 'honest' so many times that it's as though he has the lying tag, 'Honest Iago', inscribed across his jerkin like a bookie's T-shirt slogan. Then there's Othello, the black man who is the victim of racial stereotyping by Iago, Roderigo, and Brabantio, the stereotype being that of the black man as 'an erring barbarian', lustful and bestial. Othello confounds this stereotype by his inital self-presentation as civilized, composed, maturely moderate, and possibly even beyond the claims of sexual desire ('the young affects | In me defunct'). Again, the storm at sea proves to be an ironic sign. Normally in a Shakespearian tragedy, we'd associate a storm with burgeoning evil. The storm in *Othello*, however, is surprisingly benign: it allows Othello and Desdemona to emerge unscathed, while scattering the Turks who had threatened Cyprus. Later, when the play's catastrophe develops, Othello says: 'Methinks it should be now a huge eclipse | Of sun and moon'. In another Shakespearian tragedy, there might indeed be such cosmic accompaniments of disorder (Gloucester in *Lear* cites 'These late eclipses in the sun and moon'); but in this play of ironic signs, no cosmic disorder echoes the human cataclysm.

Samuel Taylor Coleridge long ago remarked that in Iago we see 'the motive-hunting of motiveless malignity'.[6] Certainly the play makes a conspicuous mystery of Iago's motives. Near the end, Othello says:

> Will you, I pray, demand that demi-devil
> Why he hath thus ensnared my soul and body?

And Iago's response is obdurate:

> Demand me nothing. What you know, you know.
> From this time forth I never will speak word.
>
> (5.2.307–10)

Iago has previously given so many explicit motives for his conduct that they almost seem to cancel each other out. He has cited thwarted ambition and hatred of Cassio, Othello's (and Cassio's) supposed adulterous union with Emilia, lust for Desdemona (as retaliation), and the desire to turn Desdemona's virtue into pitch. The last of these rings true. Iago proves to be an ingenious semiotician with a taste for cynical paradoxes. He has a radically cynical outlook, but enough intelligence to see that the world offers evidence to refute a cynic. Evidence, for example, that love is not merely a sect or scion of lust and can triumph over prejudice. So Iago seeks to transform the world around him so that it buttresses cynicism instead of refuting it; and he is expert in Riffaterre's 'praxis of the transformation'. When Iago's at work, it's a paradoxical praxis; aptly, he swears 'by Janus', the two-faced god. Roderigo is a spineless specimen of humanity; so Iago will manipulate and goad him to the point at which the puny Roderigo finds himself attacking Cassio. Cassio is an 'arithmetician' and a courtly gentleman skilled in social graces (he 'hath a daily beauty in his life'), so Iago converts him, for a while, into a drunken sot. *In vino veritas?* Desdemona is conspicuously loving and chaste; so Iago will 'turn her virtue into pitch', converting her, in her husband's imagination, into a lecherous whore. Othello is initially a living refutation of the racist association of blackness with barbarism; but Iago's scheme reduces Othello to the point at which, barbarically, he cries 'I will chop her into messes!'

Iago's plotting draws much of its energy from racial prejudice: his own, and that of others. One of the cruellest ironies in the play is that Desdemona's transcendence of racial prejudice is used by the paradox-loving Iago as evidence that she is likely to betray Othello. In Act 3, scene 3, to tempt Othello into distrust of Desdemona, Iago's method is to give Othello a lesson in semiotics. He argues on these lines: 'Look, Othello, your reading of Desdemona as virtuous and faithful is superficial; it's merely heuristic. You should note this oddity, this tell-tale anomaly: in marrying you, she betrayed her father and the white race in general. Then you will be led to the hermeneutic significance, which is that she is radically treacherous; so she is capable of betraying her husband (particularly as it's unnatural for white to marry black).'[7]

Shakespeare thus criticizes Riffaterre's *Semiotics of Poetry* 370 years before that book appeared. He does so by suggesting that sometimes the heuristic reading may be the true reading, while the hermeneutic reading may offer only an illusory significance. Alas,

Othello proves too receptive a pupil of Iago, and soon believes a fatally hermeneutic interpretation of a lost handkerchief. Worse; Othello lies to Desdemona to persuade her that the handkerchief is only to the untutored eye a pretty gift; to the tutored eye it is replete with such symbolic force that its loss is tantamount to the destruction of the marriage. But there is truth in his lie. Othello does indeed regard the handkerchief as the object which makes or breaks the marriage. When, his folly exposed, Othello prepares to kill himself, he chooses a finely appropriate way. Perhaps he's spinning a yarn again (the effect of self-regarding self-dramatization here is characteristic), but consider the dramatic body-language:

> And say besides that in Aleppo once,
> Where a malignant and a turbaned Turk
> Beat a Venetian and traduced the state,
> I took by th' throat the circumcisèd dog
> And smote him thus.
>> *He stabs himself.* (5.2.361–5)

To fit the sense of the lines, the final stabbing gesture should ideally resemble a large zigzag or curve, going away from Othello towards the imagined Turk and then back again into Othello: a most conspicuous reversed sign.[8] The stabbing of the imagined enemy of the Venetian state becomes the stabbing of the defender of the state. The image of the exotic foe, and the contrasting image of the defender of European civilization, suddenly merge. Aggressor and defender, Muslim and Christian, 'barbarian' and Venetian, fuse in death, impaled on one blade. Othello has signalled to sympathetic sign-readers one large cause of his downfall: the cultural and psychological insecurity of a man caught between two worlds and belonging fully to neither; a self crushed between conflicting stereotypes; an immigrant whose understandable insecurity has been both heightened and goaded into myth-powered violence by racial prejudice and the belief that signs are true when they are false (Iago's 'honesty') yet false when they are true (Desdemona's avowals of love). After his death we see the ultimate reversed sign of the play: a double bed which has become a bier: a bed for newlyweds which has become the resting-place of two corpses, one black, one white, united in death.

Heart-warming hermeneutics. The concluding sound-track, if sentimental, could play 'Ebony and Ivory'; if acerbic, Broonzy's

'Black, Brown and White'. Either way, for those who want a critical introduction to modern literary theory and an insight into Iago's motives, *Othello* is a play which teaches semiotics while offering warnings against the seductions of semiotics. Alternatively, it may be a warning 'to all good Wives' not to look to their linen but to look out for the male chauvinism endemic in male-dominated professions, the army being one. Emilia puts it more militantly:

> But I do think it is their husbands' faults
> If wives do fall. Say that they slack their duties,
> And pour our treasures into foreign laps,
> Or else break out in peevish jealousies,
> Throwing restraint upon us; or say they strike us,
> Or scant our former having in despite:
> Why, we have galls; and though we have some grace,
> Yet have we some revenge.

$$(4.3.85\text{--}92)$$

And her revenge, of course, will be the betrayal of Iago, whose reading of his wife had been—as Riffaterre might say—merely but fatally heuristic. Serves the semiotic ensign right.

C.W.

How much time did Richard waste?

The deposed King Richard's 'I wasted time, and now doth time waste me' is one of his memorable 'Hamletisings'. Posterity has liked to see him in the role of poet-king—like the melancholy prince, a superb actor incapable of action. Less metaphysically, chronology is hard to make sense of in this play. The solve-all convenience of Shakespearian 'double time' does not offer its usual help since—on a practical level—the principal actors in *Richard II* must, if they are to follow cues in the text, play their characters as both young and old without any clear signals as to where the switch should happen.

On its narrative surface *Richard II* has the railroad straightforwardness of the *Chronicle* (Holinshed's second edition) from which it was so clearly derived. The play also shows, in the highest degree, Shakespeare's (early) habit of compressing historical time—with all its divagations and delays—into the capsular dimensions of dramatic time, with its two-and-a-bit hours frame. The question, bluntly, is whether the dramatist does this well or badly.

The action opens with the staged trial by combat of Mowbray and Bolingbroke in front of the King and 'Old John of Gaunt', Bolingbroke's anguished and (as we are repeatedly informed by epithet) ancient parent. It is clear that Bolingbroke at this juncture is conceived as a hot, impetuous *young* man. He describes himself as 'lusty, young, and cheerly drawing breath' and talks lightly of his 'youthful spirit' before doing battle. We see him in the mind's eye (and often on the stage) as bursting to explosion point with energy—a young hothead.

Young Bolingbroke is eventually banished for six years (as the sentence is commuted by the king, after the father's intercession). Much depressed in spirit Gaunt says that he will bring his exiled son on his way to France: 'Had I thy *youth* and cause,' he says, 'I would not stay.' Nor does Bolingbroke stay even apparently long enough to pack his bag (there is no suggestion, incidentally, that he has any baggage in the form of wife and children to accompany him). He bids England's ground farewell and is off.

The dislikeable Green, a creature of the King's, also sees the young hothead on his way safely out of the country. On hearing that Bolingbroke is embarked, Richard declares that (having disposed of this upstart at home) he must deal with threats abroad, 'the rebels that stand out in Ireland.' He needs money to supply a punitive expedition. Happily (for Richard), Gaunt has been so overcome by the ordeal of just this minute saying goodbye to his son that he has promptly fallen into terminal illness. He has been taken to Ely House in London.

> The lining of his coffers shall make coats
> To deck our soldiers for these Irish wars   (1.4.60–1)

Richard gleefully declares. There have been no intervals of time in this sequence of events.

On his deathbed, John of Gaunt decides to do the state one last service. He will counsel the 'unstaid youth' of the King. 'Deal mildly with his youth,' the chronically cautious (and self-seeking) Duke of York advises, 'For young hot colts, being reined, do rage the more.' The implication, clearly, is that Richard is barely more than an adolescent, in the 'youth of primy nature,' like Hamlet—or compact with 'youthful spirit', like Bolingbroke.

Gaunt's deathbed counselling goes down very badly. The old man dies a few minutes later. Richard promptly seizes 'his plate, his goods, his money, and his lands', despite York's feeble expostulations. 'Tomorrow next | We will for Ireland' Richard declares. And to his queen, he instructs, 'Be merry, for our time of stay is short.'

Time is indeed short. After the King has left the stage, for a last conjugal encounter with his queen, as we guess (given his current rush she need not expect much foreplay), Northumberland, Willoughby, and Ross remain on stage to chew things over. Northumberland reveals that he has received intelligence from France that Bolingbroke has, with other dissident noblemen, gathered a fleet of eight tall ships and three thousand men of war and is making for the English northern coast (where Lancaster's name is a potent rallying cry) with 'all due expedience'. Perhaps they have already touched land, Northumberland says:

> but that they stay
> The first departing of the King for Ireland. (2.1.291–2)

Even in the days of telephony, the internet, the Channel Tunnel, and the hovercraft this is very good going on Bolingbroke's part. As best we can calculate, he was exiled some twelve hours ago. He has (as we later discover) none the less learned of the King's theft of his inheritance, intercepted the monarch's military plans, recruited armies in France and England, and assembled a puissant naval task force—all on a day trip to France.

Bolingbroke, as we subsequently learn, arrives at Ravenspur, on the Yorkshire coast, at just about the time that Richard leaves for Ireland (the 'next day' as he earlier remarked, after Bolingbroke's exile). Bolingbroke will thus have arrived back practically before Gaunt's body is cold. He has, however, no time for funerals, obsequies, or even CPR-resuscitation. A full-blown rebellion is afoot. York vainly tries to dissuade Bolingbroke from his treacherous act, calling him a 'foolish boy', and ascribing the rashness to his 'hot youth'. He is evidently, at this point of the play, still a 'hot colt', just like Richard.

On his return, Bolingbroke complains that 'My father's goods are all distrained and sold.' Clearly, in the few hours before he left for Ireland, Richard has also been busy. Moving the House of Lancaster's family silver two hundred miles to London and auctioning it off (not to say drawing up the necessary legal instruments to do so) has been achieved in a day.

While the King is away in Ireland (a campaign which he apparently concludes in less than a fortnight) the Welsh forces loyal to the crown muster on the west coast to await his return. The Welshmen remain ten days before giving it up for a bad job and going home. Ten days, as Harold Wilson might have said, is a long time in the world of *Richard II*.

Richard returns to Harlech, to find himself powerless. 'O, call back yesterday,' Salisbury bemoans:

> bid time return,
> And thou shalt have twelve thousand fighting men.
> (3.2.65–6)

Even York, Richard discovers, has joined Bolingbroke. Still in the region, apparently a few hours later, Richard surrenders to his opponent, who has marched the four hundred miles from the northeast coast of Yorkshire to the west coast of Wales in nine days—a feat to rival Hannibal's crossing of the Alps. Richard instantly submits, and is taken off to London the next day, as best we can reckon. 'Cousin,' he tells Bolingbroke, 'I am too young to be your father, | Though you are old enough to be my heir' (as the notes tell us, both men were born in 1367 and, historically, 32 years old at this point).

In London, following the Bishop of Carlisle's vain protest, Richard promptly abdicates. In the poignant speeches accompanying the act he no longer talks of himself as young nor acts young:

> Alack the heavy day,
> That I have worn so many winters out
> And know not now what name to call myself! (4.1.248–50)

He talks of the 'wrinkles' on his face and examines them closely in the looking-glass which he orders to be brought him. He has, we apprehend, aged years in the last few days. It is less a mirror than Dorian Gray's portrait that he looks into.

Now an ex-king, Richard is conducted to the Tower and the ex-queen removes to France. Richard curses false Northumberland:

> thou ladder wherewithal
> The mounting Bolingbroke ascends my throne,
> The time shall not be many hours of age
> More than it is ere foul sin, gathering head,
> Shall break into corruption.   (5.1.55–9)

'Hours' is an interesting usage here. Months or years would be more usual. Counter-rebellions surely take more than 'hours' to come to fruition? Not in this play, apparently.

Immediately after Bolingbroke's accession to the throne as Henry IV there occurs the most perplexing scene in the play, as regards chronology. It would seem, by the dramaturgical clock, to be not that long since the play opened so vividly with the trial by combat at Coventry.[1] The King enters with sundry nobles (the setting is now Windsor):

> KING HENRY Can no man tell of my unthrifty son?
> 'Tis full three months since I did see him last.
> If any plague hang over us, 'tis he.
> I would to God, my lords, he might be found.
> Enquire at London 'mongst the taverns there,
> For there, they say, he daily doth frequent
> With unrestrainèd loose companions—

Even such, they say, as stand in narrow lanes
And beat our watch and rob our passengers—
Which he, young wanton and effeminate boy,
Takes on the point of honour to support
So dissolute a crew.   (5.3.1–12)

This is the 'foul sin' breaking into 'corruption' that Richard
prophesied would occur within 'hours'—and so it has. But there has
been no direct mention hitherto of Bolingbroke's having a wife.[2] It is
less than a month, by count of events and sequence (and only a year
or so by Holinshed time) since the beginning of the play. Young Hal
(where did he come from?) has evidently been hanging around in
London dives long enough to form bad habits (it is even three
months since his father has seen him). Hal has clearly reached the
age of indiscretion—he must be in his late teens, at least.[3] And
suddenly Bolingbroke, the young man of the early scenes, is in the
sere and yellow leaf. Shakespeare has had him vault into middle
years—it is rather as if one saw him, in Friar Bacon's visionary glass,
many years hence: 'Old Henry,' as his father (historically 58 years
old) was 'Old Gaunt'.

But it is not many years hence. Richard is still in Pomfret Castle,
smarting from the pain of his recent abdication. In his prison
solitude he soliloquizes beautifully on time's passing with a complex
web of horological imagery:

For now hath time made me his numb'ring clock.
My thoughts are minutes, and with sighs they jar
Their watches on unto mine eyes, the outward watch
Whereto my finger, like a dial's point,
Is pointing still in cleansing them from tears.
Now, sir, the sounds that tell what hour it is
Are clamorous groans that strike upon my heart,
Which is the bell. So sighs, and tears and groans
Show minutes, hours and times. But my time
Runs posting on in Bolingbroke's proud joy,
While I stand fooling here, his jack of the clock.

                              (5.5.50–60)

Again the emphasis is on 'minutes' and 'hours'. As with Bolingbroke,
the speaker seems no longer young although we cannot, within
the dimensions of the play, find the months and years that have
made him as old as we now take him to be. In the case of both the

principals, drastic alterations of character and physical appearance
are in order.

What was Shakespeare doing with chronology in *Richard II*? It is
sometimes suggested that at this relatively early stage of his evolution, in the mid-1590s, he had not yet mastered the narrative tech-
nique of managing large tracts of linear time.[4] His art was essentially
episodic, myopic, and (in this respect) simple. Where chronological
lines had to be drawn, for linking purposes, he kept them artificially
short.

Against this one notes as significant that Shakespeare seems
to know quite well what he is doing in the play. His handling of
chronology seems sophisticated rather than primitive. In the clock
conceit, for example, he plays on the idea of minutes and hours
—but not weeks, months, or years. He seems to have *wanted* to
contract the play so as to exclude large units of time. It was less
technical immaturity than a deliberate intention.

One can find something analogous in the four generations of *Star
Trek* (all of which have had to accommodate to time frames of
between 40 and 50 minutes). The *USS Enterprise* (like its successor-
craft) is on a fire-at-will mission through the cosmos, carrying *Pax
Americana* and the American Way to the furthermost edges of
the universe. The problem for the scriptwriters of the series is the
familiar one of *vita brevis*. It would take generations of Kirks and
Spocks, thousands of generations if one wanted to be literalistic, to
cover the distance the crew is supposed to cover in one mission or
one episode.

The solution is FTL (faster than light) travel—'warp speed' as it
is called in the series. This handy device shrinks space to nothing:
millions of light-years are traversed in the twinkling of an eye and
the press of a button on the *Enterprise* bridge. Theoretical physicists
I have spoken to have many different theories about their branch of
science. But all agree that 'FTL travel' is hogwash; the SF equivalent of the fairy-tale witch's broomstick. Yet, in space opera, the
banal business of lengthy space travel has to be got over somehow.
Some means of shrinking aeons into minutes has to be devised.
Another favourite device (as in the *Alien* series of movies) is suspended animation, deep sleep, over which the narrative flashes forward to the moment of waking; Ripley, discovered in her fetching
futuristic nightwear, yawns and we perceive that decades have

passed. Bring on the monsters. Like 'warp speed', suspended animation is a way of saving valuable on-screen narrative time, authenticity be hanged. It enables the writers to cut to the chase.

In *Richard II*, Shakespeare seems to have devised something similar; a kind of 'warp time'. Clearly intervals of years could have been introduced into the play (as they are, for example, explicitly in *A Winter's Tale* and implicitly in *Macbeth*). Elizabethan dramatists were not constrained by Aristotelian rules of unity (although in *The Tempest* Shakespeare virtuosically displayed his power to do so, when he cared). But in *Richard II* it would have interrupted the moods and fluidities which Shakespeare wished to create. As with SF, all that is required is that the audience understands the rules of the game, and plays along.

J.S.

Who killed Woodstock?

Richard II holds an ominous puzzle which recurs but remains murky.

When the play begins, King Richard presides over a scene of elaborate and bewildering accusation and counter-accusation. Bolingbroke and Mowbray accuse each other, vehemently and at length, of high treason. The nub of the matter seems to be culpability for the murder at Calais of Thomas Woodstock, Duke of Gloucester, the king's uncle. Bolingbroke says Mowbray murdered him. Mowbray, rather strangely, replies:

> I slew him not, but to my own disgrace
> Neglected my sworn duty in that case.[1] (1.1.133–4)

To whom, we wonder, did Mowbray swear his duty? Surely not Richard, who is presiding so confidently over this dispute? The king urges both men to 'Forget, forgive, conclude, and be agreed', which many readers or spectators may regard as an eminently sensible recommendation, given the bafflingly contradictory nature of the accusations. But the two noblemen decline to be reconciled, and are therefore told to prepare for trial by combat at Coventry upon Saint Lambert's Day.

The following scene, to those who are ignorant of the story of Woodstock's death, provides a shock. Woodstock's widow, the Duchess of Gloucester, has evidently been urging John of Gaunt to take action against her late husband's killers. Gaunt replies:

> Alas, the part I had in Gloucester's blood [i.e. the fact that
>   he was my brother]
> Doth more solicit me than your exclaims
> To stir against the butchers of his life.
> But since correction lieth in those hands
> Which made the fault that we cannot correct,
> Put we our quarrel to the will of heaven,
> Who, when they see the hours ripe on earth,
> Will rain hot vengeance on offenders' heads.   (1.2.1–8)

At the words 'correction lieth in those hands | Which made the fault', it becomes evident that the person responsible for the killing must be King Richard himself. Gaunt should be able to put before the king the matter of a nobleman's murder, but in this case the king is himself culpable; and a monarch should be judged not by a subject (that could imply treason) but by God in his own good time. Gaunt soon confirms this reading.

> God's is the quarrel; for God's substitute,
> His deputy anointed in his sight,
> Hath caused his death . . .   (lines 37–9)

This casts a retrospectively ironic light on the previous scene. Then, the king had seemed just and patient; now, we can see that he was being utterly duplicitous. The Duchess says she hopes that at the forthcoming combat, Bolingbroke's spear will 'enter butcher Mowbray's breast'. So it sounds as if Mowbray had killed Woodstock at the king's command. But this still leaves as a puzzle Mowbray's claim that he had 'neglected [his] sworn duty in that case'.

Scene 3 takes place at 'the lists at Coventry'. With much ceremony and formality, Bolingbroke and Mowbray prepare for their combat. Just as they are about to fight, the king intervenes to say that instead of permitting bloodshed, he is going to sentence them to exile. Bolingbroke receives a ten-year sentence, rapidly commuted to six years. Mowbray (who sounds particularly indignant) is exiled for life. So the matter is vetoed rather than resolved.

In scene 4, Richard discusses with his cronies, Bagot, Green, and Aumerle, the annoying popularity of Bolingbroke and the need to raise funds for the Irish war. 'We are enforced to farm our royal realm', says Richard. If 'farming the realm' (selling the rights of taxation to various wealthy subjects) won't work, the blank charter system will be used. (People will be required to prove their loyalty by signing blank cheques to the king, the king's officers inserting above the signatures the sums to be paid: a combination of blackmail and taxation, open to corrupt practices by the royal agents.) Then Richard, hearing that old John of Gaunt is mortally ill, says:

> Now put it, God, in the physician's mind
> To help him to his grave immediately.
> The lining of his coffers shall make coats

To deck our soldiers for these Irish wars.
Come, gentlemen, let's all go visit him.
Pray God we may make haste and come too late!

(1.4.58–63)

If, in Act 1, scene 1, the king had sounded regal, wise and just, then
by Act 1, scene 4, he appears scheming, crafty, perhaps irresponsible,
certainly cynical. He seems here to be inviting the nemesis which is
soon to befall him. Indeed, when he promptly cuts off Bolingbroke's
inheritance by seizing the wealth of the dead Gaunt, he is warned
that he is, in effect, cutting the ground from beneath his own
feet. Says York: 'for how art thou a king | But by fair sequence
and succession?' To seize the wealth which should be inherited by
Bolingbroke is to deny the principle of inheritance which has
brought Richard to the throne.

Bolingbroke returns early from exile, claiming that he seeks only
to regain his rightful inheritance. Gradually, however, he gains so
much power that he is clearly heading for the throne. Richard bitterly recognizes that he is faced with a successful rebellion. In Act 4,
scene 1, the setting is Westminster Hall. Bolingbroke presides over a
parliamentary assembly at which Richard will be obliged to abdicate.
But, remarkably, before Richard appears, a confusing quarrel breaks
out among those assembled. And what's the cause of the quarrel? Yet
again, culpability for the murder of Woodstock!

Bagot says Aumerle is guilty of the deed. Aumerle vehemently
denies it. Fitzwalter (or Fitzwater) says he heard Aumerle boast of
the killing. Percy supports Bagot and Fitzwalter. Surrey says Fitzwalter is lying. Confusion worse confounded, until Fitzwalter says
that the banished Mowbray can settle the matter, because Mowbray
had actually heard Aumerle say he had sent two men to kill Woodstock at Calais. Very well, says Bolingbroke, we'll recall Mowbray
from exile and establish the truth. But now Carlisle breaks the frustrating news that Mowbray has died in Venice. So Bolingbroke says
that the matter will be put in abeyance 'Till we assign you to your
days of trial'.

The trial will be overtaken by civil broils. Richard is deposed,
Bolingbroke becomes King Henry IV, and the broils begin. Aumerle
conspires against the new regime, is betrayed by his father, but
is pardoned by the new king. Fitzwalter, Northumberland, and
Harry Percy do sterling work against the rebels; Carlisle, one of the

leaders, is captured. But the civil war continues and will rumble on throughout the two plays to follow, *1* and *2 Henry IV.*

When you look back over *Richard II*, therefore, it seems that the spirit of the dead Woodstock has had as great an influence on events as the Ghost will have on the events of *Hamlet*. It's as if his blood is crying out for revenge and is stirring up strife. But who, exactly, is guilty of the shedding of his blood? Richard? Mowbray? Aumerle? Other people?

The anonymous play *Woodstock* gives some help. There's disagreement among scholars about whether this play did or did not precede Shakespeare's *Richard II*. I think it probably did; and, either way, it offers a usefully detailed view of the king's role in events. What *Woodstock* shows is a Richard who became infuriated by Woodstock's plain speaking: in particular, his justified denunciations of Richard's fecklessness, extravagance, and eagerness to let the realm be bled financially by Bushy, Bagot, Green, and Tresilian. Accordingly, Richard connived with his crooked advisers in a plan to kidnap Woodstock and have him shipped to Calais to be killed. Richard personally took part in the kidnapping. The unfortunate Duke was murdered at Calais. A complication is that after the kidnapping but before the death, Richard repented and countermanded his own order for Woodstock's murder, but too late. Another complication is that at Calais, according to this play, one Lapoole oversees the killing; the two men who actually bludgeon and stifle Woodstock are then themselves slain at Lapoole's orders. A complicated and murky business, therefore, needing more clarification.

A source definitely used by Shakespeare was Holinshed's *Chronicles*, which reports Bolingbroke's accusation that Thomas Mowbray, 'by his false suggestions and malicious counsell', 'hath caused [Woodstock] to die and to be murdered'.[2] Holinshed says that when Woodstock was at Calais, Mowbray procrastinated, being reluctant to kill him (so that explains 'neglected my sworn duty'); but Richard sent word that Mowbray would be killed himself if he didn't act quickly. So Mowbray called on Woodstock at midnight and 'caused his servants to cast featherbeds upon him, and so smoother [*sic*] him to death; or otherwise to strangle him with towels (as some write)'.[3] Mowbray was reported to have said that the servants were sent by Richard. ('Featherbeds' and 'towels'? To leave no conspicuous marks of violence; part of a literal and metaphorical cover-up operation.)

Modern historians vary in their accounts of the matter. One of them takes the view that in 1397 Woodstock was 'mysteriously murdered, no doubt at the king's instructions':

He was, it seems, suffocated at Calais, when under the charge of the Earl of Nottingham, the same Thomas Mowbray whose position had so often been interestingly ambiguous. Mowbray, in apparent recognition of his complicity, was then made Duke of Norfolk.[4]

'No doubt', 'it seems', 'apparent recognition': the tell-tale phrases show that even the modern historian isn't certain. Another twentieth-century account, confident of Richard's culpability, suggests that the intermediaries may have been Mowbray or the Earl of Rutland, employing an 'actual agent' of the crime:

The actual agent is supposed to have been either a man called Serle, who was tried and executed for treason under Henry IV, or a certain Halle, who put in a 'confession' which had a high market value at that date, in Henry IV's first parliament, but . . . there is no decisive answer to the question.[5]

The ambiguities and confusions of the matter in the original play linger on to the present. But the predominant modern view is that Richard bore ultimate responsibility for the murder, and this, at least, tallies with what was said in Holinshed and *Woodstock*. Probably, then, for many of the original spectators of Shakespeare's *Richard II*, the opening of the play would have displayed clearly the king's hypocrisy (in apparently trying to get to the bottom of the matter) and treachery (in sending into exile Mowbray, who had been involved with him in the murder-plot). As for the later accusation in the play, that made by Bagot and others against Aumerle, Holinshed provides a small measure of clarification, for the chronicler says that 'he was the man that, to fulfill [Richard's] mind, had set him in hand with all that was doone against the said duke [Gloucester]': in other words, Aumerle had aided and abetted, and perhaps even prompted, the king's desire to kill his uncle.[6]

What makes this tangled matter important can soon be set out. First, we see that Gloucester (from the grave, so to speak) is influencing and disturbing the political life both of Richard's reign and of Bolingbroke's. Secondly, Richard is punished for shedding his uncle's blood, for Richard in turn will die violently. 'Let heaven revenge', Gaunt had said; perhaps heaven does so. To kill a blood-relative is particularly heinous, for bloodshed within a family is a small-scale civil war which may symbolically portend a large-scale civil war; and that happens: the large-scale dissension burgeons. Thirdly, Aumerle's involvement against Woodstock makes sense of his later involvement in the conspiracy against Bolingbroke: in both cases, Aumerle is loyal to Richard. On discovering Aumerle's involvement in the plot, his father (the Duke of York) informs Bolingbroke; his mother, on the other hand, begs Bolingbroke to grant mercy to the son. Yet again, we see a divided family, even as the death of Woodstock had prompted division and wrangling amongst the noblemen. Curiously, the character and spirit of Woodstock live on. In the anonymous play, he was 'plain Thomas', the devout and bluntly spoken patriot prepared to denounce corrupt favourites of the king and to warn the king against irresponsible conduct (particularly in fee-farming the realm and using the blank charter taxation-system). In *Richard II*, it is Gaunt who inherits this role: he becomes in turn the patriotic plain-speaker whose death will be gleefully awaited by the king. What you wouldn't guess from Shakespeare's play is the degree of rivalry, in real life, between Gaunt and Gloucester. The latter had once hoped to gain vast estates by marriage, his bride's sister being destined to a nunnery; but, despite his opposition, Gaunt ('the best hated man in England') had arranged for that sister to be married to his own son, Bolingbroke, thus securing ample land. Another matter which Shakespeare doesn't mention is that in 1387, Gloucester had led the Lords Appellant, a band of powerful noblemen who had actually seized power from Richard for a while. Richard had been captured and virtually deposed.[7] In *Woodstock*, Gloucester is the ever-loyal patriot who will blame the king's cronies rather than the king himself; in reality, he was a power-seeker who had incurred the king's wrath and was to pay with his life for Richard's humiliation.

One of the most famous speeches in Shakespeare's works is Gaunt's on 'this sceptred isle':

> This royal throne of kings, this sceptred isle,
> This earth of majesty, this seat of Mars,
> This other Eden, demi-paradise . . .

He ends by invoking the memory of Gloucester:

My brother Gloucester, plain well-meaning soul—
Whom fair befall in heaven 'mongst happy souls—
May be a precedent and witness good
That thou [Richard] respect'st not spilling Edward's blood.

(2.1.40–3, 129–32)

The truth behind the patriotic rhetoric of Gloucester in *Woodstock* and Gaunt in *Richard II* is rather different. Both those magnates had been ruthlessly grasping in their time. When Gaunt had gained domination of Edward III's parliament in 1376–7, for example, heading a coalition containing 'corrupt household servants, courtiers and officials',[8] he had helped to undo much of the previous administration's good work against corruption; and the courageous speaker of the House of Commons was imprisoned. Again, when Woodstock and his allies in 1387 seized control and established the 'Merciless Parliament', as it was called, these were the consequences: 'The king's chief supporters were executed, exiled, imprisoned, or otherwise removed. Their accusers or "appellants" rewarded themselves and their friends profusely with money, honours, and appointments . . . '[9]

The ultimate responsibility for the death of Woodstock certainly lay with Richard; but, in such matters of ruthless power-politics, one of Richard's mentors was Woodstock himself. Shakespeare's play *Richard II* contains passages of lyrically devout patriotism which are lacking from Christopher Marlowe's earlier *Edward II*. Nevertheless, Marlowe, in depicting English political life of the fourteenth century as harsh, Machiavellian, and dominated by egoistic power-seekers, seems to have been closer to the truth. Marlowe was violently silenced at the age of 29. An ironic postscript to *Richard II* is famous: on 7 February 1601 a performance of the play was commissioned by the Earl of Essex's supporters as the clarion-call for a *coup d'état* against Elizabeth which proved abortive. *Plus ça change, plus c'est la même chose*; or, in Rochester's words,

> Birds feed on birds, beasts on each other prey,
> But savage man alone does man betray.[10]

C.W.

Hal and Francis: what's the issue?

———

'What's the issue?' is Poins's question to Hal in Act 2, scene 5, of *1 Henry IV*, after Hal has played a baffling trick on a waiter. The reader or spectator may share Poins's puzzlement; but there ought to be a good answer, because this is one of Shakespeare's most thoroughly wrought plays.

Generically, histories lack the prestige of tragedies. Yet *1 Henry IV* is more intelligent than most of Shakespeare's tragic dramas. By obvious criteria, it's one of the finest plays in the Shakespearian canon. It has a rich array of full characterizations: Prince Henry (Hal), Falstaff, Hotspur, Henry IV, Glendower; even such relatively minor figures as Douglas, Blunt, Worcester, Northumberland, Bardolph, and Poins have their distinctive voices. The action is well arranged: initially the contrasting scenes, court versus tavern, high politics versus low machinations; the worries of state at court and the comedy of the Boar's Head and Gadshill; and gradually the convergence of the great political adversaries—and of Falstaff—on the battlefield of Shrewsbury, with the culminating fight in which Hal slays Hotspur. Thematically the play is rich, too: for instance, the theme of 'expropriating the expropriator' links the great matter of the rebellion to the minor matter of the Gadshill robbery. Again, a network of comparisons co-ordinates the work. To take a few examples of the numerous comparisons: Henry IV initially compares Hal unfavourably with Hotspur, and wishes that in their infancy 'some night-tripping fairy' had exchanged the two Harrys (Prince Harry and Harry Percy, Hotspur). To tighten the comparative network, Shakespeare makes the two seem coevals, born at much the same time, whereas the real Hotspur was old enough to be Hal's father.[1] Then in Act 3, scene 2, King Henry complains that Hal now resembles Richard II in his days of folly before his downfall. In Act 5, scene 4, on the battlefield, Henry IV has many 'counterfeits': to confuse the enemy, numerous soldiers are disguised as the king; but when the rebel Douglas meets him, a quick feat of comparison reveals the truth:

> I fear thou art another counterfeit;
> And yet, in faith, thou bearest thee like a king.[2]   (5.4.34–5)

It's clearly a play in which every detail is meant to count. And yet it contains the puzzle of the apparently feeble practical joke at the expense of Francis. At the beginning of Act 2, scene 5, a scene set at the Boar's Head Tavern, Hal boasts to Poins of his familiarity with 'a leash of drawers', a group of young bar-men or waiters; one of them has given Hal a pennyworth of sugar. The Prince then proposes this practical joke:

> I prithee do thou stand in some by-room, while I question my puny drawer to what end he gave me the sugar; and do thou never leave calling 'Francis', that his tale to me may be nothing but 'Anon'.   (2.5.27–30)

Accordingly, Poins from an inner room repeatedly calls for Francis, while the Prince engages the young waiter in conversation that the lad (understandably) finds confusing. Here's how the practical joke goes:

PRINCE HENRY Come hither, Francis.

FRANCIS My lord?

PRINCE HENRY How long hast thou to serve, Francis?

FRANCIS Forsooth, five years, and as much as to—

POINS (*within*) Francis!

FRANCIS Anon, anon, sir.

PRINCE HENRY Five year! By'r lady, a long lease for the clinking of pewter. But Francis, darest thou be so valiant as to play the coward with thy indenture and show it a fair pair of heels and run from it?

FRANCIS O Lord, sir, I'll be sworn upon all the books in England, I could find in my heart—

POINS (*within*) Francis!

FRANCIS Anon, sir.

PRINCE HENRY How old art thou, Francis?

FRANCIS Let me see: about Michaelmas next I shall be—

POINS (*within*) Francis!

FRANCIS Anon, sir. Pray stay a little, my lord.

PRINCE HENRY Nay, but hark you, Francis: for the sugar thou gavest me, 'twas a pennyworth, was't not?

FRANCIS O Lord, I would it had been two!

PRINCE HENRY I will give thee for it a thousand pound. Ask me when thou wilt, and thou shalt have it.

POINS (*within*) Francis!

FRANCIS Anon, anon.

PRINCE HENRY Anon, Francis? No, Francis; but tomorrow, Francis, or, Francis, o' Thursday, or indeed, Francis, when thou wilt. But, Francis—

FRANCIS My lord?

PRINCE HENRY Wilt thou rob this leathern-jerkin, crystal-button, not-pated, agate-ring, puke-stocking, caddis-garter, smooth-tongue, Spanish-pouch—

FRANCIS O Lord, sir, who do you mean?

PRINCE HENRY Why then your brown bastard is your only drink; for look you, Francis, your white canvas doublet will sully. In Barbary, sir, it cannot come to so much.

FRANCIS What, sir?

POINS (*within*) Francis!

PRINCE HENRY Away, you rogue, dost thou not hear them call?
> *Here they both call him; the Drawer stands amazed, not knowing which way to go.*
> *Enter the Vintner.*

VINTNER What stand'st thou still and hear'st such a calling? Look to the guests within.   *Exit Francis.*

(lines 37–78)

The Prince, now rejoined by Poins, is jubilant; but Poins still doesn't understand the prank. He says:

But hark ye, what cunning match have you made with this jest of the drawer? Come, what's the issue?   (lines 87–9)

In other words: 'What have you been doing? What crafty game are you playing by means of this prank? Come on, tell me: what's the real point?' Hal's reply is oblique:

I am now of all humours that have showed themselves humours since the old days of Goodman Adam to the pupil age of this present twelve o'clock at midnight.   (lines 90–3)

G. L. Kittredge, a scholar who believed that there was '*no point*' in the prank, interpreted that reply as: 'I am in the mood to indulge any fancy that any man has ever had since the creation'.[3] If that interpretation is correct, Hal is side-stepping the question by expressing exuberant high spirits. We move nearer the answer a little later when Hal offers these reflections on Francis:

That ever this fellow should have fewer words than a parrot, and yet the

son of a woman! His industry is upstairs and downstairs, his eloquence the
parcel of a reckoning. I am not yet of Percy's mind, the Hotspur of the
north, he that kills me some six or seven dozen of Scots at a breakfast,
washes his hands, and says to his wife, 'Fie upon this quiet life, I want
work.' 'O my sweet Harry,' says she, 'how many hast thou killed today?'
'Give my roan horse a drench,' says he, and answers, 'Some fourteen,' an
hour after, 'a trifle, a trifle.' I prithee call in Falstaff. I'll play Percy, and
that damned brawn shall play Dame Mortimer his wife. 'Rivo!' says the
drunkard.   (lines 96–108)

It's a glorious passage. Its high spirits and fluent associations are
appropriate to someone whose mind is lubricated with drink. But it
implies one of several answers to Poins's question. An editor of the
Arden edition comments, on the reflections on Hotspur, 'This
change of subject is surprising.'⁴ But really there is no change of
subject. The Prince has been preoccupied by his looming confron-
tation with the rebel leader, Hotspur. As the King had compared the
two Harrys, so now Hal himself pursues the comparison. It has been
underlying his game with Francis. And what emerges is the following thought-process. Francis is a puny, limited kind of person. In
battle, Hotspur kills many readily, indeed casually. He's hardened to
it. But 'I am not yet of Percy's mind', reflects Hal, reasoning thus:
'Trivial though Francis is, I think it's more intelligent to concentrate
on manipulating people, as I have just manipulated Francis, than to
gain prowess through repeated acts of slaughter on the battlefield, as
Hotspur does. Hotspur may have the reputation of a hero, but he can
appear a slow-witted ruffian who values a horse above a human
being. The waiters here told me "when I am King of England I shall
command all the good lads in Eastcheap"; in the long term, my
astuteness will serve me better than Hotspur's naïve and impatient
valour serves him.' In *Henry V*, that belief will be vindicated.

Hal does a good job of mimicking Hotspur: he captures that bluff,
tough, impatient tone, that mess-room combination of swagger and
down-to-earthness. He knows that to understand a person's mode of
language is to gain a sense of power over that person; perhaps, by
comprehension one may gain the reality of power. At the opening of
the scene, the Prince was gloating because he had 'sounded the very
bass string of humility', becoming popular with the humblest of the
low, the waiters; and he had learned their language, mastered their
slang. Now he displays further mimicry, of Hotspur and 'Dame

Mortimer his wife'. He wants to extend the game of mimicry (that 'counterfeiting' which extends throughout the work), and says that there shall be play-acting in which he'll play Hotspur while Falstaff plays Hotspur's wife. In the event that play doesn't happen; what we do get is, first a performance in which Falstaff plays King Henry and Hal plays himself, and secondly a performance in which Falstaff plays Hal and Hal plays King Henry. What happens then is that Falstaff pleads for the Prince's continued friendship, while the Prince warns Falstaff that banishment is in store. This play-acting sequence is not only splendid comedy, through its mimicry and the extravagance of Falstaff's self-defence and the Prince's satiric accusations; it is also a fine way of maintaining consideration of issues of state—the cares of the King and the responsibilities that Hal must one day shoulder. It extends the theme of loyalty and betrayal, alongside the related theme of paying debts and keeping or breaking promises. And those concerns, too, had been implicit in the joke at Francis's expense.

Francis had been called from opposite directions at the same time. Poins, in the inner room, had summoned him, and Francis's duty was to serve him. But the Prince had called him and engaged him in conversation, and Francis naturally deferred to the Prince's importance and the possibility of gain. Hal's glee at Francis's expense is partly the glee of someone who sees a personal dilemma farcically expressed in someone else's action. For the Prince, too, is being pulled in two directions, by the responsibilities of politics and the pleasures of the tavern-world. Of course, Hal had said initially,

> I know you all, and will a while uphold
> The unyoked humour of your idleness.
> Yet herein will I imitate the sun,
> Who doth permit the base contagious clouds
> To smother up his beauty from the world,
> That, when he please again to be himself,
> Being wanted he may be more wondered at . . .
> (1.2.183–9)

Of course, he had explained that he was spending time with low companions so that eventually, at his apparent 'reformation', he would seem the more impressive. That was partly true, but also partly false. To first defile oneself with pitch is an odd way of making eventual cleanliness seem impressive.

We know that at the end of that play-acting scene with Falstaff, he has given Falstaff warning of eventual banishment. But the intricacy and intensity of that sequence in which Falstaff had pleaded for himself against Hal's half-playful and half-monitory arguments had shown the depth of the Prince's involvement with Falstaff's world. Indeed, the very relish and enthusiasm of Hal's involvement with the tavern-world had implied more than a Machiavellian exploitation of the situation for long-term purposes. Even as Machiavellianism, it creates more problems than it solves, for certainly the King is persuaded that Hal is not merely irresponsible but positively dangerous, a possible enemy. In seeing Francis caught between the two claims on his attention, Hal had objectified as farce what for himself was a deep-seated tension. If you doubt that the Prince could see the simple Francis as a psychologically symbolic counterpart to himself, look at what happens later, in 2 *Henry IV.* In that play, when Falstaff, at the same tavern, summons Francis, the waiter who steps forward is none other than the Prince (disguised in the serving lad's outfit worn by Francis and his fellows), with Poins at his side; both replying, as Francis had once haplessly replied, 'Anon, anon, sir.'[5]

In his dialogue with Francis, Hal is a tempter: he tempts Francis to break his indenture (his legally binding long-term contract of apprenticeship): an important document of allegiance. In return, he briefly hints, Francis will receive a fortune—the vast sum of a thousand pounds.[6] After all, Francis had given him a pennyworth of sugar. The Prince continues: 'Wilt thou rob this leathern-jerkin . . . Spanish-pouch?', i.e., 'Will you rob your master, the vintner?' The robbery might simply be the matter of breaking the indenture; it might be pilfering of more sugar; more likely, it means actual theft of some of the vintner's money—taking the takings. Francis is puzzled by the oblique identification of the vintner by his garb. (So, probably, is the modern reader, who will be grateful for editorial footnotes which explain that a Spanish-leather pouch was part of a vintner's outfit.)[7] At this point, however, the Prince seems to terminate the matter with his opaque comment:

Why then your brown bastard is your only drink; for look you, Francis, your white canvas doublet will sully. In Barbary, sir, it cannot come to so much.   (lines 70–2)

This comment is probably meant to sound opaque, as the Prince enjoys confusing Francis and prolonging his bewilderment. Hal has been drinking, in any case. But 'brown bastard' is a sweet Spanish wine: the *Oxford English Dictionary* cites a book of 1616: 'Bastards ... seems to me to be so called, because ... oftentimes adulterated and falsified with honey'. Sugar, too, was sold in taverns to sweeten wine: hence Francis's gift to Hal. So the first part of the Prince's response seems to imply: 'Keep your sugar; use it for the wines you serve here'. Implication: keep your job. This seems to be confirmed by the reference to the 'white canvas doublet'. Kittredge interpreted this as: 'If you rob your master, you'll become a fugitive. A white doublet like that you are wearing will not keep clean long'.[8] As for 'In Barbary, sir, it cannot come to so much': editors point out that Barbary (a vague term encompassing much of north Africa) was a noted sugar-growing area. So the sense then may be: 'If you go on the run, you may be a loser. Sugar may be worth something here; far abroad (where it comes from) it is worth far less. Stay at home.'

Perhaps. On a small scale we encounter what might be termed 'the *Hamlet* principle'. When writing at his best, Shakespeare is so intelligent, and is capable of such subtlety, that when in a given textual area the sense seems obscure or incomplete, interpreters strive to lighten the darkness and complete the incomplete. Here the Prince intends to be baffling; but there does seem to be the implicit sense that the bribe is being annulled. What is obvious is that the Prince relished the tempting of Francis: would this fellow betray his master in the hope of gain? The vintner has taken plenty of Hal's money (for Hal often pays Falstaff's bills as well as his own); perhaps the vintner can be robbed by the treachery of Francis. The underlying preoccupation makes very good sense. Hal moves in a world of multiple treachery; a world in which that theme of 'expropriating the expropriator' seems ubiquitous. Henry IV, when Bolingbroke, had broken his 'indenture', his sworn allegiance, to Richard II. Now, as King, he has to contend with 'rebels' who can be seen both as traitors to his crown and as loyalists to the lineage of Richard (for Richard's legitimate heirs were, first, Roger Mortimer, Earl of March, and, on Roger's death, his son Edmund).[9] In seeking power, the rebels can claim that they are following Bolingbroke's example and taking the crown from someone who had seized it by force. Hal has previously participated in a double act of 'expropriating the expropriator'.

Falstaff (aided by Gadshill and Bardolph) had robbed the king's exchequer at Gadshill; but in turn the disguised Prince and Poins had robbed Falstaff, and eventually that money will be repaid—with interest, we're told—to the exchequer by the Prince. The theme is maintained at the highest level of the plot. Hotspur has been busily amassing military honours, while Hal has apparently been wasting time. Hal's ingenious defence to the King is:

> Percy is but my factor, good my lord,
> To engross up glorious deeds on my behalf.   (3.2.147–8)

Over a long period of time, Hotspur gains many honours; but he's like an agent working for Hal, in the sense that Hal has only to kill Hotspur, and the honours accumulated by Hotspur are gained at a stroke by Hal. At the battle of Shrewsbury, the dying Hotspur is bitterly aware of this irony:

> I better brook the loss of brittle life
> Than those proud titles thou hast won of me;
> They wound my thoughts worse than thy sword my flesh.
> (5.4.77–9)

The theme of expropriating the expropriator is, characteristically of this play, sounded in a largely comic, partly sinister key when Falstaff takes up Hotspur's corpse and claims to have killed Hotspur himself. Hal seems to connive:

> PRINCE HENRY Come, bring your luggage nobly on your back.
> For my part, if a lie may do thee grace,
> I'll gild it with the happiest terms I have.
>
> (5.4.151–3)

Falstaff's opportunism is a deft way of getting Hotspur's body off-stage. But Hal's promise of lying connivance with Falstaff's claim to glory is evidently not kept (perhaps only Falstaff would expect it to be kept), and in *2 Henry IV* Hotspur's father is told that the 'swift wrath' of Hal has beaten down the never-daunted Percy to the earth. The Prince had told Hotspur:

> It is the Prince of Wales that threatens thee,
> Who never promiseth but he means to pay.   (5.4.41–2)

The broken promise to Francis is deviously related to the lethally kept promise to Harry Hotspur.

To conclude. Hal's game with Francis is a sign of the astonishing richness and complexity of *1 Henry IV*. If the game has a distasteful quality (an element of exploitative manipulation), it expresses some of Hal's most durable and politically important characteristics. In revealing Hal's preoccupation with kept and broken promises, with modes of treachery, with conflicting claims of allegiance, and with 'expropriating the expropriator', it relates to themes that pervade the whole sequence of history plays from *Richard II* to *Henry V*. The very cry 'Anon, anon' ('In one instant, at once, I'm coming') reverberates loudly in these works concerned with the pressure and power of time. *Multum in parvo*: much, indeed, in little. Whether you consider what it says about Hal's psychology or what it says about Shakespeare's structural subtlety, this incident unfolds remarkably in the imagination. Poor Francis was not enriched, but we may be.

C.W.

Henry V, war criminal?

The great surprise at the Oscar awards of 1989-90 was the board-sweeping success of Kenneth Branagh's *Henry V.* Branagh's victory was what gamblers call 'a turn-up for the book'; a rank outsider had won cinema's richest prize. The odds had been stacked heavily against Branagh's film, on three counts: it was English, it was litera-ture, it was low(ish) budget. It is normally assumed that vast amounts of promotional dollars are needed to blitz the few thousand academicians who make up the electorate. None the less, *Henry V* won; propelling Branagh into world stardom, *bankrolling his follow-up productions (Much Ado about Nothing, Hamlet),* and set-ting in train a Hollywood 'Shakespeare boom' which would lead to another unlikely Oscar-winner, Tom Stoppard's *Shakespeare in Love* which hoovered up a record number of awards in 1999. It had been a wonderful decade for Shakespeare on film.

Branagh's take on Shakespeare's play was frankly antagonistic to its filmic predecessor, Laurence Olivier's 1948 production.[1] Olivier's film (the first Technicolor movie I ever saw) was conceived in a spirit of martial triumphalism, carrying as it did the on-screen dedication 'To the Commandos of England', those intrepid soldiers who, like Shakespeare's warrior-king, had daringly raided France.

Olivier's film glorified British martial spirit. Its keynotes were 'Saint Crispin's day' and 'God for Harry, England, and Saint George!' The film's design was starkly patriotic, verging on propa-gandistic.[2] Colourful its chromatics may have been, its morality was black and white. Olivier's film reminded audiences that Shake-speare's play was written within a decade or so of the Great Armada, when God had breathed and blown away England's enemies—as he would graciously do again in 1945.

Branagh came to Shakespeare's play carrying heavier baggage. In his production, grey and dirty-brown were the predominant hues. His vision was discoloured by Vietnam, residues of the 'politi-cized' 1970s infatuation with Brecht, and Orson Welles's epically muddy battle scenes in *Chimes at Midnight,* with its 'war is hell' message. My Lai, not El Alamein, was what came to mind watching the 1989 film. None the less, like Olivier, Branagh ducked what is the most contentious element in the play for British audiences, namely Henry's apparently criminal massacre of his helpless French prisoners in what seems suspiciously like an attack of pique, or at best cold-blooded strategic calculation.

Henry's conduct is, for those of a patriotic turn of mind, very troubling. If, for example, Henry had thrown Kate on the floor and raped her it would have been less heinous a war crime than what is shown on stage—if one chooses to show it. Olivier did not. In his version, the king never gives any command to kill the prisoners (as he does twice in the text of the play). Olivier's warrior-king looks at the dead bodies of the English boys whom the French have slaughtered in the baggage park, mutters that he has never till this moment in France been angry, only to throw himself into the battle again to do victorious single combat with his armoured foe. Olivier's Henry is sanitized of any war crime by no war crime happening (or at least being shown on screen). It is blanked out. Stage productions in England routinely did the same. So too, Branagh's Henry never issues any command that the French prisoners be killed. Like Olivier's king, he is shown infuriated by the massacre of the boys in the baggage park. But Branagh's Henry takes out his anger on the luckless French herald, whom he subjects to vigorous physical battery. He too is sanitized. Despite his fury, and despite Branagh's altogether harsher view of the realities of war, no French prisoner is shown harmed.

Editors are less free to prune. Although many have been unhappy with the prisoners' massacre, traditionally they put their disquiet aside with *autre temps, autre mœurs*. Herschel Baker, in the *Riverside Shakespeare*, blandly notes that 'Henry's dreadful talk before Harfleur and his command to kill the prisoners were approved procedures in fifteenth-century war'.[3] Approved? If that were the case, what foe would ever be fool enough to allow himself to be taken captive? Are we to assume that a mass offstage slaughter of prisoners accompanies the battles we see on stage in the Henry IV plays?

More persuasive are those critics who have seen the killing of the prisoners as reflecting on Harry's peculiar characteristics as a military commander. His ruthlessness appals, but—perversely—also attracts us, rather as the rabbit is attracted by the beautiful but deadly stoat. Hazlitt, in a brilliant tirade on drama's pernicious practice of glamourizing war, notes that Henry's sleek violence fascinates us. We cannot take our eyes off him. We gaze at him, safe all the while in our theatre seats,

as we like to gaze at a panther or a young lion in their cages at the Tower, and catch a pleasing horror from their glistening eyes, their velvet paws, and dreadless roar; so we take a very romantic, heroic, patriotic, and poetical delight in the boasts and feats of our younger Harry, as they appear on the stage and are confined to lines of ten syllables; where no blood follows the stroke that wounds our ears, where no harvest bends beneath horses' hoofs, no city flames, no little child is butchered, no dead men's bodies are found piled on heaps and festering the next morning—in the orchestra![4]

The 'kill the prisoners' issue is raised on a number of occasions in the play, but in such a way as to make it almost impossible to formulate any clear verdict on where Shakespeare stands. There is a comic prelude in Act 4, scene 4, when Pistol, the 'boy', and a scared-witless French soldier enter, amid 'alarms and excursions':

PISTOL Yield, cur.
FRENCH SOLDIER *Je pense que vous êtes le gentilhomme de bon qualité.*
PISTOL *Qualité? 'Calin o custure me!'*
   Art thou a gentleman? What is thy name? Discuss.
FRENCH SOLDIER *O Seigneur Dieu!*
PISTOL O Seigneur Dew should be a gentleman.—
   Perpend my words, O Seigneur Dew, and mark:
   O Seigneur Dew, thou diest, on point of fox,
   Except, O Seigneur, thou do give to me
   Egregious ransom.
FRENCH SOLDIER *O prenez miséricorde! Ayez pitié de moi!*
PISTOL 'Moy' shall not serve. I will have forty 'moys',
   Or I will fetch thy rim out at thy throat
   In drops of crimson blood.
FRENCH SOLDIER *Est-il impossible d'echapper la force de ton bras?*
PISTOL Brass, cur? Thou damnèd and luxurious mountain goat,
   Offer'st me brass?
FRENCH SOLDIER *O, pardonne-moi!*
PISTOL Sayst thou me so? Is that a ton of moys?—

Come hither, boy. Ask me this slave in French
What is his name.
BOY *Écoutez: comment êtes-vous appelé?*
FRENCH SOLDIER *Monsieur le Fer.*

(4.4.1–24)

And so it continues. It is not a very edifying spectacle of British conduct on the battle field. The boy tells the terrified Monsieur le Fer that Pistol (who is posing as a soldier of 'quality') '*me commande à vous dire que vous faites vous prêt, car ce soldat ici est disposé tout à cette heure de couper votre gorge.*' The captive's throat will be slit—unless, that is, he comes up with a ransom. Monsieur le Fer protests that he is of a 'good house', and that he can furnish 200 crowns for his life. Pistol's fury abates. Throats will not after all be slit.

The boy concludes the scene with an ominous remark about the undefended nature of the baggage park in the second-echelon lines, where this scene is apparently taking place: 'The French might have a good prey of us, if he knew of it, for there is none to guard it but boys.' (Pistol, who is evidently part of the base camp defences, is not, we deduce, a tower of strength.)

The scene after next, a triumphant Henry comes on, with prisoners in his train. The day is going the English way, 'But all's not done; yet keep the French the field', the King shrewdly notes. He receives intelligence from other fighting fronts. The scene ends with a worrying development:

But hark, what new alarum is this same?
The French have reinforced their scattered men.
Then every soldier kill his prisoners.
Give the word through.

(4.6.35–8)

A counter-attack is imminent. As commanders know, the moment of maximum vulnerability is immediately after you have won ground. Fatally, at this moment the tendency of troops is to relax their discipline, to think about plunder—or just some rest. (Shakespeare gives a fine description of how suddenly battles can reverse, and victory be lost in a moment, in the early battle scenes of *Coriolanus*.)

Henry is right to impose his leader's grip on his men at this point. But why kill the prisoners? Apart from anything else, it would be a long, bloody, and exhausting business. The French captives (many still armoured) are not going to offer their throats to their slayers' swords like so many lambs in the slaughterhouse. Apologists for Henry at this point note that Shakespeare is 'faithfully' following his source in Holinshed. The chronicler records that some of the French cavalry had circled back on the rear lines and, for motives of 'spoile', or 'revenge' had attacked the English base camp. Once they had broken in the French skirmishers slew 'such servants as they found to make any resistance'. On being informed of this attack on his undefended rear position, Henry, fearing that the enemy would regroup and attack:

contrarie to his accustomed gentlenes, commanded by sound of trumpet, that everie man (upon paine of death) should incontinentlie slaie his prisoner. When this dolorous decree, and pitifull proclamation was pronounced, pitie it was to see how some Frenchmen were suddenlie sticked with daggers, some were brained with pollaxes, some slaine with malls, other had their throats cut, and some their bellies panched, so that in effect, having respect to the great number, few prisoners were saved.[5]

In the play, there is sharp editorial disagreement as to whether, following Henry's order, the slaughter of prisoners takes place on stage or off. Witnessing the atrocity in front of its eyes, as Hazlitt points out, will materially affect the image of the English warrior king which is gradually taking shape in the audience's mind. (Olivier and Branagh protect Henry's image, and that of his soldiery, by excising the command 'Let every man kill his prisoners' and dropping the Monsieur le Fer scene altogether.)

The next scene opens with a moral justification of the slaughter of the French prisoners on different grounds. The two Welshmen, Fluellen and Gower, have evidently arrived at the English army base camp to find the evidence of carnage visited by the French raiders on their unarmed victims:

FLUELLEN Kill the poys and the luggage! 'Tis expressly against the law of arms. 'Tis as arrant a piece of knavery, mark you now, as can be offert. In your conscience now, is it not?

GOWER 'Tis certain there's not a boy left alive. And the cowardly rascals that ran from the battle ha' done this slaughter. Besides, they have burned and carried away all that was in the King's tent; wherefore the King most worthily hath caused every soldier to cut his prisoner's throat. O 'tis a gallant king.   (4.7.1–10)

The scene, after this sombre opening, then veers off in a very strange direction. The two soldiers proceed to argue—at inordinate length—whether Henry is Welsh or not, and which region of their country can claim him. (This excursus is cut by Branagh and Olivier.) We have to imagine them holding this comic-chauvinist dispute among the still-smoking corpses of the 'poys'—including Pistol's young friend of whom we have grown rather fond (where *did* he learn to speak French so fluently?).

It would, of course, seem more natural to have had this scene (or at least the first part of it) *before* Henry ordered the killing of the prisoners. It evidently preceded that dread command and to have seen it earlier would have made the point that the first breach of 'the law of arms' was French, not English. Coming as it does afterwards, it looks like *ex post facto* justification, or special pleading.

As Shakespeare has portrayed it on stage, however, Henry *cannot have known* at the point that he ordered the massacre of prisoners that the French cavalry were acting simultaneously in such an unchivalrous fashion some miles to his rear. No messenger has brought him the news—at least that we know of. It was motives of military prudence, not condign reprisal, that led him to give the fell command, 'Then every soldier kill his prisoners.'

On the next occasion on which we see him on-stage, Henry has evidently (and belatedly) been apprised of the slaughter of his rear-line innocents. It has made him very cross. He bursts on stage with the exclamation:

> KING HENRY I was not angry since I came to France
> Until this instant. Take a trumpet, herald;
> Ride thou unto the horsemen on yon hill.
> If they will fight with us, bid them come down,
> Or void the field: they do offend our sight.
> If they'll do neither; we will come to them,
> And make them skirr away as swift as stones
> Enforcèd from the old Assyrian slings.
> Besides, we'll cut the throats of those we have,
> And not a man of them that we shall take
> Shall taste our mercy. Go and tell them so.   (4.7.50–60)

This speech inspires Dr Johnson's observation that Henry is clearly in a 'sanguinary mood'; having cut his prisoners' throats once he orders that they shall be cut again. It is odd. What prisoners are there left for the English soldiers to murder?

But, we may go on to inquire, are those throats cut, on either occasion that the king gives the command to do it? A couple of scenes later, after he knows the day is unequivocally his, Henry asks his herald for a body count: 'Here is the number of the slaughtered French', the man replies (in an oddly undeferential way), passing him a paper. Henry, having scanned it, turns to Exeter:

> KING HENRY What prisoners of good sort are taken, uncle?
> EXETER Charles, Duke of Orléans, nephew to the King;
>   Jean, Duke of Bourbon, and Lord Boucicault;
>   Of other lords and barons, knights and squires,
>   Full fifteen hundred, besides common men.   (4.8.73–7)

This is puzzling. The king, not a man to be disobeyed, particularly on the battlefield, has expressly ordered the French prisoners to be killed not once, but *twice*. Now he wants to know how many they have. Coming close to those prisoners we know about, has Pistol killed craven le Fer, after Henry's command that he should do so? Or has he preserved him and pocketed the 200 crowns ransom? We never know. This detail could be shown as a piece of silent stage business. But it is hard to know what warrant a director would have for scripting it one way or the other (le Fer slaughtered, le Fer not slaughtered?).

Returning to the big picture, how is it that there remain living this huge number of captives? Fifteen hundred is the size of a small army. These French prisoners surely did not surrender *after* Henry gave his 'kill them all' command. It would have been suicide to do so. Henry issued a proclamation to the enemy that after the slaughter of the boys, no prisoner taken should 'taste our mercy'. Take no prisoners, give no quarter, in other words. And after hostilities have ceased entirely, all prudent Frenchmen would slope off home, rather than throw themselves on the mercy of the cold-blooded and vengeful Henry. There is no sign of the English mounting any pursuit of the routed French. The vanquished foe is free to slink from the field, and all sensible Frenchmen will have done so by this point of the play.

There are two ways of making sense of this apparent anomaly. The first is that Shakespeare was in two minds and was not averse to the audience being likewise uncertain. The dramatist leaves open the possibility that the bloody edict is words only—the kind of over-the-top thing that is said in the heat of battle. Rather like the *haka* (or fearsome Maori battle chant) with which the All Blacks begin their rugby games, it shouldn't be taken at face value. (The Maoris, one is told, tied wet rawhide round their testicles before going into battle, to render themselves—as the rawhide dried and shrank—berserk fighters.)

Alternatively, we may believe that only a few encumbering prisoners are *actually* killed. Things were moving too rapidly for a mass homicide. It would, as has been said, take hours of wearying labour to cut the throats of 1,500 uncooperative Frenchmen. So rapid and equivocal is the sequence of events during and after the battle that the audience may well be rather bewildered. What actually happened to those prisoners? It's hard to recall—were they killed, or weren't they? Or was the order given and there wasn't time to carry it out? It would be interesting to quiz an untutored audience as to what impression they carry away, having seen the play. Students I have quizzed, many of whom know the play well for examination purposes, are often unsure in their mind. (Of course, if one has the massacre onstage, there will be no uncertainty.)

On mature reflection, the audience may also come to the conclusion that there are prisoners and prisoners. The mind goes back to that thought-provoking pre-battle discussion between the other ranks in Act 4, scene 1. It is the small hours of the morning in the English lines. Henry himself is patrolling the lines incognito, pretending to be just another private soldier, wondering like the others if he'll still be around the following night to warm his hands at the campfire.

Michael Williams makes his moving speech 'if the cause be not good . . . I am afeard there are few die well that die in battle.' King Henry retorts with a closely argued justification for the English ruler's right to lead Englishmen to their death in battle in *his* (the King's) cause. There follows the following exchange:

BATES 'Tis certain, every man that dies ill, the ill upon his own head. The King is not to answer it. I do not desire he should answer for me, and yet I determine to fight lustily for him.

KING HENRY I myself heard the King say he would not be ransomed.

WILLIAMS Ay, he said so, to make us fight cheerfully, but when our throats are cut he may be ransomed, and we ne'er the wiser.

(4.1.178–86)

Williams's point is that, during and after the battle, other ranks' throats are of less worth than noble throats. Noblemen are booty. If le Fer, for example, had not, as he said, been a *'gentilhomme de bonne maison'* he would have been put to the sword forthwith. When Henry said, 'kill all prisoners', did he mean 'Jean, Duke of Bourbon, and Lord Boucicault', or the 'unqualitied' followers in their train? Ordinary soldiers taken prisoner are merely a logistical burden. After the battle, King Henry specifically asks 'What prisoners *of good sort* are taken' (he presumably means 'were taken, during the hostilities'). These 'gentles' have not had their throats cut, presumably because they have given their *parole.* They, after all, are of the same class as the King and his nobles (he will even marry into their ranks).

We may, then, assume one of two things. In the heat of battle Henry gives a command that may not have been carried out—at least not in full. Alternatively, only the unregarded ordinary prisoners of war have been put to the sword. And who cares about them? As well shed tears for the dead horses festering in Agincourt's fields.

J.S.

Henry V's claim to France: valid or invalid?

Henry V has a useful knack of making other people appear to take the responsibility or blame for his own actions. The play offers numerous illustrations. There's Henry's response to the Dauphin's derisive gift of tennis-balls, for instance:

> And tell the pleasant Prince this mock of his
> Hath turned his balls to gunstones, and his soul
> Shall stand sore chargèd for the wasteful vengeance
> That shall fly from them—for many a thousand widows
> Shall this his mock mock out of their dear husbands,
> Mock mothers from their sons, mock castles down;
> Ay, some are yet ungotten and unborn
> That shall have cause to curse the Dauphin's scorn.
>
> (1.2. 281–8)

As alliterative rhetoric, this is stirring. As retaliation for a poor jest, it is somewhat excessive. In effect, Henry is saying that joke will rebound in the form of devastating warfare by England against France—and the blame will fall not on Henry for the warfare but on the Dauphin for the jocular gift. Then, in Act 2, there's the odd circumstance of the arrest of the conspirators, Cambridge, Scrope, and Grey. Instead of arresting them straightforwardly, Henry lulls them into a sense of security by seeking their views on the impending war. He then remarks that he is inclined to pardon a man who had railed against his person. Cambridge, Scrope, and Grey rise to the bait and urge the King to be severe rather than merciful. Henry then gives them documents denouncing them as traitors; and, when they appeal for mercy, he can say:

> The mercy that was quick in us but late
> By your own counsel is suppressed and killed   (2.2.76–7)

—in effect, 'Blame yourselves and not me for the death-sentences you are about to receive'.

Later, at the siege of Harfleur, Henry makes the blood-curdling threat to the governor and citizens that, if they continue to offer resistance, the British troops will be utterly ruthless when they break in. There will be 'licentious wickedness', rape, and slaughter; the people will see the aged massacred and 'naked infants spitted upon pikes'. And who's to blame? The governor and citizens, of course: 'you yourselves are cause'! So 'Take pity of your town and of your people.' They open the gates, and the promised massacre is averted: 'Use mercy to them all', says Henry. (Actually, important citizens who refused to take an oath of allegiance were sent to England for ransom, while the poorer citizens, women and children were 'forcibly evacuated'.)[1] Eventually, on the eve of the Battle of Agincourt, this matter of responsibility for the king's actions becomes the subject of debate between Henry, Bates, and Williams. The arguments rattle Henry badly. As soon as he is alone, he utters the long, anguished speech beginning:

> Upon the King.
> 'Let us our lives, our souls, our debts, our care-full wives,
> Our children, and our sins, lay on the King.'
> We must bear all. O hard condition . . .   (4.1.218–21)

Looking back over this sequence, we might conclude that Henry's tendency to place on others the blame for the consequences of his own decisions and actions is his habitual way of coping with the psychological pressures and stresses of kingship. But there is also a question of moral and political guilt which had been raised at the outset of the play. In Act 1, scene 2, Henry asks the Archbishop of Canterbury whether he, the king, has a just claim to France. Characteristically, Henry stresses that Canterbury bears a heavy burden of responsibility:

> For God doth know how many now in health
> Shall drop their blood in approbation
> Of what your reverence shall incite us to.   (1.2.18–20)

Canterbury explains that the Salic law, denying succession through the female line, is invalid in France, and therefore the king has a just claim to the French throne. That explanation, however, takes so long (extending over more than eighty lines) and is so involved that it presents obvious problems in staging. The famous Olivier film made the explanation into a farcical palaver in which a buffoonishly effeminate Bishop of Ely, struggling to manage an unwieldy pile of documents which Canterbury needs to consult, gets them in a muddle, annoys Canterbury, and drops the heap on the floor, so that both churchmen scramble absurdly among the papers, causing general mirth. That seems a sensible way of giving entertainment-value to what, on the page, looks like a tedious and well-nigh incomprehensible rigmarole. But was it *meant* to be a rigmarole?

Gary Taylor (in a scholarly introduction to the text) says that in Shakespeare's day this long speech would have been taken very seriously. Elizabeth's claim to the throne depended on the legitimacy of female succession, so it would have been 'indiscreet' for the Archbishop's argument to appear parodic. Taylor continues:

Shakespeare's audience would have been interested in the Salic Law (as we are not) and accustomed to listening to long and intellectually complex sermons (as we are not); . . . the legitimacy of a king's (or a nobleman's) inheritance was the foundation of the entire political and social system . . .[2]

It may be objected that even if all the members of the audience were accustomed 'to long and intellectually complex sermons' (which seems questionable), it is certain that that was not what they paid for when they went to the theatre. Whether they were interested in the Salic law would surely depend in large part on whether the actual presentation of it was interesting; after all, one can be keenly interested in the amount of tax one pays but still find the completing of an income-tax form a tedious chore. It seems to me that the speech contains clear signs that it's meant to be regarded not just as tedious but as comically tedious. In the first place, the length is excessive for the purpose; the evidence could have been presented much more concisely. The archbishop is so prone to needless digression that Polonius, in comparison, seems a model of succinctness. The details of locations, names, and legal jargon seem designed to induce bafflement; an early foretaste of the legalistic prolixity comes with ' "*In terram Salicam mulieres ne succedant*" — | "No woman shall succeed in Salic land" '; and repetitiveness soon sets in:

> Which 'Salic land' the French unjustly gloss
> To be the realm of France, and Pharamond
> The founder of this law and female bar.
> Yet their own authors faithfully affirm

> That the land Salic is in Germany,
> Between the floods of Saale and of Elbe . . .
> Which Salic, as I said, 'twixt Elbe and Saale,
> Is at this day in Germany called Meissen.
>
> (1.2.40–5, 52–7)

The remainder is a mind-numbing catalogue of locations, names, dates, and fussy details. Confirmation of comic intent comes when, after nearly fifty lines of the speech, Canterbury reaches the line 'So that, as clear as is the summer's sun,'—a line which customarily, in stage and film productions, provokes mirth both from the courtiers on stage and from the audience. When Henry breaks in with 'May I with right and conscience make this claim?', the appropriate tone is exasperated impatience ('Come to the point, man!').

Taylor says we are meant to conclude that Henry's claim seems valid. But spectators with memories of *2 Henry IV* will recall the Machiavellian advice given by the dying Henry IV to his son: 'Be it thy course to busy giddy minds | With foreign quarrels' (4.3.343–4). In any case, the very first scene of *Henry V* pointedly shows Canterbury discussing with Ely the fact that a bill in the House of Commons threatens to take away half the Church's lands, half their wealth; and the way to avert this threat, says Canterbury, is to promise the king that the Church will generously subsidize the war in France; for then the king will 'mitigate' the bill. (The Branagh film, in which the churchmen appear sinisterly conspiratorial, seems closer to the spirit of the text at this point than does the Olivier version.) Shakespeare, who gave Brecht lessons in 'alienation effects', didn't have to provide that opening; but he chose to provide it, and it makes a foregone conclusion of Canterbury's eventual assurance to the king that the claim to France is valid. He *would* say that, wouldn't he?—and our foreknowledge again increases the sense that the long justification is rigmarole rather than elucidation.[3] John Fletcher seems to have thought so: his play *The Noble Gentleman* (*c.*1624–6) contains the following direct parody. The speaker is a *madman*, Shattillion, who (forgetting that 'the law *Salicke* cuts him off from all') advances his crazy claim to the French throne:

> Sir, you shall know
> My love's true title, mine by marriage.
> Setting aside the first race of French Kings,
> Which will not here concerne us, as *Pharamond*,

With *Clodion, Merov,* and *Chilperik,*
And to come down unto the second race,
Which we will likewise skip . . .
      . . . . of *Martell Charles,*
The father of King *Pippin,* who was Sire
To *Charles,* the great and famous *Charlemaine;*
And to come to the third race of *French* Kings,
Which will not be greatly pertinent in this cause . . .[4]

Fletcher's parody thus amplifies the prolixity and needless naming
which are tell-tale signs in the original. In any case, modern readers
may recall Tom Paine's remark, in *The Rights of Man,* that British
people who derive their ancestry from William the Conqueror are
claiming as forebear 'the son of a prostitute, and the plunderer of the
English nation'.[5]

Gary Taylor has said that the legitimacy of a king's inheritance
was the foundation of 'the entire political and social system'. In Act 4
of *Henry V,* after the debate with Williams, after the reflections that
the king's burden of responsibility is so great that he cannot enjoy
the sound sleep of 'the wretched slave . . . crammed with distress-
ful bread', Henry worries about the battle that will ensue on the next
day. The British are outnumbered, so God's help is needed. But will
God feel inclined to grant it? There is one huge obstacle:

> Not today, O Lord,
> O not today, think not upon the fault
> My father made in compassing the crown.
> I Richard's body have interrèd new,
> And on it have bestowed more contrite tears
> Than from it issued forcèd drops of blood.
> Five hundred poor have I in yearly pay
> Who twice a day their withered hands hold up
> Toward heaven to pardon blood. And I have built
> Two chantries, where the sad and solemn priests
> Sing still for Richard's soul. More will I do,
> Though all that I can do is nothing worth,
> Since that my penitence comes after all,
> Imploring pardon.[6]

> (4.1.280–93)

What price now, the churchman's argument that since the Salic
law did not apply, Henry had a rightful claim to France? What price
now, his injunction to Canterbury – 'And God forbid, my dear and

faithful lord, | That you should fashion, wrest, or bow your read-
ing'? His own soliloquy proclaims the hypocrisy; for it reminds us of
what the churchman's lore and the patriotic rhetoric have concealed.
Being the son of a usurper who had gained the throne by the over-
throw and murder of Richard, Henry V did not have a legitimate
claim to the throne of *England*, let alone that of France.[7]

Like father, like son. Henry IV had felt such guilt after the killing
of Richard that he had planned a penitential pilgrimage to the Holy
Land; but he never made that pilgrimage because (as though
Richard's and Carlisle's prophecies of divine wrath were being
fulfilled) he appeared to be punished by God, the punishments
mainly taking the form of repeated incursions by rebels who could
claim that they were avenging the slain monarch. (Henry IV
eventually notes the irony that he reaches Jerusalem after all: the
chamber called Jerusalem, in which he will die.) Henry V has
inherited that guilt, and he knows it; hence, in part, that repeated
desire to cast on others the responsibility for his own violent acts.
Hence, also, the attempt to buy grace. Yes, he has interred Richard's
body anew, he has paid the needy for intercessionary prayers, and he
has hired priests to sing for the repose of Richard's soul—but

> all that I can do is nothing worth,
> Since that my penitence comes after all,
> Imploring pardon.

The best gloss on these lines is suggested by Claudius in *Hamlet*,
when he, kneeling, strives to pray for forgiveness:

> but O, what form of prayer
> Can serve my turn? 'Forgive me my foul murder'?
> That cannot be, since I am still possessed
> Of those effects for which I did the murder—
> My crown, mine own ambition, and my queen.[8]

When Henry says 'Though all that I can do is nothing worth, |
Since that my penitence comes after all', he surely means something
very similar. To be truly penitent would entail giving up the ill-
gotten throne. (Richard's true heir was Edmund Mortimer, Earl of
March, in whose interest that abortive conspiracy by Cambridge,
Scrope, and Grey had taken place.) But having come this far, having
helped to consolidate his father's usurpation and having proudly

inherited the fruits of usurpation, Henry isn't going back. And, of course, on the next day, the Battle of Agincourt results in a well-nigh miraculous victory for the British. The Lord moves in mysterious ways, but it looks as if God, having punished the usurper by civil wars, has come to regard the usurper's son as worthy of a helping hand. When the huge French losses and the few British losses are reported, Henry's response is characteristic:

> O God, thy arm was here,
> And not to us, but to thy arm alone
> Ascribe we all . . .
>   Take it God,
> For it is none but thine.
>   (4.8.104–6, 109–10)

It's not only the appropriately pious response; it's also the morally and psychologically salutary response. To give God the credit is to give God the responsibility. At last, Henry can reconcile the apparently irreconcilable: to be a warmonger and a Christian, to be the son of a rebel who killed the Lord's Anointed (Richard), and yet a ruler who demands loyalty and executes rebels. The victory could even be seen as part of a providential pattern. Indeed, the historical events as portrayed by Shakespeare in the 'second tetralogy' of history plays (*Richard II*, 1 and 2 *Henry IV*, and *Henry V*) intermittently bring to mind the Christian paradox of the Fortunate Fall. The Fall of Adam was bad, yet in the long term good in the sense that it led to the Atonement. The downfall of Richard ('a second fall of cursèd man', as his queen calls it) was bad in bringing about a period of further civil warfare but good in the sense that it led to the emergence of Henry V, probably the most charismatically successful British monarch known to the Elizabethans. That charisma is splendidly rendered and magnified by Shakespeare's eloquence. So, however, is the shrewd Machiavellianism—albeit 'White' (e.g. patriotic) Machiavellianism—which in Shakespeare's works is usually a characteristic of the successful political leader. Observed through half-shut eyes, the second tetralogy can look like an epic entitled 'The Evolution of the Ideal Monarch'. Richard was legitimate but feckless; Henry IV was politically astute but guilty and tainted; Henry V was astute, stirringly eloquent, and, it seems, eventually cleansed of the inherited taint by God. Apparently, Henry V has succeeded triumphantly not only in uniting his realm but also in conquering France and achieving, through marriage, amicable union with the French dynasty. Princess Katharine's English lesson wasn't just an excuse for a couple of filthy puns; it was part of the political-cum-linguistic theme: whether they have Irish accents (MacMorris), Scottish accents (Jamy), Welsh accents (Fluellen), or even French accents (Katharine shocked by '*de foot* et *de cown*'),[9] Henry unites them. Just now I said 'Observed through half-shut eyes'; Shakespeare, however, keeps his eyes wide open. After the triumphalism of the last Act comes this Epilogue:

> Thus far with rough and all-unable pen
>   Our bending author hath pursued the story,
> In little room confining mighty men,
>   Mangling by starts the full course of their glory.
> Small time, but in that small most greatly lived
>   This star of England. Fortune made his sword,
> By which the world's best garden he achieved,
>   And of it left his son imperial lord.
> Henry the Sixth, in infant bands crowned king
>   Of France and England, did this king succeed,
> Whose state so many had the managing
>   That they lost France and made his England bleed,
> Which oft our stage has shown—and, for their sake,
> In your fair minds let this acceptance take.

It makes the point that though Henry's achievement was splendid, it was short-lived. He died early, and in the reign of Henry VI the gains were lost and England was riven by civil war again. The sense of history as progressive is replaced by the sense of history as cyclical: after civil war, peace, then civil war again; after losses abroad, gains abroad, then losses again. And the cyclical pattern is reflected in the very order of the plays. This sonnet, the epilogue of the final play in the second tetralogy, links the ending of *Henry V* to the opening of *1 Henry VI*, the first play in Shakespeare's first tetralogy of history plays (*1, 2, 3 Henry VI* and *Richard III*). Like a snake swallowing its tail, the two tetralogies are thus bound together as a cyclical octology—an infinite group of eight. Commentators on James Joyce point out that the last words of *Finnegans Wake* begin a sentence completed by that novel's opening words; and Samuel Beckett's 1964 drama entitled simply *Play* contains, a few lines from the apparent end, the daunting direction, '*Repeat play*'. There are few modern experimentalists whom Shakespeare has not anticipated.

To return to the original question. Henry's claim to the throne of France, made suspect by the self-interest of its appointed validators, is invalidated by the illegitimacy of Henry's title to the British throne. And, in a larger sense, it's invalidated by that Epilogue. The capture of Harfleur, the victory at Agincourt, the marriage to Katharine: it all came to nothing. France was lost and England bled again. Machiavelli once remarked: 'In the affairs of all men, and especially of princes, where there is no tribunal to which we can appeal, we judge by results.'[10] A bleaker gloss is provided by Henry IV:

> O God, that one might read the book of fate,
> And see the revolution of the times
> Make mountains level, and the continent,
> Weary of solid firmness, melt itself
> Into the sea. . . .
>   O, if this were seen,
> The happiest youth, viewing his progress through,
> What perils past, what crosses to ensue,
> Would shut the book and sit him down and die.[11]

C.W.

What happens to Viola's 'eunuch' plan?

———

Shakespeare's enigmatically named comedy *Twelfth Night* (what has the feast of the Epiphany to do with it?) opens with a briskness that promises pace throughout. After Orsino's deceptively languorous love-drunk eulogy on music and the ambiguous 'play on' (echoing, as it does, a cricket umpire) the action switches to the sea-coast as the strains of music give way to the surge of (still violent) waves.

'What country, friends, is this?' Viola asks, having just been plucked from death by drowning. The captain of the ship on which they were sailing, from Messaline (wherever that may be—Mitylene has been suggested) to who knows where, answers her. They have been cast up on the shore of Illyria. The captain knows the country well. He is in fact Illyrian—was 'bred and born' there, and has been absent for only a month. (Geographically, Shakespeare's Illyria seems to be where modern-day Dalmatia and Bosnia are; their current associations are, luckily, absent from modern productions.)

Illyria is governed by 'a noble Duke' (or 'Count'—the titles are interchangeable in the play). His name is Orsino, as the captain tells Viola. Orsino's name is known to Viola from her having heard her father use it in conversation. (Viola's father is the ill-named Duke of Messaline—was his wife a whore?) Oddly, Viola already thinks of this potentate as a sexual target. Orsino was, she musingly recalls, 'a bachelor then'. The captain, who clearly has active contacts, has picked up gossip about Orsino's obsessive infatuation with 'fair Olivia'. This noblewoman has lost the brother who was her protector. Despite Orsino's grandeur she will admit no suitor and has 'abjured the . . . company of men'. There are no nunneries in Illyria, apparently; or perhaps it is just this one man, not the sex, she wants to avoid.

Her brother, Viola learns, may have drowned or may have been saved. She, like Olivia (as she thinks), has probably lost a protective brother. Sebastian was last seen clinging to a spar. She muses about what she should now do:

> O that I served that lady,
> And might not be delivered to the world
> Till I had made mine own occasion mellow,
> What my estate is.   (1.2.38–41)

Peremptorily Viola forms a strange plan. She is, as a disapproving Johnson observes, 'an excellent schemer'.[1] She instructs the captain to 'conceal me what I am':

> I'll serve this duke.
> Thou shalt present me as an eunuch to him.
> It may be worth thy pains; for I can sing,
> And speak to him in many sorts of music
> That will allow me very worth his service.
> What else may hap, to time I will commit,
> Only shape thou thy silence to my wit.   (lines 52–8)

He will do what she requests, the Captain says: 'Be you his eunuch, and your mute I'll be.' Being a sailor who has travelled to the Levant (Turkey is not far, by ship, from Illyria) he knows about harems, and their attendants—some of whom have their testicles removed, others their tongues. There is a tinge of bawdry in his joke about mutes (as in Cleopatra's, 'I take no pleasure | In aught an eunuch has').

Viola's mind is probably moving in other directions. She has come from civilized urban Italy and has landed in wildest Illyria. The Italy that she left was all abuzz with the latest artistic fad, 'opera'—the first regular performance of which took place at Florence in 1600 (around the time that Shakespeare was, it is thought, writing *Twelfth Night*). Eunuchs had been, for some time previous, part of the musical companies at the Popes' palaces. They were recruited for the new musical form.[2]

What one assumes is that Viola picked up from her father's comments that Orsino was mad about music, and she sees an opportunity of using that passion to have herself appointed to his entourage. Johnson is dubious about the ethics of this: 'Viola', he notes, 'seems to have formed a very deep design with very little premeditation; she is thrown by shipwreck on an unknown coast, hears that the prince is a bachelor; and resolves to supplant the lady whom he courts.' It is, as he misogynistically terms it, the act of an unscrupulous 'schemer'.[3]

This may be to take things too seriously. As Anne Barton points out, arbitrariness is the law of the universe in *Twelfth Night*. This, if it means anything, is the burden of the title:

The words 'Twelfth Night' not only suggest a carnival world; they warn an audience that it is not to ask too many awkward questions about the miraculous resemblance of boy and girl twins who, on the stage, will almost invariably look less than identical. Nor are we to question love at first sight, a duke who accepts as his wife a servant he thought, only five minutes before, was a boy, or the feasibility of persuading a man that he can make his fortune forever by way of yellow stockings and crossed garters. In a world that is ritually upside down, almost anything can happen.[4]

In this topsy-turvy world one should not expect strict canons of psychological realism to apply. None the less, the sequence of events at the opening of the play remains disturbingly odd. There seems lacking even a film of probability over Viola's 'scheme'. In fact it seems in some ways to be obstinately perverse. In the first instance, there is no present danger to the lady—certainly nothing to warrant deep cover. There is no textual evidence for believing Illyria to be at war with Italy. It is true that the Duke does not like pirates such as Antonio, but what law-abiding maritime authority does? Modern Bosnia, of course, would be something else. An attractive young girl who found herself in that hapless region might well be advised to disguise herself from the licentious soldiery.

It would, at first sight, seem logical for the captain to make known his (and his passengers') plight—if only to alert Illyria's coastguard to keep an eye out for survivors. It would seem similarly logical for Viola, who is not hard up (she offers to pay the captain 'bounteously' and gives 'gold' to the sailor who tells her that her brother may not after all be drowned), to throw herself, as a gentlewoman of means, on the hospitality of the Illyrian gentry. She might then continue her journey to wherever she was originally travelling. Albeit with a heavy heart and dressed in mourning black.

It may be, of course, that she wants to kill time waiting for news of her twin, Sebastian. He *may*, she hopes, have been saved. But in that case it would be sensible to do so in her own person, in some local hostelry appropriate to her gentility.

Other explanations for her scheme can be hypothesized:

1. As a man, Viola will find it easier to inherit her family's money (the remark about being uncertain of her 'estate' suggests this). If she is known to be an inheritrix, she will become a target for predatory males, like Olivia.

2. On board it may have been agreed that if the vessel were taken by pirates she would pretend to be a man, to escape a fate worse than death. Now she intends to go through with it, just to be on the safe side.

3. As an identical twin, she has always wondered what it would be like to travel the short distance into Sebastian's gender and an exciting zone of sexual liberation (this may also be presumed to be part of Portia's motive in *The Merchant of Venice*).

4. As a eunuch, if she fails to get admission into Orsino's entourage, she will be admitted into Olivia's. Being a eunuch is a passport, enabling her access to both the man's and the woman's protectorates.

The most likely explanation, however, is connected with Orsino's music-madness, something which is notorious even beyond Illyria's borders. The duke will be naturally curious about these castrati about whom everyone in Italy is raving and whom he has not yet heard with his own ears.

What follows in the play is perplexing. There is no further reference to Viola–Cesario's being a eunuch. He/she appears in Act 1, scene 4 as a 'page'. She is, apparently, taken to be at (or just before) that threshold point at which the boy's voice 'breaks'. As Orsino observes, her voice belies 'thy happy years | That say thou art a man.' The more suspicious Malvolio observes that Cesario's voice is 'not yet old enough for a man, nor young enough for a boy'. The voice has not yet broken.

Getting an appointment as a page would be tricky, depending on favours and patronage. Some pedigree would also be necessary; noblemen's pages were, traditionally, the scions of other noblemen. No one in Illyria is nobler than Orsino. How did Viola, with the aid of the sea-captain, achieve this appointment so expeditiously?

It has been suggested that the disappearance of the 'eunuch' ruse from the remainder of *Twelfth Night*'s text indicates hasty revision on Shakespeare's part.[5] One can, however, knit it into the subsequent action. Eunuchs, trained from early childhood as singers, were unoperated on during their boyhood years. The operation came at some point before it was judged their voices would break. Cesario's (Viola's) cover story is, one may propose, that he (she) was a singer in Italy selected for a future career as a castrato. As the ominous date approached (this, incidentally, was well before the invention of anaesthetics) he (she) resolved to escape the surgeon's knife. Since a potential castrato would be well below the age of majority— effectively subject to the decisions of parents or guardians—the only recourse would be flight. This is the plot of Kingsley Amis's 'alternative universe' novel, *The Alteration* (1976). A boy soprano, in the Pope's musical entourage, confronting castration at the age of puberty, goes on the run.

This is, one guesses, Cesario's cover story to Orsino. He lost his nerve at the thought of the gelding shears and made a bolt for it. It would explain both his musical skills and the flight from Italy. It would also explain why he must be incognito—lest his parents track him down and drag him off, while his voice is still pristine, to a fate worse than death. Cesario's story would appeal to the Duke on two grounds. This refugee from the cutting edge (literally) of the Italian musical world could bring him up to date as to what was happening there. Cesario would have gossip, the latest melodies, and could tell him all about opera. There would also be an irresistible appeal to the Duke's protectiveness.

J.S.

Malvolio: vengeful or reconciled?

In the world of comedy, a rather puritanical and joyless figure is likely to receive comic humiliation; but in *Twelfth Night* the humiliation is severe and protracted. A sense of sympathy with the underdog—in this case, the duped Malvolio—complicates one's loyalties. 'Poetic justice' here seems unpleasantly ruthless. The role can be played in many ways, but the text certainly provides warrant for seeing tragic possibilities in the character

What, after all, is Malvolio's offence? If he's a kill-joy, it's partly because that's his job. We readily recall the early scene in which he attempts unavailingly to end the noisy drunken revelry of Sir Toby Belch, Sir Andrew Aguecheek and Feste the Clown:

My masters, are you mad? Or what are you? Have you no wit, manners, nor honesty, but to gabble like tinkers at this time of night? Do ye make an ale-house of my lady's house, that ye squeak out your coziers' catches without any mitigation or remorse of voice? Is there no respect of place, persons, nor time in you? (2.3.81–7)

The question 'Are you mad?' will later be turned against him; but the main point to be noted here is that his complaint makes very good sense. The late-night revellers in the house of Viola—who is mourning her brother's death—are indeed noisy, thoughtless, and besotted. Maria, who is no friend to Malvolio, had herself remarked a minute or two previously:

What a caterwauling do you keep here! If my lady have not called up her steward Malvolio and bid him turn you out of doors, never trust me. (lines 68–70)

The second point is that Malvolio is acting not as an independent person, but as Countess Olivia's dutiful employee (a steward responsible for the household economy), here obeying orders:

Sir Toby, I must be round with you. My lady bade me tell you that though she harbours you as her kinsman she's nothing allied to your disorders. If you can separate yourself and your misdemeanours you are welcome to the house. If not, an it would please you to take leave of her she is very willing to bid you farewell.   (lines 89–94)

Sir Toby's response has become justly famous: 'Dost thou think because thou art virtuous there shall be no more cakes and ale?';[1] but what may be forgotten is that those words are preceded by Toby's scornfully snobbish remark: 'Art any more than a steward?' Without stewards like Malvolio, no cakes and ale would be available for such parasitic consumers. Malvolio has to work for his living, as errand-boy, general manager, and unarmed policeman; and in this scene he suffers humiliation at the hands of a pair of idle knights (one of whom is the Countess's cousin) and their cronies. It is his unavailing errand at the behest of Countess Olivia that provokes Maria, Toby, and Andrew to hatch the plot in which Malvolio is duped by the forged letter into the conviction that Olivia loves him. In accordance with the directions in the letter, he enjoys delusions of social promo-tion, pleasure, and power, and both dresses and behaves grotesquely; and consequently he is mocked, derided, and eventually incarcerated as a madman. Of course, the scene in which he appears as a doting lover, cross-gartered in yellow hose and simpering inanely (Act 3, scene 4) is one of the most celebrated farcical scenes in Shakespear-ian comedy. The protracted torment of Malvolio which follows, however, and which entails the mockery of the incarcerated 'lunatic' by Feste posing as 'Sir Topaz [or Topas] the curate' (Act 4, scene 2) while Sir Toby and Maria gloat at their victim's wretchedness, may today seem not only unfunny but distasteful; our sympathies are likely to move strongly towards Malvolio and against his tormentors. The First Folio stage direction, '*Malvolio within*', suggests that he may be partly or wholly out of sight; which does not necessarily mitigate the sense of protracted bullying; indeed, it may emphasize cruel detachment or cruel relish in Feste's performance as Sir Topaz. If Malvolio is visible, he may display desperation. An account of Henry Irving's Malvolio includes these remarks:

The mental and physical horror of darkness and the longing yearning for deliverance from a prison cell were never so realized, I think, before. . . . [T]here is the sense of the grievous wrong done to him, and the utter hopelessness of redress.[2]

The same reviewer, Edward Aveling, remarked that the effect was one of 'intense tragedy'. The Oxford editors, Roger Warren and

Stanley Wells, offer the warning that 'Shakespeare's contemporaries were notoriously cruel in their attitude to madmen';[3] but, to Olivia, Malvolio is the 'poor gentleman' in his derangement. (King Lear's madness is no comic turn.) Malvolio has indeed, as he claimed, been 'notoriously abused'; and Olivia concurs precisely: 'He hath been most notoriously abused.' Malvolio's resonant last words in the play, 'I'll be revenged on the whole pack of you!',[4] can be uttered in a variety of ways, ranging from the sinister to the pathetic, from the malicious to the petulantly self-pitying.

For Laurence Olivier, it was 'the cry of a man unmade', followed by a tearful exit; Beerbohm Tree in 1901 angrily tore off his steward's chain; Donald Sinden returned it to his mistress with dignity; Edward Sothern in 1907 (followed by many actors since) tore the forged letter in pieces. Some of these interpretations suggest frustration, some heartbreak . . .[5]

Even if his cry of revenge is venomously vindictive, that could be either proof of the underlying nastiness of his character (true to his name: 'Malvolio'—'Ill-will') or evidence of the psychological damage inflicted on a naïvely egoistic person (even one 'sick of self-love') by his tormentors.

If Malvolio was readily deluded into thinking he was loved by Olivia, he was demonstrating that capacity for deception and self-deception which others share. Orsino initially believes himself to be in love with Olivia, but eventually he will marry Viola, who has deceived him so easily in her masculine guise. Olivia, also deceived by that guise, falls in love with 'Cesario' but eventually marries Sebastian; and she subsequently mistakes Cesario for her husband. Antonio confuses Cesario with Sebastian, and bitterly reproaches his supposed friend for ingratitude. Sir Andrew challenges Sebastian, thinking he is Cesario; and so forth. Various characters, confused by disguise, show themselves capable of acting sanely in their own belief but crazily in the eyes of others. When Sebastian finds that a stranger (Olivia) is welcoming him lovingly, he remarks:

> What relish is in this? How runs the stream?
> Or I am mad, or else this is a dream.
> Let fancy still my sense in Lethe steep.
> If it be thus to dream, still let me sleep.   (4.1.58–61)

And later:

> I am ready to distrust mine eyes
> And wrangle with my reason that persuades me
> To any other trust but that I am mad,
> Or else the lady's mad.
>
> (4.3.13–16)

Malvolio is one of many dupes in this comic world, in which even the noblest figures may be possessed by the benign lunacy of sexual love; except that in his case it has been malign and his duping more destructive.

The text does, however, extend the possibility that Malvolio will follow the course not of revenge but of reconciliation. Consider how, in that final scene, his plight is recalled to Olivia. Viola says:

> The captain that did bring me first on shore
> Hath my maid's garments. He upon some action
> Is now in durance at Malvolio's suit,
> A gentleman and follower of my lady's.

Olivia responds:

> He shall enlarge him. Fetch Malvolio hither—
> And yet, alas, now I remember me,
> They say, poor gentleman, he's much distract.
>
> (5.1.268–74)

So, what prompts people to remember and summon Malvolio is the need to persuade him to withdraw his lawsuit so that the captain (Viola's helper, and therefore—it appears—presumed innocent without more ado) can be 'enlarged', set free. There follows the dénouement in which the matter of the forged letter and the fooling of Malvolio is outlined. Olivia then says that the steward will have retribution:

> This practice hath most shrewdly passed upon thee,
> But when we know the grounds and authors of it
> Thou shalt be both the plaintiff and the judge
> Of thine own cause.
>
> (lines 343–6)

At this point, Fabian seeks to persuade her that the trick was a matter of 'sportful malice' which should 'rather pluck on laughter than revenge'. Olivia seems sympathetic to this view, to judge from her immediately ensuing remark to Malvolio:

> Alas poor fool, how have they baffled thee!   (line 360)

Feste, sensing victory, adds to Malvolio's present humiliation by gleefully recalling his past humiliation and suggesting that the steward had asked for all he got: 'And thus the whirligig of time brings in his revenges.' It's that reference to 'revenges', coupled with Malvolio's realization that Olivia's promise of retribution has been rescinded, that provokes Malvolio's 'I'll be revenged on the whole pack of you!', followed by his exit. Orsino, perhaps prompted by Olivia's remark that the steward 'hath been most notoriously abused', then says:

> Pursue him, and entreat him to a peace.
> He hath not told us of the captain yet.
> When that is known, and golden time convents,
> A solemn combination shall be made
> Of our dear souls.

(lines 370–4)

In other words, the wedding of Orsino and Viola will take place only after two conditions have been met. One is that 'golden time' must 'convent': an appropriately favourable time must arrive—which may mean no more than that the couple must agree on the most suitable date for the wedding. The other condition is that Malvolio must be 'entreated to a peace' (persuaded to reconciliation with the others), a matter related to Olivia's desire that the captain be liberated. And to liberate the captain, Malvolio must be persuaded to withdraw his lawsuit, which again implies reconciliation. If Orsino is to be believed, then, the event he most desires, his marriage, will depend crucially on the pacification of Malvolio. Such pacification *could* happen. Stranger things have happened, offstage, in the world of Shakespearian comedy. (In the last Act of *As You Like It*, it is reported that the wicked Duke Frederick, usurper and would-be murderer, has been speedily converted to virtue after a chance encounter with 'an old religious man'.)

A sceptic could remark, of course, that Malvolio's lawsuit against the captain, of which not a word had been said (by Malvolio or anyone else) before the final scene of *Twelfth Night*, was written into the dénouement merely as linkage-material, just to provide a cue for the recalling of the unfortunate steward. In the ensuing dialogues, the matter is ignored. Alter Malvolio's exit, Orsino's line 'He hath not told us of the captain yet' could then be a way of dealing with the resultant loose end: not by tying it up but by at least recalling it and raising a prospect that it may be tied. In any case, the sceptic must concede that someone has been sent to 'entreat' Malvolio. The Folio text does not specify the identity of this emissary. The Oxford text nominates Fabian, and annotates the nomination thus:

As one of the conspirators against Malvolio, he might be thought unlikely to *entreat him to a peace*, but as a would-be peacemaker . . . he stands as much (or as little) chance as anyone else.[6]

The 'or as little' may be a shade pessimistic, for if Orsino means what he says, the Duke could, via the emissary or directly, bring to bear on Malvolio all the powers (of persuasion and doubtless of bribery) that he can wield in order to ensure that the marriage takes place.

Malvolio is, of course, 'a kind of puritan'. Perhaps in 1642, when the theatres were closed down, and in 1649, when Charles I was beheaded, the triumphant Puritans and Parliamentarians included some previously victimized stewards. The whirligig of time brings in his revenges.

C.W.

Does Bottom cuckold Oberon?

———

In Act 3, scene 1, of *A Midsummer Night's Dream*, Titania takes Bottom away to her bower. Are we to believe that they actually have sexual intercourse? Professor Harold F. Brooks, erudite editor of an Arden text of the play, says No. He argues: '[E]ven a controlled suggestion of carnal bestiality is surely impossible: jealous Oberon will not have cast his spell to cuckold himself. Her dotage is imaginative and emotional.'[1]

One answer might be Prince Florizel's:

> Apprehend
> Nothing but jollity. The gods themselves,
> Humbling their deities to love, have taken
> The shapes of beasts upon them. Jupiter
> Became a bull and bellowed; the green Neptune
> A ram and bleated . . .[2]

But Harold Brooks's phrase 'carnal bestiality' seems unfairly prejudicial, since what is at issue is rather the possibility of sexual intercourse between a man and a woman. Bottom wears an ass's head, but the text makes clear that his body remains that of a man; and the entranced Titania sees him not as beast but as 'gentle mortal'. Brooks says that Oberon 'will not have cast his spell to cuckold himself'; well, Oberon will not have *intended* such an outcome, but it makes the play funnier and (arguably) *morally better* if he is cuckolded, since his own conduct is morally suspect.

Titania has been cherishing a 'changeling boy'. Oberon, jealous, demands that the boy should become 'Knight of his train, to trace the forests wild', but she refuses. As revenge, Oberon tells Robin Goodfellow (Puck) to drug her with a love-potion, the juice of the flower love-in-idleness; and, eventually, while she is still subject to the bemusing magic of the juice, Oberon taunts her and makes her agree to hand over the child. He thus wins the bizarre 'tug-of-love' dispute by taking advantage of Titania's entranced state. If, meanwhile, he has been cuckolded, that serves him right for having acted as a manipulative bully. We know that his schemes *can* miscarry: his plan to reconcile Demetrius and Helena went wildly wrong as a result of Robin's mismanagement. So it's feasible that he's deservedly fooled by the outcome of the meeting of Titania and Bottom.

'Bless thee, Bottom, bless thee. Thou art translated.' So says Quince, soon after Robin has transformed Bottom's head into that of an ass. The most celebrated modern production of the play, by Peter Brook (Royal Shakespeare Company, 1970), certainly suggested that Bottom's translation was, among other things, translation to a realm of sexual bliss with Titania. Much of the action took place in an austerely white setting, a kind of gymnasium with climbing-frames. As Oberon talked to Puck, the two sat on trapezes which swung steadily to and fro, over the stage and out over the orchestra-pit. In contrast to this austerity, as the voluptuous Titania conveyed Bottom away, Bottom joined her triumphantly (grossly tumescent) in a vast crimson bed, a huge soft nest of brilliant feathers; the bed ascended heavenwards, and, simultaneously, the stage erupted into festivity and wild joyous noise: a jazz band played a wedding march, while rejoicing figures scattered bright streamers into the audience. Brook's production was influenced by the Japanese theatre and by circuses featuring acrobats and gymnasts; but the biggest influence was the sexually hedonistic spirit of those 'permissive' times, when the counterparts of the juice of 'love-in-idleness' were marijuana and lysergic acid diethylamide; and the heart of the play, in Brook's version, was the orgasmic joy as Bottom and Titania embraced.[3]

One fault of that production, I thought, was that Bottom wore no ass's head but merely a clown's red nose and a cap whose dangling flaps vaguely suggested long ears. This contradicted the text (which specifies a realistically hairy ass's head), and accordingly reduced the absurd comedy and muffled the theme of love's blindness. Partly for that reason, the most enjoyable production of *A Midsummer Night's Dream* that I've seen was not Peter Brook's but a local production with amateur performers.[4] It took place in a Sussex village; the location was the garden of Rudyard Kipling's former house. The walls, trees and bushes of the garden sufficed as scenery, and the audience consisted of variegated villagers, who turned out with picnic hampers and bottles of wine or beer. Such a production lends to the dramatic endeavours of Bottom and his friends a topical aptitude and charm that no professional cast can match. Bottom, played with panache by Mr Ken Spalding, wore a realistic ass's head with large ears operated by concealed strings, so that when Titania declared her love for him, the ears grew instantly erect, indicating both astonishment and sexual excitement. By gesture and intonation, this actor strongly suggested that Bottom's abduction by Titania would have its sexual consequence. Consider what Titania says at the end of Act 3, scene 1:

> Come, wait upon him, lead him to my bower.
>   The moon, methinks, looks with a wat'ry eye,
> And when she weeps, weeps every little flower,
>   Lamenting some enforcèd chastity.
> Tie up my love's tongue; bring him silently.[5]   (lines 187–91)

The comedy here derived partly from the vocal counterpoint of Titania's pensive lyricism and Bottom's semi-articulate half-braying sounds, as well as from the visual contrast between the regal beauty of Titania and the ludicrous clumsiness of an ass-headed weaver. At the words 'Lamenting some enforcèd chastity', Spalding's Bottom made brayings of excited consternation (implying his apprehension of being forcibly 'deflowered' by her); and some such comical noises are indicated by the line 'Tie up my love's tongue; bring him silently.'

The lengthy scene 2 of Act 3 represents a period of time ample for leisurely offstage copulation by Bottom and Titania. Towards the end of that period, Oberon, having discovered Titania 'seeking sweet favours' for Bottom, had become jealously angry:

> I did upbraid her and fall out with her,
> For she his hairy temples then had rounded
> With coronet of fresh and fragrant flowers . . .   (4.1.49–51)

This is evidence that Titania has been well gratified; and it certainly proves that Oberon has not been aware of all that Bottom and Titania have done together, for he is disconcerted to see that this coronet has been made—a crown for a king's rival.

At Act 4, scene 1, when Bottom and Titania reappear, it's clear that there has been an amatory interim. Bottom (her 'gentle joy') is now relaxed and at ease, ready for food and sleep, while Titania lovingly embraces him. They resemble a slightly absurd and intoxicated, yet patently gratified, honeymoon couple.

TITANIA Sleep thou, and I will wind thee in my arms. . . .
O how I love thee, how I dote on thee!
They sleep. (4.1.39, 44)

The notion that the unwitting Oberon has been cuckolded, there-fore, has some interesting support in the text; and, indeed, it has been heralded by the song from Bottom that had first awakened the enchanted Titania:

> The finch, the sparrow, and the lark,
> The plainsong cuckoo grey,
> Whose note full many a man doth mark,
> And dares not answer 'Nay' . . . (3.1.123–6)

In other words, when a married man hears the cuckoo utter its warning that he may be a cuckold, he cannot with certainty offer a denial. In future, can Oberon? Perhaps that serves him right for his love of Hippolyta, his 'bouncing Amazon' and 'buskined mistress'.

Bottom is 'translated' in various senses: transformed, enraptured, removed, conveyed to a heaven. He is translated not only to a region of sexual bliss but also to one refined and spiritualized by magic and fantasy. Titania had promised: 'I will purge thy mortal grossness so | That thou shalt like an airy spirit go.' In Milton's *Paradise Lost*, the archangel Raphael explains to Adam that when spirits embrace, a perfect merging ensues: 'Total they mix' and 'obstacle find none | Of membrane, joint, or limb'.[6] Furthermore, the post-interim dialogues of Bottom with Peaseblossom, Cobweb, Moth, and Mustardseed (fairies often played on stage by young children) give a quality of childish innocence and fairy-tale fantasy to the situation. What is implied in the Bottom–Titania sequence is a translation into a tran-scendent realm of dream-like experience. At the centre of that realm may well be a blissful sexual union, but one rendered both innocent and, eventually, ineffable. By 'ineffable' I simply mean 'beyond expression', for that is what Bottom later finds to be the case:

I have had a most rare vision. I have had a dream past the wit of man to say what dream it was. Man is but an ass if he go about to expound this dream. Methought I was—there is no man can tell what. Methought I was, and methought I had—but man is but a patched fool if he will offer to say what methought I had. The eye of man hath not heard, the ear of man hath not seen, man's hand is not able to taste, his tongue to conceive, nor his heart to report what my dream was. (4.1.201–10)

Well, I—as expounding ass and patched fool for the occasion—will
venture to say that what he had was a sexual union with Titania, but
one that was no more like ordinary coitus than Mozart's *The Magic
Flute* is like Jagger's 'Honky-Tonk Woman'. The point is made by
Bottom's synaesthetic half-remembrance of the Bible. In 1 Corin-
thians 2: 9–10 we read:

The eye hath not seen, the ear hath not heard, neither have entered into
the heart of man, the things which God hath prepared for them that love
him.
   But God hath opened them unto us by his spirit. For the spirit
searcheth all things, yea, the bottom of God's secrets.[7]

Bottom is not, or has not plumbed, 'the bottom of God's secrets', for
he's part of a fantasia with a different metaphysic; but his tangled net
of allusion catches short-lived memory of an ineffable fusion of the
base and the exalted: of the mortal, human, animal, grotesque, and
male, with the female, beautiful, regal, superhuman, and immortal.
He and Titania will soon forget it, of course; but in several ways they
have made fools of Robin and Oberon. Bottom wore the ass's head
but Oberon wears the horns. More importantly: Oberon is mocked
by an event which transcends his knowledge and his capacities.
Commentators who worry about whether the union of Bottom and
Titania is *either* sexual *or* innocent seem to be trapped in the very
false disjunction that the play centrally mocks. It's not 'either/or':
it's at least 'both/and'.
   The bliss of Bottom and Titania provides the concealed but tantalizing centre of the whole drama. The lyrical fantasia which is *A
Midsummer Night's Dream* has an underlying strength which derives
from its readiness to translate into shimmering images and lyrical
poetry several platitudes of the emotional life. One platitude is that
sexual love can make bedfellows of the most unlikely partners
('What on earth does she see in him?'). Another is that while, to
outsiders, it may seem childish or ludicrous ('She made an ass of
him'), such love can at best reconcile 'mortal grossness' with experience which resembles enchantment and seems to elude the grasp of
language. Bottom says that his experience should be called 'Bottom's
Dream', 'because it hath no bottom'—suggesting both that it has no
solid foundation and that it is unfathomably profound.
   His name means 'core (or spool) of yarn' (appropriate to a weaver)

as well as suggesting 'buttocks'.[8] 'Titania' was one of the ancient names of Circe, the seductive enchantress who turned men into beasts, and of Selene or Diana, goddess of the moon; and, as commentators customarily note, imagery of the moon proliferates in this play, for that planet is associated with femininity, chastity, procreation, and change: the moon-goddess is tutelary deity of 'translation'. The union of Bottom with Titania is partly a burlesque counterpart of the trysts of Endymion, the shepherd, with Selene, the goddess; and it is partly a transcendent contrast to the literally bestial fornication-acts in Apuleius' *The Golden Ass*. It is a union of mortal with immortal, of the socially low with the supernaturally high, and of the knowable with the ineffable: carnal knowledge becomes incorporeal insight. It's a translation into radiant truth of the old platitude that sexual love can give intimations of immortality, even if such intimations prove no more durable than a dream.

As Bottom says, 'This was lofty.'

C.W.

Never act with dogs and babies

A number of puzzling aspects in *A Midsummer Night's Dream* have attracted learned exegesis over the centuries. How large are the fairies? Small enough to snuggle into a cowslip, or large enough to embrace a monstrously ass-headed man? (Or to copulate with an ass-headed man, if one goes along with the 1999 RSC production that scandalized some sections of the theatre-going public.) How do the four days which Theseus and Hippolyta repeatedly mention in the opening speeches mysteriously become shrunk to two and a bit days? (And in the title to one night?)

Here I want to focus on a very minor puzzle, Theseus's choral pack of hounds. The entrances of Theseus, Duke of Athens, frame the play. He symbolizes power, reason, and order. Arguably—at least in the arguments of subversive twentieth-century critics—his attempts to impose some discipline should be viewed as comically futile. As futile, that is, as the attempts of the mechanicals to achieve absolute realism in their masque. The harder they try (by having a character with a lamp play 'moon', for example), the less realistic their play becomes. So, too, the more authoritatively Theseus imposes order the more hilariously disorderly the play becomes.[1]

Theseus is, mythologically, an ambiguous figure. Legend portrays him as a rapist and a serial deserter of wives. He has won his latest bride, the taciturn Amazonian Hippolyta, by force: 'I wooed thee with my sword', he says. During the course of the play Theseus appears extraordinarily, not to say callously, engrossed with his personal affairs. Having briskly condemned Hermia to death or immurement in a nunnery, he bucks up his intended (who is clearly not looking forward to her impending nuptials) and demands the attention of Hermia's father Egeus and her lover Demetrius:

> Come, my Hippolyta; what cheer, my love?
> Demetrius and Egeus, go along.
> I must employ you in some business
> Against our nuptial, and confer with you
> Of something nearly that concerns yourselves. (1.1.122–6)

This 'something', we apprehend, is the programme of entertainment for his wedding celebrations. The fact that it may coincide with Hermia's being hanged—seems not to occur to Theseus. First things first.

It is feasible to conceive Theseus's authority and dignity as deliberately undercut by Shakespeare at moments like this. The Duke comes on only to preside at the beginning and the end, providing a framework of Athenian rationality around the madness of the wood. (His absence from the stage has led to convincing speculations that Shakespeare was allowing his cast to double up—Theseus and Oberon, Duke and King, would both be played by the same actor, for instance.)

At the end of the action, at dawn, the lovers are discovered sleeping off their night in the wood. Enter Theseus and Hippolyta hunting. There is the accompaniment of foresters' cries and the winding of horns. As it transpires, however, Theseus and Hippolyta are not actually involved in the hunt, they are merely spectators (or auditors). There ensues a series of speeches which seem rather beside the point (unless one assumes that they are principally designed to allow actors time to change role, makeup, and dress). Theseus goes on at great length about his wonderful dogs. He sends for the keeper of his animals in order, as he says, that 'My love shall hear the music of my hounds'.

To this end he instructs that the dogs be let loose by his foresters into a valley. He and Hippolyta, meanwhile, will listen to the tuneful echo of their barking:

> We will, fair Queen, up to the mountain's top,
> And mark the musical confusion
> Of hounds and echo in conjunction.   (4.1.108–10)

While they make to ascend the mountain (gathering their 'train'), Hippolyta—in an unusually long speech for this sullen bride-to-be— recollects an earlier occasion hunting with Hercules and Cadmus:

> When in a wood of Crete they bayed the bear
> With hounds of Sparta. Never did I hear
> Such gallant chiding; for besides the groves,
> The skies, the fountains, every region near
> Seem all one mutual cry. I never heard
> So musical a discord, such sweet thunder.
>   (lines 112–17)

(The last phrase was brilliantly drawn on by Duke Ellington as the title for his Shakespearian jazz suite.)

Theseus, not to be outdone by Hercules (and clearly nettled by the allusion to these other strong men) is driven to further encomiums on his pack:

> My hounds are bred out of the Spartan kind,
> So flewed, so sanded; and their heads are hung
> With ears that sweep away the morning dew,
> Crook-kneed, and dewlapped like Thessalian bulls,
> Slow in pursuit, but matched in mouth like bells,
> Each under each. A cry more tuneable
> Was never holla'd to nor cheered with horn
> In Crete, in Sparta, nor in Thessaly.
>
> (lines 118–25)

This dog-fancying line of thought is broken up by the sight of the sleeping lovers. By the time explanations have been made (as best they can be) the morning is 'something worn' and everyone returns to Athens for the great day. Nothing has been caught in the hunt. The day will be crowned by a wedding of Revd Moon-like numerousness.

As commentators have pointed out, hunting was a well-developed recreation in Elizabethan and Jacobean England and was as ritualized a pastime as even Roger Scruton might desire. The musical qualities of baying hounds were cultivated. H. H. Furness cites Gervase Markham's *Country Contentments* (1615):

If you would have your kennel for sweetness of cry, then you must compound it of some large dogs, that have deep, solemn mouths and are swift in spending, which must (as it were) bear the bass in the consort; then a double number of roaring and loud ringing mouths, which must bear the counter-tenour; then some hollow, plain, sweet mouths, which must bear the mean or middle part; and so with these three parts of music you shall make your cry perfect.[2]

Theseus, however, goes even further. Each of his overbred Spartan hounds has been selected for its having a different bay, so that the effect of the pack in full cry is that of a peal of bells, each with its separate note. Something important (all important in hunting dogs, one might think) has been sacrificed for this tunefulness. Theseus's dogs are 'slow in pursuit'.[3] I am no huntsman, but I would have thought that the last thing that you would want if you went a-hunting in the Athenian woods was slow dogs. But, as is made clear, Theseus and Hippolyta are not hunting. They are merely watching and listening, as one might at a play or a concert. Does Theseus, perhaps, not trust his Amazonian bride with a bow and arrows, or with a horse?

One might argue that having been bred as a Warwickshire boy (and possibly a poacher) Shakespeare had the countryman's contempt for the gents' sport and their fancy get-up. He is mocking the effeteness of the nobility at their Nimrod play. There is another possible explanation. Hunting scenes are wonderfully exciting narrative episodes. One thinks of the opening stag-hunting stanzas in Scott's *The Lady of the Lake*, the fox hunt (with its innovative hand-held camera work) in Tony Richardson's film of *Tom Jones*, the pig hunt in Peter Brook's film of *Lord of the Flies*, and any number of scenes in Trollope and Surtees. But the hunt is virtually impossible to do in any realistic way onstage. For one thing, dogs are often uncontrollable. Never act with dogs or babies, as W. C. Fields sagely warned. One dog may be manageable: Lance and his four-legged friend are a star-turn in *Two Gentlemen of Verona*. But a pack of them? Never.

Even if the dogs (or little eyases) *are* well behaved, and play their parts without mischief, the audience is so distracted by the sheer skill of the fact that they ignore the main business of the play. Like women preaching (to echo Dr Johnson) the wonder is that it is done at all. But most likely the beasts will embarrass the production by defecating on stage, chasing something or other, or just frisking around.

In the opening scene of Act 4 of *A Midsummer Night's Dream* Shakespeare's composition is driven by a number of imperatives. There has to be some plausible reason for Theseus and Hippolyta to be in the forest on the morning of their wedding day. A celebratory hunt was satisfactorily plausible. On the other hand, dogs were not to be thought of. Shakespeare finesses the problem by having Theseus and Hippolyta 'spectate' the hunt from a distance. How to rationalize this? They want to listen to the 'sweet thunder'—they do not want to exhaust themselves, with a wedding night in prospect. It will, of course, be quite possible to create the necessary tuneful baying using the repertoire of stage effects, although a certain restraint will be necessary. One does not want to create the ludicrous effect of that record, once beloved on the radio requests programme, *Children's Favourites*, of harmonious canines barking out 'How much is that Doggy in the Window?' The way round this secondary problem is to drive the super-phallic Theseus to transparent hyperbole, and unconscious self-satire, with the business about his wonderful melodious hounds. But then, having raised our expectations, Shakespeare dashes it. 'Judge when you hear,' Theseus tells Hippolyta. But then he breaks off ('what nymphs are these?'—being Theseus, he does not notice the swains). We never do hear; she never does judge.

J.S.

Why is Shylock unmusical?

———

> And others when the bagpipe sings i'th'nose
> Cannot contain their urine . . .   (4.1.48–9)

We don't expect *The Merchant of Venice* to offer an account of Jews
in Venice which, in detail, is historically accurate. On the other hand,
as readers and spectators of the play, we may well assume that
in some obvious respects the play is accurate enough. We may
assume, for example, that in the historical Venice of the late sixteenth
century, business-minded Jews were confined to money-lending,
whereas the many occupations of Christians included mercantile
venturing; that Jews might be more mercenary and less inclined
to financial generosity than were the Christians; and that Jews
maintained an austere and joyless cultural separateness. All these
assumptions are demonstrably wrong. Brian Pullan's *Rich and Poor
in Renaissance Venice* provides the historical facts.

In the play, Shylock, who clearly prefers to charge high interest
rates, is angered because Antonio, by lending gratis, reduces the
rates. In fact, the Jews of Venice were subject to elaborate and often
punitive controls by the authorities. Those Jews were obliged by law
to maintain charitable and unprofitable banks to provide loans to
needy Christians at strictly controlled low rates: 5 per cent to cover
expenses.[1] In order to supply such banks, Jews took to foreign trade.
At a time (1590 to 1610) when many Christian merchants, finding
trade too risky, preferred to invest in estates on the mainland, the
Jews sent merchandise across the sea, particularly to the Turkish
empire between Dalmatia and Constantinople. In some respects
their risks were greater than Antonio's, for, in addition to the hazards
of storm and tempest, their cargoes were subject to depredations by
anti-Semitic Christian pirates, among them the Knights of St John
of Malta.[2] During this period, the magistrates of Padua reported to
the Venetian Senate that Jewish merchants were markedly less
rapacious than Christians:

[T]he Jew is forbidden to invest his money in anything other than merchandise, and so long as he knows that trade is progressing and multiplying he is content with smaller gains than the Christian, who wishes to invest his money in estates, houses and other real property, and is not content with a little, but develops a voracious desire for gain.[3]

We may recall incidentally, that (nearer to home) John Shakespeare, the playwright's father, had once been found guilty of usury, his interest rate apparently being an extortionate 25 per cent.[4]

Venetian Jews were confined to a ghetto and were subject to many humiliating restrictions. Numerous occupations were legally denied to them; they were prevented from infringing the Christian guilds' monopoly of manufacturing. They were forbidden, for instance, to become tailors or to import new clothes:

Behind these regulations, though it was never expressly acknowledged, there probably lay the desire to deny the Jews the satisfaction of creative work, and to thrust them into a position in which they appeared to be social parasites—dealers, middlemen and moneylenders, never producers. Anti-semitism itself foists upon the Jews the characteristics it later ascribes to their innate depravity.[5]

Nevertheless, occupations which remained open to them included those of physician, printer, bookseller, greengrocer—and musician. *The Merchant of Venice* suggests that Christians (rather than Jews) appreciate music, and are thus attuned to the celestial harmony which lies beyond this 'mortal vesture'. Shylock's daughter, Jessica, is 'never merry' when she hears pleasant music; but Lorenzo lyrically explains that to dislike music is to be untrustworthy, and, indeed, to be out of touch with the divine:

> How sweet the moonlight sleeps upon this bank!
> Here will we sit and let the sounds of music
> Creep in our ears. Soft stillness and the night
> Become the touches of sweet harmony. . . .
> There's not the smallest orb which thou behold'st
> But in his motion like an angel sings,
> Still quiring to the young-eyed cherubins.
> Such harmony is in immortal souls . . . .
> The man that hath no music in himself,
> Nor is not moved with concord of sweet sounds,
> Is fit for treasons, stratagems, and spoils. . . .
> Let no such man be trusted.[6]   (5.1.54–7, 60–3, 83–5, 88)

Such a man without music is clearly Shylock, who had commanded
Jessica thus:

> Lock up my doors, and when you hear the drum
> And the vile squealing of the wry-necked fife,
> Clamber not you up to the casements then . . .
> But stop my house's ears—I mean my casements:
> Let not the sound of shallow fopp'ry enter
> My sober house.

(2.5.29–31, 34–6)

In the historical Venice, the contrasting facts were these:

[A]t the turn of the century, Jewish dancing masters, musicians and players
were obviously sought-after by Christian pupils and audiences—as
witness a licence prepared in September 1585 to authorize a Jew to
enter the houses of eleven noblemen and five other persons 'to teach their
children to sing, dance and play musical instruments, freely and without
restraint'.

Pullan adds that during the Carnivals of 1594 and 1595, Don Livio
of Ferrara, a Jewish resident in the Venetian ghetto, received permis-
sion to take his pupils or 'company' to dance in the houses of noblemen, while one Iseppo, with two fellow lute-players, was allowed to
perform for the nobility until 'the sixth hour of the night'. In
November 1590, a company of fourteen Jewish players obtained a
licence to leave the Ghetto during the Carnival 'to try out and
perform *una opera premeditada* [*sic*, a planned work]'.[7]

Shylock has a Christian servant, Lancelot, but Patriarch Priuli
had insisted in a memorandum of 1596–7 that Jews should not
employ Christian servants or workmen, must not invite Christians to
eat with them, and must wear yellow caps to mark them out as
members of an accursed race.[8] Yet these reviled pariahs were nevertheless obliged to maintain the charitable banks and to provide
finance for the Venetian navy. Within their ghetto they still managed
to organize fraternities for almsgiving, clothing the poor, lodging
foreigners, and running a children's school and an academy.[9]

In short, the myth further propagated by Shakespeare (at a time
when riots against aliens were not uncommon in London) offers
some remarkable contrasts to what is now regarded as the historical
truth. Probably few readers or spectators of the play appreciate the
full extent of the ironic disparity between what Shakespeare suggests
and what the life of Jews actually was. Whether Shakespeare actually

travelled in Italy and to Venice has long been a matter of scholarly debate. Like *Othello*, *The Merchant* has sufficient local colour: Portia even refers to the 'traject' (i.e. the *traghetto*, the local ferry). The biographer Samuel Schoenbaum remarks, though, that Shakespeare had a loose grasp of Italian topography:

Characters in land-locked Verona (in *Two Gentlemen*) take ship; Milan, in *The Tempest*, is conceived as connecting with the sea by a waterway. In *The Taming of the Shrew* inland Bergamo has a sailmaker, and Biondello comes ashore in Padua . . .[10]

Shakespeare could have learnt of Italian matters from various Italians resident in London. Schoenbaum mentions some of them, notably 'numerous Bassanos, natives of Venice', who were musicians to the Queen. Perhaps a recollection of them suggested the name 'Bassanio' in *The Merchant*.[11]

Of course, Shakespeare was drawing on a long sequence of source-tales featuring the avaricious Jew who seeks a pound of flesh, as payment of a debt, from his unfortunate Christian defaulter. That tradition includes the thirteenth-century *Cursor Mundi*, fifteenth-century translations of the *Gesta Romanorum*, and Ser Giovanni's *Il pecorone*. But the Jew's hostility to music appears to be a distinctively Shakespearian addition to the source-materials. There is a broad thematic reason for this, as we have seen: Shakespeare is (un-historically) associating the Christians with the cosmically harmonious, and this Jew with those who are by nature 'discordant' and untrustworthy. Frequently Shakespeare associates music with healing, with the restoration of order to a disordered self: sweet harmonies are part of the therapy for Lear and for Pericles. Within *The Merchant of Venice*, the playing of music is required on two occasions. The first is when Bassanio is choosing one of three caskets. If he chooses the correct casket, made of lead, he will win the hand of the wealthy lady whom he loves, Portia. The two rival suitors were not accorded this musical aid; Bassanio, granted it, chooses correctly and his love is fulfilled. Perhaps cheating is involved: some commentators have suggested that the song, 'Tell me where is fancy bred, | Or in the heart, or in the head?', while not specifying the word 'lead', still offers three rhyming syllables – 'bred', 'head', and 'ed' at the end of 'nourishèd'—which may subliminally guide Bassanio's choice.[12] If the commentators' suggestion is correct, music is the means to the defeat of Shylock; for when Bassanio wins Portia, she learns of Antonio's plight, and proceeds to intervene victoriously at the court of justice. The second occasion for music arises, of course, in that Belmont scene in which Lorenzo emphasizes the healing, harmonizing power and that responsiveness to concord which Shylock lacks.

But there seems to be another reason for Shylock's unhistorical unmusicality. In characterizing him, Shakespeare has given Shylock not only supposedly Jewish traits but also Puritanical traits. He has acquired some of the killjoy characteristics which will be found in other Puritanical figures: the Malvolio of *Twelfth Night* and the Angelo of *Measure for Measure*. At a time when the Puritans were leaders of the campaign against the theatres, dramatists retaliated by depicting Puritans as hypocritical and sometimes ruthless bigots. Music, of course, was a staple of the Elizabethan theatre; not only was it frequently incorporated within plays, it frequently formed a coda to the play—even of such a political tragedy as *Julius Caesar*.[13] To make Shylock unmusical was to ally him with the inveterate enemies of the theatre, and thus with enemies of the theatre's regular patrons.

Anti-Semitic stereotypes form part of the source-materials of *The Merchant of Venice*, though the extent to which Shakespeare's play is anti-Semitic has long been a topic of debate. (In the 1930s, the Nazis thought it served their purposes; in the 1970s Arnold Wesker felt that it needed an antidote, his own play *The Merchant*.) What complicates the debate is that *The Merchant of Venice* is also, intermittently, anti-Puritanical. And what actors of the part of Shylock have long recognized is that it is the most impressive role in the play. In his wrongheaded intensity, and his final humiliation at the hands of Christians whose various responses include the jeering and the vindictive, he gains some of the sympathy we extend to the underdog ('You . . . foot me as you spurn a stranger cur', he had formerly remarked); and, in addition, he approaches the stature of the self-destructively misguided, yet beleagueredly intense, tragic hero.[14] Shakespeare frequently associated music with cosmic harmony, with healing, and with genial hedonism; but, just as he could sometimes express disgust at his own chosen profession ('And almost thence my nature is subdued | To what it works in, like the dyer's hand'; 'Alas, 'tis true, I have gone here and there | And made myself a motley to the view'), so occasionally he could associate music with the subversively importunate claims of the sensual appetite. One may think of the drunken wassailing on Pompey's barge in *Anthony and Cleopatra*; and, in *Twelfth Night*, it is the self-indulgent and dangerous Orsino (here sounding like a forerunner of decadent Aesthetes) who says not only 'If music be the food of love, play on', but also 'Give me excess of it, that surfeiting, | The appetite may sicken and so die'.

Commentators on Othello have referred to 'the *Othello* music', that distinctive romantic eloquence enriched by exotic place-names (the Pontic sea, the Propontic and the Hellespont, the Arabian trees that drop their medicinal gum).[15] Shylock, in contrast, has 'the Shylock discordancies': his characteristic utterances are tinged with harshness; they tend to the doggedly argumentative and to illustrations which jar or embarrass: one thinks, for example, of his story of Jacob and the 'woolly breeders'; and even his celebrated plea for equality (the speech in Act 3, scene 1, beginning 'Hath not a Jew eyes?') degenerates into an abrasive vindication of revenge. A characteristic minor discordancy is his odd reference, with which this essay began, to the diuretic quality of bagpipe music. Shylock was not alone in this curious belief. Edward Kno'well, a character in Ben Jonson's *Every Man in His Humour* (a play in which, in its early version, Shakespeare acted), asks Wellbred: 'What ails thy brother? Can he not hold his water at reading of a ballad?'; and Wellbred replies: 'Oh no; a rhyme to him is worse than cheese or a bagpipe.'[16] The explanation of this multiple slander (on bagpipes, cheese, and ballads) is, however, matter for a different discussion.

C.W.

Is Portia a virgin at the end of the play— and will she stay one?

Bassanio's triumphant lovemaking at Belmont is interrupted immediately after the business of the trial-by-casket. A letter arrives from Venice delivered in person by Salerio. The news is as bad as can be. Antonio informs his 'Sweet Bassanio' that 'my ships have all miscarried'. His bond is consequently forfeit. Shylock will surely demand his pound of flesh. Death, of an exceedingly painful and public kind, is certain. Let their 'love' urge Bassanio to return to Venice, for a last farewell.

Bassanio is visibly distraught. Portia is amazed at his anguished reactions, suspecting some awful disaster. When she learns it is just 'business' she promptly proffers her fortune, multiplying what she will give this stranger, on behalf of her lover (almost as much a stranger to her at this point as Antonio), to fabulous amounts of ducats. 'Double six thousand, and then treble that'—she says, magnificently; 'Pay the petty debt twenty times over.' It's not clear how much Shakespeare thought a ducat worth. But since a major business loan on the Rialto is 2,000 ducats the lady is clearly talking a lot of money.[1]

Portia's money is, we gather, 'old money'. And it is still hers, of course. After marriage (which is imminent) it will be her lucky husband's to do what he wills with it (unless, of course, her smart lawyer friends in Padua have tied it up by some kind of settlement). Bassanio must, he says, hie off to Venice at once. But first, Portia decrees (still commander of her fortune, she has—for a few hours more—the authority to give orders), they must be married. All four of them, she means (Portia and Bassanio, Nerissa and Graziano). While their new-minted spouses are away, she declares:

> My maid Nerissa and myself meantime
> Will live as maids and widows.[2]   (3.2.307–8)

By this paradox she means that they will not consummate the union. Why, then, marry? To create a bond as arbitrary and symmetrically binding as Shylock's? Or perhaps, as a married man (and lord of Belmont's wealth), Bassanio will be financially empowered to buy his bosom friend's reprieve, before that bosom is ripped open and the beating heart torn out of his ribcage. Or, perhaps, Portia does not trust Bassanio and wants to test him (as indeed, she eventually does)?

Bassanio and Graziano rush away in admired disorder. Whether by carriage (which is what Portia and Nerissa will employ when they follow) or on horse is not clear. 'No bed,' Bassanio promises, will be 'guilty of my stay' before he returns to the marriage bed. There follows the trickery of Portia's letter to Bellario, her learned lawyer friend and kinsman in Padua. He (she knows in advance) will agree to conspire with her in the impersonation of the 'civil Doctor' from Rome, 'Balthasar' (the name is mischievously that of her slow-witted servant). Portia's relationship to the Paduan lawyer is never spelled out nor does he ever appear on stage. But it must be remarkably close for him to join with her in an act of what will be—to the cold eye of any appellate court—criminal fraud. One does not know how the Bar was regulated in seventeenth-century Italy; but Bellario's flagrant misconduct would invite disbarment in any legal system with the slightest pride in its own legality.

One assumes, incidentally, that it was Bellario who devised the casket business (a process which Portia is manifestly in a position to rig; *she* knows, as is clear, which casket contains her counterfeit, and nudges suitors which way it suits her). As with Penelope's weaving and the bow of Ulysses, the test is designed less to select suitors than to keep them at bay. It is also, one assumes, Bellario who instructs Portia (who can scarcely be a legal scholar) in the pettifoggery about 'no jot of blood' (is there no 'de minimis' restriction in the Venetian legal code?).[3] By all the evidence we have in the play, Portia's cousin Bellario is in the same lawyer class as 'my cousin Vinnie'. Shylock meets shyster.

One thing, however, is very clear. Portia is resolved to go to any length to save her lord's 'bosom lover' (the term she uses, rather than the more conventional 'bosom friend'). To cover the ladies' clandestine jaunt to Venice it is given out that she and Nerissa will go to a holy house ('a monastery two miles off'). The ladies would not, of course, qualify for entry to this convent unless they were still virginal. To prepare for their jaunt to Venice they cross-dress as men, with much ritual bawdry (something, incidentally, that would not be fitting were they bedded wives; they have a borrowed lease of a few hours in which they can revel in such girlish high jinks).

There follows the great business of the trial and the anti-climax of the ring-exchange game. Timing is significant at this juncture and rather vexing. The audience, alerted by the business with the wedding-rings, must be nervously aware that there is some unfinished (or unstarted) marital business to perform. Consciously, or unconsciously, we are led to wonder when the business of the bed will take place and where it will take place. There is a threshold beyond which sexual excitement becomes sexual frustration. The audience is poised awkwardly on that threshold for the last hour of *The Merchant of Venice*.

In the geography of the play, Belmont is apparently twenty miles distant from Venice by road. They will, presumably, be good roads (there is no mention of bandits in the play) and the journey will take some three to four hours at a horse's normal pace. When, outside the court, the Duke invites her to dinner (after Shylock has been disposed of), Portia–Balthasar politely declines: 'I must away this night toward Padua' (to report in person to her mentor, Bellario, as the Duke will apprehend). Later to Nerissa she says more candidly:

> We'll away tonight,
> And be a day before our husbands home.   (4.2.2–3)

Away where? Are they going directly home to Belmont? If so, they will be back before next daybreak.

On his part, Bassanio is not in the home-wending vein; not tonight, at least. He intends to spend the night in his bosom-lover Antonio's house and in the morning 'early . . . Fly toward Belmont' (what about his promise that no bed, other than Portia's, should be guilty of his stay?). Graziano is instructed to stay with him. 'We'll rush to our wives—to-morrow'. It's an odd mixture of delay and urgency. It reminds one of the old 'Laugh-in' joke: 'Do you believe in sex before marriage? Not if it makes you late for the ceremony.' Bassanio, apparently, doesn't believe in sex after marriage. At least, not too soon after the ceremony.

We do not witness the celebrations in Antonio's house—lavish they will be, we can be sure. The scene shifts to Belmont, and the post-coital crooning of Lorenzo and Jessica (there have been no delays in that quarter; they are like a couple of cats gorged on cream). It is, as we are repeatedly informed, the small hours of the morning—some eight hours after Nerissa and Portia left Venice, as we may at first think.

But, on second thoughts, the audience will reckon that it is more likely to be around 36 hours—a full day and a bit. This longer interval is suggested by the fact that, only a minute or two after Nerissa and Portia arrive, Antonio, Bassanio, Graziano, and their followers come on the scene. There is no indication that they have forgone their great dinner, or have not had a good post-prandial rest to recover from it. They say nothing about being exhausted or having hurried themselves.

When the married (but still oddly maiden) ladies arrive it is towards morning ('This night,' Portia says, 'is but the daylight sick. | It looks a little paler'). The note of disappointment is understandable. She may have expected greater things of the darkness of this night than an empty bed and a burned-down candle. She might also reasonably have expected her husband to be waiting, in his night-clothes, for her, impatiently stalking up and down the bedchamber in his lover's ardour. Brides like to be carried across the thresholds of their marital home—a symbolic rapture. Portia walks in lonely virginity across hers.

The empty house is still illuminated by candles ('so shines a good deed in a naughty world'). But the moon is down, a sign of imminent daybreak.[4] To validate their 'monastery' cover story the ladies have (according to Portia's servant, Stefano) brought with them a 'holy hermit'. This chaperone says nothing. Perhaps he has taken a vow of silence. The ladies have, perhaps, stopped by the monastery, and remained there some hours, composing themselves. At least, this is what they want the world to suppose.

There is, however, a more plausible explanation which the audience can arrive at, if they remember Portia's earlier reply to the Duke, turning down his invitation to dinner. It connects neatly with another rather mysterious piece of evidence. Just before the play ends, Portia hands Antonio a letter in which he will find:

> three of your argosies
> Are richly come to harbour suddenly.
> You shall not know by what strange accident
> I chancèd on this letter.　　　　(5.1.276–9)

Antonio is dumbstruck. How on earth did she come by the letter? In Padua, of course, we apprehend. In short, what Portia told the Duke was true. She *did* return there, to square things with Bellario. He, of course, could be badly compromised if it came out that he had forged 'Balthasar's' credentials and connived in a legal fraud. Bellario will have been on tenterhooks—what if they are unmasked in the Venetian court as girl-impostors? Will he have to compound his lies by denying any involvement? The custodians of Venetian law—who are prepared to witness one of their most esteemed merchants legally disembowelled in their august presence—may not be forgiving of a Paduan lawyer who makes such a mockery of their legal system.

Having soothed Bellario's anxieties the ladies then came back via the nearby monastery, picking up the dumb and pliant 'holy hermit' to cover their tracks. That functionary will, of course, have been instructed to back them up in whatever falsehoods they come out with. (If the monastery is two miles distant from fabulously wealthy Belmont it will be entirely dependent on the great house's beneficence.)

At Padua, news from the port of Genoa would arrive before it reached Venice, on the east coast. When it was known that Portia was riding at all speed towards Belmont, and would there meet Antonio, she might very plausibly have been asked to act as courier. Antonio, on his part, would have left urgent messages in Genoa that any good news as to his ships coming in should be rushed to him as fast as horse could gallop. His life might depend on the speed with which letters could reach him. It is quite likely that his good news would be entrusted to someone travelling post-haste eastwards.

The best estimate is that the Portia/Nerissa detour via Padua (some forty miles from Venice) has taken the best part of the day after the trial. (One should, of course, not over-estimate Shakespeare's grasp of Italian geography: in the opening scene of *Two Gentlemen of Verona* he assumes you can get from Verona to Milan by canal.) Assuming, however, that Shakespeare had a map of Italy to hand, we can estimate that the ladies left Venice for Padua in the early evening of day one. They arrived in Padua in the morning of day two. They left Padua around lunchtime on day two—having conferred with Bellario—then made for the monastery, and bundled the holy hermit into their carriage. They finally reached Belmont in the early hours of day three; around three or four o'clock in the morning. Still night-time, that is, but only just.

A few minutes later, almost at dawn on day three, the husbands arrive from Venice. Their timetable goes thus: they spent the night of day one and the early morning of day two carousing and feasting. So merry was the event that despite the good intention to 'fly toward Belmont' next morning, they spent most of day two sleeping off the night before, and nursing their hangovers. They set out, with a considerable entourage (Antonio, and all their 'followers'), in late afternoon, and have arrived, as has been said, in the wee small hours of day three.

And what of the bed-business? At the end of the play, Bassanio says very little on this matter. Portia and Graziano are left to wrap the proceedings up:

> PORTIA   It is almost morning,
> And yet I am sure you are not satisfied
> Of these events at full. Let us go in,
> And charge us there upon inter'gatories,
> And we will answer all things faithfully.
> GRAZIANO Let it be so. The first inter'gatory
> That my Nerissa shall be sworn on is
> Whether till the next night she had rather stay
> Or go to bed now, being two hours to day.
> But were the day come, I should wish it dark
> Till I were couching with the doctor's clerk.
> Well, while I live I'll fear no other thing
> So sore as keeping safe Nerissa's ring.   (5.1.295–307)

The bawdy joke makes quite clear that Graziano is going to waste no time ('two hours' seems a hopeful over-estimate). But what about Portia and Bassanio? They, apparently, are going to *talk things over*— answer a few questions, mull over the events of the previous days. There is not enough night left for decent lovemaking, is the implication. They, of course, are gentlefolk. They will not go to't like the soiled fitchew, the gilded wren, or Graziano and Nerissa. And so the consummation of the great marriage will be put off yet another day. The wedding-night will be a full five days after the ceremony. If then.

Portia ends the play, as she began, a virgin. For the audience, that intact hymen is like a sneeze that doesn't come. It is oddly frustrating. It needn't have been. Without damage to the structure of the play's narrative, Bassanio could have galloped hell for leather from Venice to Belmont immediately after the trial, spurred on by testosterone and desire for his conjugal rights. On her part, had she known that was his intention, Portia would certainly have put off her Padua visit to be waiting for her hot lord at Belmont. As it is, she knows all about Antonio's feast (she was after all, invited to it). She knows her husband would, apparently, rather feast with his friend than on her. Hence she has time for her duty call to Bellario (he, at least, will be eager to see her).

What, we are driven to ask, would Bassanio rather do?—spend the night with Antonio and enjoy *another* bachelor party, or spend the night (of nights) with his newly wedded wife? To have the stag-night *after* the wedding is odd indeed. Can one imagine Romeo putting off his wedding-night with Juliet to carouse with the Montague boys one more time?

More than feasting may be involved. Commentators have plausibly hypothesized that Antonio and Bassanio are, as Portia puts it, 'bosom lovers'. Hence the otherwise enigmatically 'love-sick' opening speech of Antonio's:

> In sooth, I know not why I am so sad.
> It wearies me, you say it wearies you;
> But how I caught it, found it, or came by it,
> What stuff 'tis made of, whereof it is born,
> I am to learn;
> And such a want-wit sadness makes of me,
> That I have much ado to know myself.   (1.1.1–7)

This may be the love that cannot know (or name) itself. Bassanio enters shortly after, anxious about his business interests. His first mention of Portia is not that she is 'fair' but that she is a 'a lady richly left'. Were she not rich would he still be her suitor? She is, he says, a 'golden fleece'. A worthy prize—but not a woman to be won for herself.

In brief, we may surmise that Bassanio loves Antonio and vice versa. Just how much vice must be a matter of speculation.[5] There is substantial food for speculation in the nationality of the two men. As Alan Bray records, homosexuality, like the pox, was conventionally seen to be a (nasty) Italian thing by your average Englishman of Shakespeare's time:

Le bougre Italien, according to Thomas Browne was the national character of the Italians; and it was the Lombards, or so at least claimed Edward Coke, who first brought homosexuality into England. Coke also solemnly reminded his readers that 'bugeria is an Italian word'.[6]

And, we may suspect, an Italian practice.

Even more speculatively we may note that the name 'Antonio' seems in Shakespeare's mind to have been associated with homoeroticism. In *Twelfth Night* there is, as commentators have often observed, a 'time problem'. Viola is saved from drowning, and a few days later the business of the play—culminating in the double marriage—occurs. But Antonio comes to Illyria on the grounds of a 'love' which has been flourishing for 'three months' following his rescuing Sebastian from drowning. Yet, the twins Viola and Sebastian were shipwrecked at exactly the same time—a few days or three months ago? The solve-all of 'double time' cuts through this (as it does through the 'time problem' in *The Merchant of Venice*, the three months term of Shylock's bond, which is overleapt in a couple of days).

More interesting from the psychological point of view is the observable fact that in *Twelfth Night* Shakespeare *needs* the three months to render plausible the 'deeper' love of Antonio for Sebastian (another couple of Italians). Deeper, that is, than the 'love of the eye' which leads Olivia to fall in love with the young man (or his look-alike sister) at first sight. Antonio's love for Sebastian is a truer love (he will give his life for it). Antonio's love for Bassanio, we may assume, is greater than Portia's. He will, literally, give Bassanio his heart. She can only come up with ducats.

The ending of *The Merchant of Venice*—with the consummation of the Bassanio/Portia relationship hanging unresolved—wreathes the whole triangular relationship in further enigma. What, the innocent audience might think, is Antonio doing at Belmont anyway— what kind of man would take his best friend on his honeymoon? Graziano brings no friend with him to assist in the business of Nerissa's other ring. Will Bassanio, Portia, and Antonio take breakfast together after the wedding night? Will they sleep in adjoining rooms? Portia's suspended condition of virginity leaves worms of uneasiness writhing in the audience's mind as they leave the theatre.

J.S.

Muddle or method?

——

At the end of *Troilus and Cressida*, Troilus goes out to fight, but
we are not told what happens to him; we don't know what befalls
Cressida or Helen; and (for all the hints that the death of Hector
seals Troy's fate) we aren't told the outcome of the war. If we turn to
Chaucer we can learn that Troilus was spitefully slain by the fierce
Achilles; from Henryson we can learn that Cressida become a
leprous beggar; and Homer tells us that Helen returned with her
husband Menelaus to his palace in Lacedaemon. The defeat of the
Trojans by the Greeks is and was reasonably general knowledge.
Shakespeare's audiences would know that the history of Britain
began with the fall of Troy; indeed the name 'Britain' supposedly
meant 'The Land of Brutus' (Brutus or Brute being a descendant of
Aeneas, Trojan refugee and boat-person; London's old name being
supposedly Troia Nova, New Troy). Yes, we can supply the stuff to
fill the gaps, or find editors obsequiously willing to save us the effort;
but why does Shakespeare leave *Troilus and Cressida* in such a conspicuously gappy state? You could drive a coach and Trojan horses
through the holes in this ending. Instead of doing that, past audiences found it less effort to vote with their feet and walk away from
the box-office.

'He was not of an age, but for all time', said Ben Jonson (thus
providing an epigraph for thousands of essay-writing students and
a provocation to half a dozen New Historicists and Cultural
Materialists). The stage histories of Shakespeare's works suggest
something rather different. Some plays die for centuries but are
then resurrected when cultural changes provide congenial circumstances. *King Lear*, famously, vanished from the stage between
1681 and the early nineteenth century, the gap being filled by
Nahum Tate's notorious adaptation with the happy ending (in
which Cordelia, alive and well, blushingly takes the hand of Edgar,
while Lear, Gloucester and Kent prepare for meditative retirement
in the Sunset Home of 'some cool cell'). Badly recited by lecturers
to win an easy laugh, the Tate *Lear* can sound like a strong con-

tender for a 'Springtime for Hitler' prize, awarded by the ghost of William McGonagall to works so dire as to be thoroughly entertaining. But Dr Johnson, whose errors are usually more informative than other critics' accuracies, felt that on balance, using the democratic criterion of popularity, Tate's version was preferable to Shakespeare's. *Troilus and Cressida* had an even more protracted death. Between Shakespeare's day and 1907, there is no record of any British performance; but since 1907 it has been revived with gradually increasing frequency. In 1898 George Bernard Shaw said of Shakespeare: 'In such unpopular plays as *All's Well*, *Measure for Measure*, and *Troilus and Cressida*, we find him ready and willing to start at the twentieth century if the seventeenth would only let him';[1] and Shaw was right. By 1974 (the year after US troops withdrew from Vietnam) Anne Barton, in the *Riverside Shakespeare*, could remark:

More than any other play by Shakespeare, *Troilus and Cressida* is the discovery of the twentieth century. Its unconventional form, neither comedy, tragedy, history, nor satire, its intellectualism, savagery, and disillusion[,] speak forcefully to contemporary audiences naturally sceptical about ideas of honor, nobility, and military glory.[2]

Though 'neither comedy, tragedy, history, nor satire', the play has to be pigeonholed by publishers, and accordingly the *Riverside Shakespeare* places it in the 'Comedies' section. *Troilus and Cressida* had been generically problematic from the outset. In 1609 the First Quarto's title-page called it a 'Historie', but the preface to the same Quarto called it a 'Commedy'; and the First Folio proclaimed it on the title-page as 'The Tragedie of Troylus and Cressida'.

By 1679 John Dryden regarded it with exasperated bafflement:

[T]he later part of the Tragedy is nothing but a confusion of Drums and Trumpets, Excursions and Alarms. The chief persons, who give name to the Tragedy, are left alive: *Cressida* is false, and is not punish'd.

Yet, after all, because the play was Shakespeare's, Dryden gallantly undertook 'to remove that heap of Rubbish, under which many excellent thoughts lay wholly bury'd'.[3] The result was his *Troilus and Cressida, or, Truth Found too Late; A Tragedy*, in which Cressida is faithful to Troilus all the time, and proves her fidelity by committing suicide; and Troilus, realizing that he has wrongly thought her

unfaithful, dies heroically fighting the Greeks. Stage direction: '*All
the Trojans dye upon the place*, Troilus *last*.' That's more like it: that's
how a tragedy should end; or so he and audiences of his time must
have thought.

The main reason for the problems of how to label Shakespeare's
Troilus and Cressida and how to understand its unconventional
ending was given clearly enough in the play itself. For all its suffering
and slaughter, central characters in the play are too stupid and hypocritical to *deserve* tragedy. Black comedy, savage farce, theatre of
cruelty; yes, they might deserve something like that. But tragedy, no.
Ulysses makes the point early on, in his famous 'degree' speech.
That's the long lecture to the Greek leaders in which he says that
there's a divinely-ordained hierarchy extending from the lowest to
the highest, and this hierarchy must be respected, otherwise there's a
progressive collapse of order:

> Take but degree away, untune that string,
> And hark what discord follows. . . .
> Then everything includes itself in power,
> Power into will, will into appetite;
> And appetite, an universal wolf,
> So doubly seconded with will and power,
> Must make perforce an universal prey,
> And last eat up himself.[4]   (1.3.108–9, 118–23)

Having insisted that all the weary warriors should preserve order by
respecting the divine hierarchy and its moral basis, Ulysses goes out
to rig an important lottery. This is a world in which people do a lot
of preaching but don't practise what they preach, much like the
political world today. If there's corruption among the Greeks, the
Trojans are no better. They've been fighting for seven years because
Helen, wife of the Greek Menelaus, eloped adulterously with Paris,
the Trojan prince. Countless men have died as a result. 'Fools on
both sides', says Troilus;

> Helen must needs be fair,
> When with your blood you daily paint her thus.   (1.1.88–9)

Yet he advocates continuing the war instead of sending the runaway
wife back. Hector sounds more sensible: at the great debate in Act 2,
scene 2, he argues that

> these moral laws
> Of nature and of nations speak aloud
> To have her back returned   (2.2.183–5)

—but then, at the end of his speech, with total inconsistency, he recommends fighting on as before. In a glorified version of 'We're 'ere because we're 'ere', he opines: ''tis a cause that hath no mean dependence | Upon our joint and several dignities.' (Roughly, 'We'll look fools if we stop now.') The loathsome but astute Thersites sums up the matter: 'All the argument is a whore and a cuckold.' While many die, little changes; and the war has a rotten centre: a Helen (or 'Nell') who, to judge from her leering gags, belongs less to the world of Homer than to the more dated world of the Carry On films. In contrast to such bawdry, the play contains so much learned and intricate debate on moral topics that some critics speculate that originally it might have been drafted for performance before young lawyers at one of the Inns of Court, the lawyers' colleges. The dramatic context of such debate, however, is sensual self-indulgence, vanity, sloth, indiscipline (Paris won't fight because Nell won't let him; Achilles won't fight because he loves not only his 'sweet Patroclus' but also the Trojan princess Polyxena), and a general atmosphere of sleaze relieved by a pointlessly archaic chivalric challenge.

In *The Elizabethan World Picture*, which several decades ago was a widely recommended guide to the great orthodoxies of the Elizabethan period, E. M. W. Tillyard quoted at length that 'degree' speech by Ulysses and linked it with a range of Elizabethan homilies on the importance of order. 'It is what everyone believed in Elizabeth's days', says Tillyard. 'The conception of order described above must have been common to all Elizabethans of even modest intelligence.'[5] But equally modest intelligence might lead the reader to reflect that if the principle of the great hierarchy, 'the Great Chain of Being', was 'what everyone believed', the doctrine would not have been so insistently and anxiously propagated by the authorities of that day. Magistrates don't read the Riot Act to worshippers at prayer. What Ulysses implies is that the grand hierarchy is a bootstrap job: like the Stock Market and the rope in the Indian Rope Trick, it stays up while people believe in it but collapses when people don't. And he doesn't say that all the king's horses and all the king's men can put this cosmic Humpty Dumpty together again. When it smashes, it smashes for good. 'And appetite . . . Must make perforce an universal prey, | And last eat up himself', Ulysses had said; and near the end of the play, during the chaotic battle-scenes, Thersites says: 'What's become of the wenching rogues? I think they have swallowed one another.'

When Dryden 're-modelled' the play in 1679, Ulysses' line 'And appetite, an universal wolf' became 'For wild ambition, like a ravenous wolf'. The substitution of 'wild ambition' for 'appetite' is clarifying but limiting. 'Appetite' links the sexual appetite (the cause of the war, and the cause of Troilus's infatuation with Cressida) with the ambition and egotism; it thus emphasizes the linkage of the 'war theme' and the 'love theme' in Shakespeare's play. In 1935 Caroline Spurgeon, in *Shakespeare's Imagery*, found that *Troilus and Cressida* had a large number of images of disease and an exceptionally large number of images of food.[6] It doesn't take long to see the connection. Both series are images of appetite: the sexual appetite, which so often is linked to venereal and other diseases; and the alimentary appetite, which, from the outset of the play, is linked, again, to sexual desire. The first exchange between Troilus and Pandarus, for example, elaborates at length the connection between, on the one hand, preparing Cressida for her sexual encounter with Troilus, and, on the other hand, the making of a cake for consumption (the grinding, the bolting, the leavening, the kneading, etc.); and, famously, in a passage that Keats loved, when Troilus is within minutes of his sexual fulfilment, he thinks:

> What will it be
> When that the wat'ry palate tastes indeed
> Love's thrice-repurèd nectar?—death, I fear me . . .
> (3.2.18–20)

And, when he learns of Cressida's infidelity, he says:

> The fragments, scraps, the bits and greasy relics
> Of her o'er-eaten faith are given to Diomed.
> (5.2.157–8)

When all is orderly, Sol's 'med'cinable eye' (the sun's curative power) checks disease. When Hector is ambushed, 'the sun begins to set'. As order collapses, appetite prevails, we were told; and it does so in various ways in various parts of the diseased world of *Troilus and*

Cressida. Instead of a clarifying conclusion, Pandarus sings a song about how 'Sweet honey and sweet notes together fail', refers jeeringly to the prostitutes in the audience, and promises to bequeath us his diseases.

In the history of literature, *Troilus and Cressida*, with its confused and confusing last Act, must therefore be one of the best examples of metaphoric structure. The moral disorder within the fictional world is reflected by the structural disorder in the textual depiction of the fictional events. We encounter ordered disorder; thematically dictated form and deformation. A more recent example of this kind of conclusively inconclusive ingenuity is *Waiting for Godot*. Pandarus's epilogue ushers in the Theatre of the Absurd.

C.W.

The mystery of the putrefièd corpse

The local evening paper, in front of me now, offers a report of a not unfamiliar kind on the theme of 'loneliness in a crowd'.

MAN LAY DEAD IN HOUSE FOR 4 MONTHS

A man's body lay undiscovered in a house for four months.

A spokeswoman for Brighton coroner's office said she believed the man had died last November.

The body was discovered [in a house in Hove] after a telephone call to the council complaining about a smell coming from the building.

The body was so badly decomposed it has not yet been possible to identify, although the man is thought to be in his mid-fifties . . .

At a dinner-party, when the meal-time conversation is beginning to flag, a sure way of enlivening the flow and eliciting the interests of one's guests is to ask: 'How long does a body take to putrefy?' Of the guests who choose not to make an early departure, the more scientific may be identified by their considerations of climate, temperature, humidity, body mass, multiplication of maggots, and so forth; the more literary by their citation of, perhaps, Edgar Allan Poe's 'The Facts in the Case of M. Valdemar'. That's the tale of a dying man who is the subject of a mesmeric experiment to preserve him. Though apparently dead, he remains physically unchanged for months, and intermittently replies to the hypnotist's questions, until at last his sepulchral voice utters the words: 'For God's sake!—quick!—quick!—put me to sleep—or, quick!—waken me!— quick!—*I say to you that I am dead!*' And though the hypnotist attempts to waken him, he, within the space of a minute or less, 'absolutely rot[s] away', so that 'Upon the bed . . . there lay a nearly liquid mass of loathsome—of detestable putridity'.[1]

The literary guests are unlikely to cite Shakespeare's *Troilus and Cressida;* yet that play contains an oddly Poe-ish incident. You'll remember how it comes about. At the height of a battle between Trojans and Greeks, Hector, the Trojan champion, sees a foe 'in sumptuous armour'. The Quarto and Folio stage directions merely specified one 'in armour', but, from Edmund Malone in the eighteenth century onwards, many editors have added the word 'sumptuous', inferring this detail from source-materials and from Hector's words. For Hector says:

> Stand, stand, thou Greek; thou art a goodly mark.
> No? wilt thou not? I like thy armour well;
> I'll frush it [batter it] and unlock the rivets all,
> But I'll be master of it. Wilt thou not, beast, abide?
> Why then, fly on; I'll hunt thee for thy hide.[2]
>
> (5.6.27–31)

There follows a short sequence (roughly 25 lines; perhaps two to three minutes) which shows Achilles bossing his Myrmidons and Thersites declining to fight Margarelon. Then, after that brief interval, we see Hector again. He is looking down at the (presumably just offstage) corpse of the warrior he has pursued and killed, and he says:

> Most putrefièd core, so fair without,
> Thy goodly armour thus hath cost thy life.
> Now is my day's work done. I'll take good breath.
> Rest, sword; thou hast thy fill of blood and death.   (5.8.1–4)

'Most putrefièd core' means 'thoroughly putrefied corpse': the rotten centre within the resplendent armour.[3] There's a stark contrast between what is 'fair without' and disgustingly rotten within. But the death has only just taken place: we are hearing the immediate valedictory words from the vanquisher. And if the death has only just taken place, the corpse has not had time to become conspicuously putrefied. Nor is this just an insulting way of referring to a dead enemy. The contrast between the fair outside and the loathsome inside is too marked for that. Hector isn't making a derogatory metaphorical comment on his victim's moral character, for he knows nothing about the man's history. Neither do we. So what's happening here?

Of the various sources, the only two to have a bearing on the matter seem initially to offer little help. William Caxton's *The Recuyell of the Historyes of Troye* says that Hector captures 'a much noble baron of Greece much quaintly and richly armed', and 'for to lead him out of the host at his ease [Hector] had cast his shield behind him'.[4] In this version, the showy opponent is not killed at all, but taken prisoner (obviously for ransom, since the fellow appears wealthy). John Lydgate's account says that Hector, motivated mainly by 'covetyse', covetousness, pursued and killed the fellow, put him on Hector's horse, and then, being vulnerable, was speared by Achilles.[5] So Shakespeare seems to have invented the matter of the apparently instantaneous decomposition of the richly armoured man.

The main figures in the play's plot are Troilus and Cressida: we follow the progress and collapse of their love-relationship. Nevertheless, the play's political emphasis, and arguably its moral emphasis, is placed on Hector, if any character can be singled out of the theme-driven *mêlée*. He is the greatest warrior among the Trojans, and he is notably chivalrous. He is the person who is expected to give the moral lead. In Act 2, scene 2, when the leading Trojans debate whether to continue the war or not, his voice is clearly the most important. And up to a point he talks sound moral sense, arguing that it's pointless to continue a war which has an immoral basis; but, then, as we have seen, he votes for continuation of the conflict. Next, he offers an absurdly chivalric challenge to the Greeks. He says he'll fight a duel to prove that the love of his life, Andromache, is better than any woman loved by a Greek. As a result of the ensuing rigged lottery, Ajax is chosen to answer his challenge. Eventually, after much verbal huffing and puffing, there is an inconclusive combat. Ajax wants to resume it, but Hector declines, pointing out that since Ajax is a relative (a nephew) of his, 'the obligation of our blood forbids | A gory emulation 'twixt us twain'. (He should have thought of that in the first place, before issuing his challenge, or at least before half-heartedly starting to fight. He's consistently inconsistent.) Hector then fraternizes agreeably with the Greek leaders. The next day war resumes, and he goes out to battle, ignoring Cassandra's prophecies of his death, and ignoring the pleas of his wife and father.

It is well known that Hector is magnanimous to opponents. Unlike Troilus, who is ruthlessly vindictive, 'Hector in his blaze of wrath subscribes | To tender objects': the phrasing is tricky, but the gist seems to be that even in the heat of battle he is merciful to the weak or inexperienced. The point is clarified in Act 5, scene 3.

TROILUS Brother, you have a vice of mercy in you,
  Which better fits a lion than a man.
HECTOR What vice is that? Good Troilus, chide me for it.
TROILUS When many times the captive Grecian falls,
  Even in the van and wind of your fair sword,
  You bid them rise and live.
HECTOR O, 'tis fair play.
TROILUS   Fool's play, by heaven, Hector. (5.3.37–43)

Hector belongs to a bygone era of chivalry and 'fair play'; Troilus belongs to the modern world in which you play to win and play dirty if necessary. Troilus's principle is most clearly endorsed by Achilles among the Greeks. At one point in the battle, Achilles rushes at Hector, gets the worst of the fight, becoming disarmed and exhausted, but tells Hector to go away until he (Achilles) is in better condition; which Hector, gallantly, or foolishly, does. But it's then that Hector sees the knight 'in sumptuous armour'. That knight runs off; and Hector, instead of sparing the scared fellow chivalrously, is tempted to pursue and kill him merely for 'his hide', the valuable covering. Having killed him, Hector rests; and at that point Achilles returns, accompanied by the Myrmidons. 'I am unarmed; forgo this vantage, Greek', says the dismayed Hector. 'Strike, fellows, strike; this is the man I seek', replies the callous Achilles. Hector is then butchered by the Myrmidons, who are ordered to acclaim Achilles (who has merely looked on) as the vanquisher; and the corpse will be dishonoured by being dragged through the dust.

There's a neat double irony. If Hector had been less chivalrous to Achilles, Hector would have lived; and if (consistently with his usual conduct) he had been more chivalrous to the fleeing opponent, Hector might have lived. Pursuit of the opponent brought him back into Achilles' path, and despatch of the opponent made him tired enough to have a rest and sheathe his sword, making him particularly vulnerable to the Greeks. But there is a large thematic irony which culminates here. One of the main themes of the play is 'true and false valuation'. This theme is introduced in the very Prologue and resounds loudly during the Greek debate of Act 1, scene 3, and at length during the Trojan debate of Act 2, scene 2. Should a war be protracted when its cause is so petty, namely the adultery of Helen with Paris? The point is made that judgement should be based on moral principles rather than on appetite or egotism.

HECTOR Brother, she is not worth what she doth cost
 The keeping.
TROILUS   What's aught but as 'tis valued?
HECTOR But value dwells not in particular will:
 It holds his estimate and dignity
 As well wherein 'tis precious of itself
 As in the prizer. 'Tis mad idolatry
 To make the service greater than the god.   (2.2.50–6)

Hector is surely right. If his principle were adopted, the war would
be ended and many lives saved. If Troilus had remembered those
words, Troilus might have been less infatuated with Cressida and
less dismayed by her infidelity.

And if Hector had remembered his own words, he might have
lived; for he would not, then, have let his desire for showy armour
defeat his customary decency. The war is rotten at the core. Among
the Greeks and the Trojans, behind the shows of civilization, hero-
ism, and hierarchy, there is the reality of moral corruption. This
theme of false valuation, of over-valuation of the surface, and under-
valuation of the essence, has precipitated one of Shakespeare's most
starkly symbolic scenes.[6] When Hector opens his vanquished foe's
resplendent armour, he does indeed see not an intact dead man, not a
pallid and spotty dead man, but a truly putrefied corpse. If he doesn't
sound surprised, perhaps it's because he's been living in a world
which contains plenty of putridity already. Like Shakespeare's pen,
Hector's sword has here probed the real and found the symbolic.

There's obvious proof of the symbolism. The clue is the *déjà vu*
feeling that the scene evokes. We've been here before. In Act 2, scene
7, of *The Merchant of Venice*, to be precise. That's when the Prince
of Morocco chooses the gold casket rather than the silver or lead one.
Of course, he thinks, the splendid gold casket must hold 'the angel
within'. He unlocks it, and:

> O hell! What have we here?
> A carrion Death, within whose empty eye
> There is a written scroll. I'll read the writing.
> All that glisters is not gold;
> Often have you heard that told.
> Many a man his life hath sold
> But my outside to behold.
> Gilded tombs do worms infold.[7]   (lines 62–9)

Hector is a clear example of 'a man [who] his life hath sold' for a seductively valuable container of corruption. Indeed, much of *Troilus and Cressida*, epitomized in Hector's vanquished yet avenging victim, is this casket scene writ large.

C.W.

Shakespeare's feminist play?

The long last scene of *Love's Labour's Lost* holds a plethora of puzzles, some large, some small. 'Jack hath not Jill', says Biron: the expected betrothals don't materialize: is this the apt culmination of an exceptionally feminist play? Can Jaquenetta really be pregnant by Armado? What do the gnomic closing words mean? And what is the bearing on *Love's Labour's Lost* of the frustratingly lost *Love's Labour's Won*? This essay tackles all these puzzles and finds that the solutions interlink.

Before that final scene, the main events have been these. The King of Navarre (Ferdinand) and his three lords, Biron, Longueville, and Dumaine, have resolved (in spite of misgivings expressed by the shrewd Biron) to withdraw from society for three years in order to gain fame by study. Almost as soon as their resolution is made, Biron reminds them that they are bound to receive an embassage from the French Princess and her three ladies, Rosaline, Katharine, and Maria; so an exception must be made to the rule of retreat. Armado, the vainglorious and impoverished knight, has contrived the arrest of Costard and Jaquenetta for consorting together (contrary to the King's edict); but Armado himself is soon smitten with love for Jaquenetta. The Princess and her ladies arrive to pursue a disputed claim involving a debt of money and land; the King and his lords become their suitors. Armado rescinds Costard's punishment in return for help in the courtship of Jaquenetta. Armado's love-letter to her is muddled up with Biron's to Rosaline. In a scene of multiple eavesdropping, the King and his lords learn that each of them is forsworn, being in love: all are 'moon-like men, men of inconstancy';[1] Biron persuades them that love is a better mentor than study: women's eyes transcend all academes.

In the final scene, Ferdinand, Biron, Longueville, and Dumaine, disguised and masked, seek to court their ladies; but the ladies, forewarned and also masked, have exchanged the 'favours' or tokens which identify them, so that each lord courts the wrong lady and is consequently humiliated. Armado and his friends then attempt to present a pageant of the Nine Worthies. The lords mock the show. Costard, playing Pompey, is repeatedly interrupted. The curate, Sir Nathaniel (representing Alexander the Great), is humiliated, and Costard speaks gallantly in his defence; Holofernes, the school-master (representing Judas Maccabeus), is similarly humiliated by the mockery (responding 'This is not generous, not gentle, not humble'). Armado, as Hector, is derided; with unexpected dignity, he responds:

The sweet war-man is dead and rotten. Sweet chucks, beat not the bones of the buried. When he breathed, he was a man. (5.2.651–3)

His dignity, however is rapidly deflated when Costard announces that Jaquenetta is two months pregnant by Armado. After that reve-lation comes a graver shock: Marcadé, a messenger from the French court, suddenly arrives to tell the French Princess, in few words, of her father's death; and 'the scene begins to cloud'. '*Et in Arcadia ego*': Marcadé mars Arcady. As the Princess[2] and ladies prepare to return (for, in any case, their lawsuit has been victorious), the King and lords attempt to persuade the ladies to marriage. The Princess tells the King to go into retreat in some 'forlorn and naked hermi-tage' for a year; if he can stand that, then she will accept him as a husband. Katharine tells Dumaine he must be patient for 'a twelve-month and a day'; Longueville receives the same shrift from Maria. Rosaline gives detailed instructions to Biron. As he has been so satirically eloquent, he must spend a year visiting the sick and dying, endeavouring to make them smile. He says that's impossible; she responds that if he doesn't succeed, he'll be less prompt to gibe. It's then that Biron epitomizes the unconventionality of the plot. In *A Midsummer Night's Dream*, Puck will make the accurate prophecy, 'Jack shall have Jill'. Biron, in contrast, says:

> Our wooing doth not end like an old play:
> Jack hath not Jill. These ladies' courtesy
> Might well have made our sport a comedy. (5.2.856–8)

Then, as if to imply criticism of the lords' reluctance to accept a year's patient waiting, Armado announces that to prove himself to Jaquenetta, he has vowed 'to hold the plough for her sweet love three year'. There follow two songs, which may be sung by the rustic characters. The first, the Cuckoo's Song, is mildly paradoxical, for though it opens as a song celebrating the delights of spring, it provides a warning that marriage does not solve all problems: the cuckoo, whose young are raised unwittingly by other birds in their nest, is a reminder that married men may be cuckolds; that's why its call is 'unpleasing to a married ear'. The reference to 'cuckoo-buds' reinforces the point. The Owl's Song, in turn, holds the mild paradox that though winter is a time of labour in inclement weather, the owl's hooting is—the singers assert—a merry sound. And the concluding words of the play are these:

The words of Mercury are harsh after the songs of Apollo. You that way. We this way.   (lines 911–12)

Even this brief plot-summary may suggest ways in which *Love's Labour's Lost* can be seen as—for its times—a strikingly feministic play. Perhaps the most obvious feature is that the play doesn't end with wedding-bells. Normally, in a Shakespearian comedy, love triumphs over obstacles and the lovers' story concludes with marriage; here it doesn't. More importantly, repeatedly in this play the King and lords display hubris, excessive confidence linked to insufficient self-knowledge, and are put in their place by the women, who, generally, are seen as more constant and circumspect than the men; indeed, the men often resemble overgrown children. In Shakespearian imagery, women are sometimes associated with the inconstant moon; in this play, it's the men who are so associated: as we have seen, they are indeed 'moon-like men, men of inconstancy'. The King's group prides itself on linguistic display, on puns and 'taffeta phrases'; the women beat them at 'a set of wit' and teach the value of 'honest plain words'. The pageant of the Nine Worthies raises the question 'Who are the true worthies here?'; and the treatment of the humbler characters by the lords invites the reflection that the lords are capable of displaying unworthiness: their mockery comes close to bullying, as Holofernes suggests, and to disrespect for the illustrious dead, as Armado points out. By interweaving the nobles' contretemps in love with that of Armado (particularly when Armado's love-letter is transposed with Biron's) the point is made that the difference between the love-smitten men, be they high or low, is not so great after all. At any rate, the King and lords earn the check that they eventually receive from the more astute Princess and ladies.

One might conclude that this is the only unequivocally feminist work that Shakespeare created. (Curiously, Lisa Jardine's feminist study, *Still Harping on Daughters: Women and Drama in the Age of Shakespeare*, ignores *Love's Labour's Lost*.) Like Ibsen later, Shakespeare had a strongly dialectical imagination; he could progress by challenging in one play ideas offered in a previous play. Just as Ibsen followed *An Enemy of the People* with the contrasting play *The Wild Duck*, so, it seems, Shakespeare decided to provide a contrast to *The Taming of the Shrew* in *Love's Labour's Lost*. Here it's the women, not the men, who adopt the controlling, mentoring role; and here, indeed, Jack hath not Jill. This light, effervescent, elegantly formalized, and exuberantly witty comedy proves finally to be much more unconventional, more challenging, more questioning, than it initially seemed to promise. Even its opening lines, with their invocation of the fame through study that will enable the men to triumph over 'cormorant devouring Time', proves in retrospect to be but the hubris that invites rebuke, notably the rebuke provided by Marcadé and his reminder of mortality. It thus appears that Shakespeare, who could be radically experimental elsewhere (notably in *Hamlet*, *Troilus and Cressida*, and *King Lear*), was here radically experimental in combining feminism with formal unconventionality.

There is, however, a further stage in the unravelling of this puzzle. Long ago Francis Meres, in his *Palladis Tamia* (1598), won literary immortality not for any reflective sagacity but merely by listing some works by Shakespeare that he knew. The list included, among the comedies, 'his *Loue labors lost*, his *Loue labours wonne*'. This reference became a puzzle for scholars, since no work called *Love's Labour's Won* (as '*Loue labours wonne*' is normally modernized) had survived.[3] Some speculated that Meres's *Loue labours wonne* might simply be an alternative title of one of the surviving comedies, perhaps *The Taming of the Shrew*.[4] Then, in 1953, a fragment of a bookseller's list was found. The fragment seems to date from 1603. The list includes 'taming of a shrew' as well as 'loves labor lost' and 'loves labor won'. Thus, *Love's Labour's Won* is not another title of *The Taming of the Shrew;* we know that it was classed as a comedy; and, significantly, both Meres and the bookseller place it immediately after *Love's Labour's Lost*.

By now you can guess the direction of this argument. A recent editor, noting that *Love's Labour's Won* existed, was published, and disappeared, declares: 'Further than that it is not possible to go.'[5] It is not only possible to go further; to do so is a temptation that it seems sinful to resist. Readers who value *Love's Labour's Lost* as a refreshingly feministic comedy by Shakespeare might experience a twinge of ideological disappointment if *Love's Labour's Won* were to surface. The former play is clearly open-ended: it points forward to a sequel. Various Shakespearian works point to sequels: *1 Henry IV* ends by reminding us of matters to be resolved in *2 Henry IV*, and that play in turn ends with a very explicit advertisement for *Henry V*. It seems to me that we can reasonably foresee the plot of *Love's Labour's Won*. After the year of waiting, the King and lords would meet again and compare experiences; each would, in various ways, have failed to be as diligently faithful and austere as he had been enjoined by his lady to be. (You can tell that from the way they behave in *Love's Labour's Lost*.) Each would, again, seek to conceal failings and to impress the ladies; the ladies would, once again, out-wit the men; but, after comic complications, all would be forgiven, and the long-deferred wedding celebrations would provide the cul-mination of the play. Jack would, after all, have Jill. The same rustic characters would enliven the action, and the nuptials might be accompanied by their farcical play-within-the-play, on the lines of that in *A Midsummer Night's Dream*, and perhaps by further concluding songs by the rustics. In short, the open-endedness of *Love's Labour's Lost* anticipates the harmonious closure provided by *Love's Labour's Won*. This thesis cannot be confirmed until such time as *Love's Labour's Won* comes to light; but neither can it, until then, be refuted.

Meanwhile, what of the laconic closing lines of *Love's Labour's Lost*? The First Quarto text (1598) has, after the two songs, the statement 'The wordes of Mercuries, are harsh after the songes of Apollo.' (Then 'FINIS.') This statement appears in unusually large type, and it is not immediately attributed to a speaker, though it may be linked to the last speaker to be specified (before the introduction of the songs), '*B*.', i.e. Braggart, i.e. Armado. Perhaps the large type indicates that some comment later added to the script has errone-ously been printed as the final statement of the play. Editors gener-ally ascribe the words to Armado. But what do those strange words mean? Mercury is the god of language, commerce, gain, merchants, travellers, scholars, quick-witted people, liars, even thieves: the rogue Autolycus in *The Winter's Tale* is 'littered under Mercury'.

'Apollo' is easier; among many other attributes, he is the patron of shepherds and of song, particularly pastoral song. So the statement may mean: 'After the two songs we have just heard, any reminders of reality will seem harsh.' But no 'reminders of reality' follow; the sense seems incomplete. John Dover Wilson once suggested that the statement was originally 'a mere reader's comment on the play as a whole': the reader having noted the contrast between the light-hearted and the sombre.[6] This suggestion could be supported by claiming that Mercury is a messenger, and the conspicuous messenger in the play has been Marcadé, who brought news of death. Mercury was associated with Hermes, conductor of dead to the underworld. In Robert Wilson's play *The Cobbler's Prophecy* (*c.*1590), Ralph the cobbler repeatedly refers to Mercury as 'Markedie', a name remarkably like 'Marcadé'. So the sense now would be: 'The message about mortality seems particularly harsh in the context of pastoral lyricism.' The trouble with this interpretation is, of course, that Marcadé's message *preceded* the songs that we have just heard; once again, there seems to be an odd mismatch. One commentator suggests that the 'songs' are 'the courtier's sonnets and Biron's praise of love in 4.3'; but who, within twenty seconds of the two songs, would reasonably think that the reference is to poetry uttered half an hour previously? A reading proposed by John Kerrigan is: '[T]he true study which the scholars must now undertake in the *harsh* world outside the park . . . is in contrast to their life within it'.[7] But the phrase 'words of Mercury' is a strained way of referring to 'true study'; and, in any case, the tasks imposed on the King and lords have not specified scholarly study, but rather penances involving (in the King's case) retreat to an austere hermitage, (in the case of Longueville and Dumaine) simply a year's patience, and (in Biron's case) visits to hospitals.

The First Folio (1623) gives this ending:

> BRAG. The Words of Mercurie,
>   Are harsh after the Songs of Apollo:
>   You that way; we this way.
>   *Exeunt omnes.*

Some modern editors retain the words 'You that way; we this way.'; others omit them. Richard David, in his notes to the 1956 Arden text,[8] speculates that this line was perhaps added 'by the stage-manager to ensure a tidy *Exeunt*'; which implies that without some such explicit guidance the singers might have left the stage in an amateurishly untidy way, perhaps colliding with each other. In fact, 'You that way; we this way' makes very good retrospective sense of 'The words of Mercury are harsh after the songs of Apollo'. Now the meaning of the combined statements is: 'A message about reality is harsh after such sweet singing; but it is nevertheless my duty to tell you that you must leave the theatre and re-enter the streets, while we go offstage into the tiring-house.'

Even better sense can be lent by an imaginative stage-production: notably, by the 1969 National Theatre production directed by Laurence Olivier.[9] The songs were sung by the rustic characters, led by Armado. As they sang, the stage gradually darkened; but the singers were lit by Armado's lantern. A few snow-flakes drifted down during the singing of the wintry 'Owl's Song'. At the end of that, the courtly spectators and all the singers quietly walked off-stage, leaving Armado alone, holding up the lantern amid the surrounding darkness. In his solitary patch of light, he murmured sadly and reflectively, 'The words of Mercury are harsh after the songs of Apollo': as if to say, 'After such music, I have harsh news for you.' Then, pointing to the audience, he said apologetically, 'You—*that* way', and gestured towards the exits at the rear of the auditorium; as if meaning: 'Now you must re-enter the world of everyday realities'. Next: he declared, 'We—*this* way!'; and, immediately, he turned his back, his lantern was at once engulfed in his dark swirling cloak, and instantly he vanished into total blackness. It seemed that he had meant: 'While you return to the noisy streets of London, to the everyday and the mundanity of mortality, we, the players, re-enter the dark silent limbo of fictional characters from which we may re-emerge, immortally and magically, down the ages.' It was a strikingly effective and appropriate ending to a drama about the impingement of harsh realities, of partings, work, disease, and death, upon an Arcadian world of elegantly artificial amusement. After sunlight, darkness; after verbal exuberance, silence.

The apparently banal line, 'You that way; we this way', was thus given reverberating significance; and, in turn, it vindicated the previous puzzling remark, 'The words of Mercury are harsh after the songs of Apollo.' Now, the play had its perfect coda. Even the most puzzling and prosaic of lines may be rendered rich and resonant by imaginative theatrical practice. It's a quotidian miracle; the punter's money buys rough and smooth magic.

A sceptic might object that Shakespeare's plays were commonly performed in broad daylight, in the afternoon at the open-roofed theatre. Well, there were plenty of exceptions. Shakespeare's plays, even before his company leased the Blackfriars indoor theatre in 1608, were often played indoors: sometimes at Whitehall; occasionally in some nobleman's house; sometimes at the Inns of Court; and even (if Quarto title-pages are to be believed) in halls at Oxford and Cambridge. As F. E Halliday has remarked, *Love's Labour's Lost* 'certainly seems to be written for a courtly rather than a popular audience'.[10] This is indicated by its elegance, erudition (puns in Latin, French, and Dutch, as well as English), formalism, virtuosic celebration and mockery of fashon, and its anticipations of Poussin and Mozart; though the popular audience's intelligence shouldn't be under-rated. Other signs of an indoor production are that the play does not require elaborate staging or props: a simple dais in a hall and a few stage trees and bushes can accommodate the action.[11] The evidence that it was staged indoors is more than adequate. The title-page of the First Quarto says that the play 'was presented before her Highnes [*sic*] this last Christmas' (i.e. 1597–8. Contrary to the film *Shakespeare in Love*, Queen Elizabeth would not have joined the throng at the public theatre.). John Dover Wilson suggested that *Love's Labour's Lost* might originally have been acted at the Earl of Southampton's house in the plague year of 1593–4. There is evidence in the *Revels Account* and in two related letters that the play was privately performed for Queen Anne at either Lord Cranbourne's or the Earl of Southampton's house in January 1605. The Second Quarto title-page says it was staged at the Blackfriars (indoor) Theatre.[12] So, in the days when indoor theatres often depended on candle-light, it is possible that some effect resembling that at the end of Olivier's production (the apparent vanishing into darkness) might have been achieved. But the imparting of vivid meaning to the closing lines does not depend on that vanishing-trick. It's sufficient that those lines mutually enrich each other and, in keeping with the thematic direction of the play in the final scene (impingement of sombre realities on the Arcadian artifice), offer the parting paradox: one way, reality and mortality; the other way, fantasy, enacted death, and immortality. Like Dionysus, who in many disguises invades the modern world of Thomas Mann's *Death in Venice*, Mercury and Apollo are deities who are recurrent figments and perennial mentors of imagination. But you can guess what Autolycus (that commercially minded entertainer littered under Mercury, god of commerce) would say to all this. He'd say that the words about Apollo and Mercury simply mean: 'After being entertained by songs, you, the patrons, have definitely had your money's-worth and must now depart so that Shakespeare and the other "sharers" (backers, investors) can count and divide the takings.' Being a singer, actor, and avaricious pedlar, he should know. 'Sure the gods do this year connive at us', he observes. But, being Autolycus, he could be lying.

And what about Armado? He falls in love with Jaquenetta, Costard's partner, in Act 1, scene 2. Her responses to his overtures are drily deflationary, though he remains inflated.

> ARMADO I will tell thee wonders.
> JAQUENETTA With that face?
> ARMADO I love thee.
> JAQUENETTA So I heard you say.
>   (1.2.132–5)

In Act 5, scene 2, Armado is informed (by Costard) that she is two months pregnant by him: 'two months on her way ... the child brags in her belly already. 'Tis yours.' After initial consternation at this embarrassing declaration, he gallantly accepts the responsibility, and will even become a ploughman for three years to win her hand. Once again, we seem to encounter an impossible Shakespearian chronology. The French Princess's embassage had aimed to resolve a matter of land and money. That matter was soon concluded, we are told in the final scene; indeed, the time-references concerning the embassage make clear that from the start of the negotiations to their conclusion only a couple of days, at most, elapse. Armado is phenomenally innumerate (he can't multiply one by three), but even he must realize that Jaquenetta cannot, in a day or so, have become two months pregnant by him. Indeed, he hadn't even 'enjoyed' her on the morning of Costard's revelation.[13] There are various possible solutions. One is that, as elsewhere, Shakespeare is using at least two different, and incompatible, time-schemes, and is hoping that the audience won't notice or won't particularly mind. Another is that

Jaquenetta is not pregnant but is conspiring with Costard (and a double time-scheme) to dupe Armado into marriage. Another is that Biron instructed Costard to slander Armado.[14] Yet another, and this by far the most satisfactory, is that Costard is really the father of Jaquenetta's unborn child ('This maid will serve my turn', he had leeringly explained), but Armado, though guessing this, is willing to make her an honest woman nevertheless. This gives sharp point to the references to cuckoldry in the Cuckoo's Song. It also suggests that the jealous Biron of Act 3, scene 1 (who, confusing his Rosaline with Shakespeare's Dark Lady, had complained that he loved 'one that will do the deed | Though Argus were her eunuch and her guard') could learn lessons in tolerance from Armado. By gladly undertaking to serve Jaquenetta for three years, Armado is arguably superior to those lords (Longueville and Biron) who complain that a year is long to wait, and whose original scheme to embark on a three-year retreat had collapsed so rapidly. Armado as ploughman serving a pregnant countrywoman is an improvement on Armado the absurdly word-obsessed egoist; his metamorphosis fits the drama's concluding thematic emphasis on the value not of ornate rhetoric but of rural realities and homely simplicities; and the prospect of a new birth complements Marcadé's reminder of death.

Jaquenetta and Armado indicate, therefore, that *Love's Labour's Lost* is already two months pregnant by *Love's Labour's Won*. There is 'bragging in the belly' indeed.

C.W.

Why does the Duke leave town?

Of all the 'problem plays' *Measure for Measure* is the most problematic. The audience is forewarned by the Duke's opening speech, an utterance of daunting opacity:

> DUKE Escalus.
> ESCALUS My lord.
> DUKE Of government the properties to unfold
>   Would seem in me to affect speech and discourse,
>   Since I am put to know that your own science
>   Exceeds in that the lists of all advice
>   My strength can give you. Then no more remains
>   But that, to your sufficiency . . .
>   . . . as your worth is able,
>   And let them work. The nature of our people,
>   Our city's institutions, and the terms
>   For common justice, you're as pregnant in
>   As art and practice hath enrichèd any
>   That we remember. There is our commission,
>   From which we would not have you warp.   (I.I.I–I5)

The play opens with an imperative—indicating absolute power. The key words of the speech—'government . . . city's institutions . . . common justice . . . terror . . . power'—make it clear that this will be a play about 'polity': how to run a city (the literal meaning of the term). But what audience—even a Jacobean audience trained by years of listening to rhetorically complex sermons—could understand what the Duke is saying here? Modern students can only decode it through the eye with the assistance of notes. And some lines (such as those around 'sufficiency') defeat even the most ingenious annotators.

Linguistically opaque, the *mise en scène* is, in other ways, enigmatic. The Duke, we apprehend, is bent on leaving Vienna, the city-state in his charge. We do not know whether he holds an elective post (like the Doge, or Duke, of Venice) or enjoys hereditary rule (like Duke Orsino, apparently, in *Twelfth Night*). Whichever, it seems an odd dereliction of duty, unless higher duty calls. What duty? Why *is* the Duke leaving? Neither the ostensible nor (as it gradually emerges) the underlying motives add up. He gives no reason to his aides as he departs, saying only that he has a horror of public display:

> I'll privily away. I love the people,
> But do not like to stage me to their eyes.[1] (1.1.68–9)

In fact, as it emerges, he very much likes play-acting ('staging himself to the eyes of his citizens'). Passing over that: where is he going, and for how long, and on what 'commission'? He says nothing to his delegates and plenipotentiaries on the matter that we know of.[2]

After he has gone underground we get some tantalizing hints. In Act 1, scene 3, we discover the Duke (now in some sort of un-ducal disguise or mufti) in conversation with Friar Thomas, in a monastery which has given him 'secret harbour'. The holy brother, as the scene opens, has apparently just asked the Duke (he is evidently as mystified as we are) whether it is perhaps an affair of the heart. The Duke pooh-poohs this:

> No, holy father, throw away that thought.
> Believe not that the dribbling dart of love
> Can pierce a complete bosom. (1.3.1–3)

No, the Duke goes on to explain. He has always loved 'the life removed' and hated 'assemblies'. Possibly he wants a spell of recuperation, a kind of detox from the responsibilities of high office? He then, for the first time, indicates what his cover story is:

> I have delivered to Lord Angelo,
> A man of stricture and firm abstinence,
> My absolute power and place here in Vienna;
> And he supposes me travelled to Poland,
> For so I have strewed it in the common ear
> And so it is received.
>
>   (lines 11–16)

This picks up a throwaway remark by Lucio, the brothel-crawling 'fantastic', in the previous scene: 'If the Duke with the other dukes come not to composition with the King of Hungary, why then all the dukes fall upon the king.' By the usual Chinese Whispers process,

Poland has become Hungary in the 'common ear'. But no one cares very much. It's simply matter for a pun by Lucio ('Hungary . . . hungry') and there is no more speculation. The cat's away, and the mice will play. Or perhaps not, if Angelo has his stern way.

If it is supposed and has been put about that the Duke has gone on a political mission to Poland a host of other questions crowd in. He would not, surely, travel alone on such an affair. Rulers do not go on high business of state unaccompanied. There is, judging by a number of passing remarks in the play, some international conflict currently brewing. Mistress Overdone, for example, complains: 'Thus what with the war, what with the sweat, what with the gallows, and what with poverty, I am custom-shrunk.' If Vienna is embroiled in war, it is amazing that the Duke would desert his post. If, as this first brothel scene implies, Vienna is in the grip of an epidemic of venereal disease ('the sweat') it would, at least, explain Angelo's edict against fornication (in 1999, the People's Republic of China banned fornication—sex outside marriage—in the world's most populous state, principally as a prophylactic against AIDS).

On the level of how politics are conducted in a modern state like Vienna's in the early seventeenth century (this seems to be a 'modern' play), the Duke's leaving in the midst of an international crisis, without retinue, without any arrangement as to communiqués, without any indication as to when he will return—all combines to create a black hole at the centre of the play's opening scene. It seems improbable and—if conceivable—grossly irresponsible.[3]

But it may be that wise spirits in Vienna see through it as a blind, or cover story. Lucio—who alone of the dramatis personae seems at all curious about the Duke's motives (and shrewdly suspects he is still present in the city in the disguise of a beggar)—tells Isabella that:

> The Duke is very strangely gone from hence;
> Bore many gentlemen, myself being one,
> In hand, and hope of action; but we do learn,
> By those that know the very nerves of state,
> His givings-out were of an infinite distance
> From his true-meant design.   (1.4.50–3)

'Action' here means 'military action'—war. Who are those who know 'the very nerves of state'? Does Lucio imply that the Duke has gone on some Chamberlain-like mission of diplomacy to avert war? ('I have, my fellow Viennese, a piece of paper in my hand . . .') Are we to deduce some separation of powers by which Angelo will take care of the domestic management of the city (particularly its moral hygiene) while the Duke deals with its foreign affairs?

One can speculate about other private motives. The Duke observes that over the last fourteen years, laws have become slack. Angelo is the man to reimpose what will be very unpopular laws.

> We have strict statutes and most biting laws,
> The needful bits and curbs to headstrong weeds,
> Which for this fourteen years we have let slip,
> Even like an o'ergrown lion in a cave
> That goes not out to prey.
>
> (1.3.19–23)

Apparently, this aspect of domestic government is much on the Duke's mind. He expatiates on the subject to Friar Thomas, saying it would be inappropriate for him to reinstate these biting laws, 'Sith 'twas my fault to give the people scope.' The Duke would seem to have discovered the hard cop/soft cop routine. Does he mean to rule—on his return—with Angelo the pit-bull by his side? Angelo will geld and spay the libidinous malefactors of Vienna while the Duke mutters, 'how sad, how sad, how necessary' alongside him.[4]

We may indeed suspect, from a couple of throwaway remarks, that the Duke is both using Angelo as a catspaw, to run a social experiment (can the ratchet of liberalization be wound back?) and—as another experiment—is seeing whether his 'precise' plenipotentiary is indeed incorruptible. If Angelo passes the test, will the Duke quietly fade from the scene—or does he *know* that Angelo's preciseness—men not being angels—is doomed to failure?

It is odd that the Duke, if he did have these deep-laid plans in mind, seems to have made no preparations for his experiments. He apparently has not brought money with him (which is why he has to disguise himself as a mendicant), and does not have his ducal seal (he has conveyed to Angelo 'absolute' power). When Lear so divests himself, it is seen as an act of madness. What is the Duke's motive? From his explanatory exchanges with Friar Thomas, it appears that he is making up his plans as he goes along:

I will, as 'twere a brother of your order,
Visit both prince and people. Therefore, I prithee,
Supply me with the habit and instruct me
How I may formally in person bear
Like a true friar.

                                                    (1.3.44–8)

A prudent Duke would have made these arrangements and rehearsed his part *before* going underground. What if Thomas—as he strictly should—were to reply 'No: I cannot prostitute the ordinances of my holy order by allowing you to impersonate a friar. Out of the question. As outrageous as my impersonating a Duke.' In fact, high level impersonation, of a very criminal kind, is in prospect. In his assumed identity, the Duke will take confession from those about to die. This is troubling. Suppose, after marrying Romeo and Juliet, Friar Lawrence had said: 'I am not a friar after all—the marriage is invalid.'

It is common for critics to short-circuit this futile questioning with the explanation that the Duke is to be understood not as a man, with human motivations, but as a device: a function in the play's moral design. As well ask why he does it as why the rain it raineth every day. Vincentio is 'Providence' in the play, and Providence is traditionally inscrutable ('If the Duke is an image of Providence,' Anne Barton tartly notes, 'there would seem to be chaos in heaven'[5]).

Being human, and not critics, actors and audiences tend to be very sceptical about reducing Shakespeare's principal characters to the level of so many plot devices. They want, in their obstinate way, to know what makes these fascinating (if enigmatic) people 'tick'. In 1999, as preparation for his playing Leontes in the Royal Shakespeare Company's forthcoming production of *The Winter's Tale*, Anthony Sher consulted psychiatrists and wrote a jubilant article for the *Guardian*, reporting the professional opinion of one expert who had diagnosed a clear case of 'morbid paranoia'. Now he knew how Leontes ticked. For the concurrent RSC production of *Measure for Measure*, a similarly explanatory campaign was undertaken (although it was not written up in the papers). The director evidently recalled the *cause célèbre*, a couple of years before, when Stephen Fry at the last moment ran away from the opening of a Simon Gray play, in which he had a starring role. He sent a letter of apology couched in psycho-analytical explanation. Combined with the associations of

Vienna (Freud's town) this hypothesis was adopted. The Duke (like Fry) had lost his nerve and bolted. As it was staged, his first speech was delivered in the form of a gramophone record (the 1998 RSC *Measure for Measure* was done in modern dress).

Other hypotheses can be put forward, equally persuasive and equally provisional. Vienna, as Shakespeare pictures it, is a large modern conurbation, much like London ('a recognizable image of almost any big city,' as Anne Barton observes[6]). Does such a city *need* a Duke, any more than 1604 London needed a 'ruler', or 1980s London needed a GLC and Red Ken Livingstone, or London 2000 needs Lord Archer as mayor? This may be a third experiment that Vincentio is running. Angelo's regime of moral terror reinforces the sense that you cannot 'govern' a city like Vienna or London—at least with the traditional machineries of power. The Duke leaves Vienna because it no longer needs dukes.

J.S.

Why Barnardine?
and: Angelo: guide to sanity?

———

If you summarize the plot of *Measure for Measure*, Barnardine is, in one obvious respect, unnecessary. An emergency requires his presence, but in the event he is not needed at all. The emergency arises from the following sequence. Angelo has said that he'll spare Claudio's life—but only if Isabella submits to Angelo's lust. Duke Vincentio, disguised as Friar Lodowick, gets Mariana (Angelo's former fiancée) to act as substitute, so that Angelo copulates with Mariana instead, believing—the night being peculiarly dark—that she is Isabella.[1] The Duke then confidently expects Angelo to keep his word and spare Claudio. Instead, Angelo proves to be a ruthless double-crosser: he orders by letter the speedy execution of Claudio, and, what's more, he wants to see the severed head as proof. That's the pressing problem, and the Duke has to improvise rapidly. Another prisoner, the murderer Barnardine, has also been sentenced to death; so the Duke persuades the Provost that Barnardine should be executed early in the morning and *his* head sent to Angelo. 'Angelo hath seen them both, and will discover the favour', opines the shrewd Provost; 'O, death's a great disguiser', is the confident reply. So Barnardine's dramatic function is obvious: he lives to die, or, more precisely, to provide the substituted head. But, when the Duke confronts him, Barnardine proves recalcitrant:

Friar, not I. I have been drinking hard all night, and I will have more time to prepare me, or they shall beat out my brains with billets. I will not consent to die, that's certain.[2] (4.3.50–3)

No arguing; he's not ready, and that's that. The Duke is obliged to accept that the convict is simply 'unprepared, unmeet for death'; the stratagem is frustrated; the plot reaches stalemate. Then, providentially, the Provost announces a remarkable coincidence:

Here in the prison, father,
There died this morning of a cruel fever
One Ragozine, a most notorious pirate,

> A man of Claudio's years; his beard and head
> Just of his colour. What if we do omit
> This reprobate till he were well inclined,
> And satisfy the deputy with the visage
> Of Ragozine, more like to Claudio?
> DUKE O, 'tis an accident that heaven provides.   (4.3.66–74)

A heavenly accident indeed, to inflict a mortally cruel fever on a man; but certainly the timing is lucky. The trick succeeds and Angelo is fooled. From the point of view of plot-construction, therefore, the Barnardine encounter seems to be a needless digression. A dramatist aiming for deft plotting would have gone straight from Angelo's letter to the revelation of Ragozine's death. Ragozine does the job, and off-stage too.

One explanation of what's happening here is that in this play Shakespeare has become preoccupied by a pattern of substitutions. Destructive substitutions are being symmetrically balanced by constructive substitutions. The 'destructive' list might be this: Angelo deputizes for the Duke; a maidenhead (Isabella's) is required instead of a head (Claudio's); Angelo's warrant confirming the execution is sent instead of the expected reprieve; Barnardine's head is to be substituted for Claudio's. In symmetrical opposition, the 'constructive' list is this: the Duke supersedes Angelo; a maidenhead (Mariana's) is substituted for Isabella's; the Duke's warrant (ensuring Claudio's reprieve) is substituted for Angelo's; Ragozine's head is substituted for Claudio's. Elegant, that. But there are less abstract explanations.

In stage productions, it is usually evident that the role of Barnardine is a plum role, a memorable cameo, an incursion of an almost lovable brute. He's this play's Caliban, the underdog we feel for. He appears late in the play (Act 4, scene 3), after we are accustomed to the other characters, so his entry is a welcome theatrical surprise. He is drunken, surly, defiant, and a law to himself. Executioner, Pompey, and Duke together can do nothing to persuade him to the block for death. In spite of the Provost's assurance that he is fearless of futurity, Barnardine's resistance stems partly from residual Christian piety: the belief that only a sober person is in a fit state to make the act of contrition before death.[3] (This is implied by his 'I have been drinking . . . I will have more time to prepare me'.) It also stems

partly from boozers' bloody-mindedness: when you read the line
'I will not consent to die this day, that's certain', you can easily
hear the sibilants slurring. But he is more subversive than this
suggests.

Barnardine's sheer distinctive individuality, and his community of
attitude with anyone in the audience who has ever been pigheadedly
drunk and hung-over, or who has been pestered with authority's
demands at a totally inappropriate time, not only wins sympathy but
also, in this dramatic context, challenges the principle that the law
has the right to kill. Saying 'Off with his head' may be relatively easy
if you don't see the head and shoulders to be severed; once you
encounter the living, arguing individual, the command becomes
harder. This play has maintained a running discussion of two inter-
linked topics. One is 'What is the right attitude to sexuality? Puritanical or permissive?' The other is 'What is the right form of
justice in the state? Severe or lenient?' Barnardine may be a killer,
but he may, all the more effectively for that fact, be an embodied
argument against capital punishment. How dare any human being
approach another and say 'Come on, hurry up, time for death, get
moving'? Naturally we sympathize with the underdog in a given
dramatic situation. The brief alliance against Barnardine of the
Friar–Duke, the pimp Pompey, and the ghoulish Abhorson offers
the sudden and visually stark suggestion that the power of the state
depends on unsavoury and paradoxical complicities. Of course, one
of the joys of the encounter between the Duke and Barnardine is
simply the pleasure of seeing a spanner shoved into the Duke's
works, of seeing that just as the Duke's fertility in mendacious invention has been briefly outwitted by Angelo's celerity in treachery, so
also can his glib improvisations be checked by Barnardine's stubborn
resistance to manipulation.

Barnardine also exposes the craziness of the Duke's judicial system. The Provost says that Barnardine has been languishing (or
sprawling) in prison for *nine years*. The news astonishes the Friar–
Duke: 'How came it that the absent Duke had not either delivered
him to his liberty or executed him? I have heard it was ever his
manner to do so.' The Duke's judicial system, if this statement is to
be believed, is little better than Russian roulette. He kills them or
he frees them. What of all the intermediate punishments which
might be appropriate? (Such Alice-in-Wonderland justice sometimes

operated in reality: at Newark in April 1603, King James sentenced a cutpurse to immediate death, without trial, but simultaneously amnestied most of the prisoners in the castle.[4]) We now have a clearer idea of what the Duke meant when he explained that, before his hand-over of power to Angelo, the laws had been so slackly maintained (for either fourteen or nineteen years—the text says both) that 'liberty pluck[ed] justice by the nose'. So Angelo has been given the job of enforcing a range of laws and penalties which, if draconian, may bring order after the arbitrariness and predominant lenience of the previous decadent era. Of course, Angelo proves to be corrupt, lustfully exploitative, and ruthlessly unjust. But when the Duke eventually reveals himself and at last administers justice in the public street, we see what has been termed an 'orgy of clemency',[5] even if it is a little more selective than that phrase suggests. The Duke does bark, though his bark proves worse than his gummy bite. Angelo is spared after having been publicly humiliated. Lucio, too, is spared provided he makes an honest woman of Kate Keepdown. Claudio is pardoned. So is Barnardine, who is furnished with a counsellor in the form of that fluent liar, Friar Peter. Whether Isabella is rewarded for her services, or deeply insulted, or left undecided, by the offer of the Duke's hand in marriage, is a matter which, in the theatre, varies according to the preferences of the particular director.[6] A fruitful crux has been created by the combination of the Duke's odd duplication of his proposal and Isabella's unconventional lack of verbal response to it.

Where the administration of the law is concerned, there has been a big gap in this play. We have seen a kind of magistrate's court in action: that was in Act 2, scene 1, when Escalus presided with some difficulty over the unruly case of Elbow *versus* Froth and Pompey. Having listened to the garbled accusations of Constable Elbow, Escalus shrewdly concludes that what's really needed is a change of constable. We know that Claudio has been sentenced to death for fornication, and that various denizens of the brothel-world (notably Pompey and Overdone) are sentenced to periods in prison which may be enlivened by flogging. When the Duke, after causing as much confusion as possible, re-emerges to deliver his judgements, he is at once prosecutor and judge; no jury here. His dispensations may finally elicit our approval (after all, he is remarkably lenient, and *perhaps* one or two of the marriages may work), but also, in

retrospect, the sense that justice is too important to be entrusted to
paternalistic autocrats.

What's missing from the play is evidence of the operation, in
practice, of proper high courts with juries. Such courts exist in
theory: Angelo knows about them. In Act 2, scene, 1, he says to
Escalus:

> I not deny
> The jury passing on the prisoner's life
> May in the sworn twelve have a thief or two
> Guiltier than him they try.   (2.1.18–21)

Nevertheless, insists Angelo, the law must take its course. The contrasting view, taken by Escalus and Isabella, when arguing for mercy,
is that since we are all sinners, we should be merciful. G. Wilson
Knight famously argued (in his essay '*Measure for Measure* and the
Gospels'[7]) that the basis of the play is 'the sublime strangeness and
unreason of Jesus' teaching'; 'The play must be read . . . as a parable';
it 'tends towards allegory or symbolism'. Thus 'Isabella stands
for sainted purity, Angelo for Pharisaical righteousness, the Duke
for a psychologically sound and enlightened ethic'. We learn that
'"justice" is a mockery: man, himself a sinner, cannot presume to
judge.' This Christian interpretation exerted a pervasive influence
on various critics or directors of the play: on, for example, F. R.
Leavis, Henri Fluchère, Roy Battenhouse, and Nevill Coghill. I
remember listening to a BBC radio production in March 1955
(director: Raymond Raikes; adviser: Nevill Coghill; Duke played by
Deryck Guyler). This broadcast used various means to suggest that
the Duke was God in disguise. An echo-chamber lent numinous
authority to his more choric pronouncements, and his final dispensa-
tion of justice seemed to take place not in the streets of Vienna but
somewhere between Heaven and earth: a joyous background-music
was provided by pealing bells and by an angelic choir singing a
Magnificat. Enough to turn you into a Lucio, but for the fact that
Lucio was represented as a metallic-voiced Lucifer.

Wilson Knight's essay also provoked a variety of counter-attacks,
of which the most adroitly penetrating and theologically insolent was
A. D. Nuttall's (in *Shakespeare Studies*). Nuttall summarized the
play's main range of ethical options. First, there is a 'tender' Christian ethic: 'No man who is not himself perfect has the right to judge

a fellow creature. Man can only forgive . . .' Secondly, there is a related 'tender' but non-Christian ethic: 'anybody without a bit of generous vice in him isn't properly human'; like the former, this advises us to forgive. Against these, the play offers a third way, a 'tough' ethic: '*of course* none of us is perfect but *of course* we must judge':

Now, do we really think that because none of us is perfect so no one should judge—that is, in hard terms, there should be no law-courts, no penal system, no juries, no police? Certainly judges are imperfect, but equally certainly it is a job that someone has to do. Men of tender conscience may preserve their charity intact, but only so long as others are willing to tarnish theirs a little.[8]

Angelo's ethic naturally lacks the tender ethic's power to 'give us warm feelings', but it is practical, it is supported by the play's depiction of the sordid brothel-world, and it is *ours*.

Angelo generally gets a bad press, much of it deserved. Certainly he is over-qualified for high political office, being a liar, hypocrite, blackmailer, would-be rapist, double-crosser, and slanderer. Nuttall may be multiplying by one or two too many when he says that Angelo is ('on a modest computation') worth about six Dukes. Nevertheless, just as Barnardine exposes the craziness of the Duke's justice from one side (exposing the doctrine of 'kill or liberate' and revealing the Duke's ignorance of what goes on within his own system), so Angelo exposes it from another. By referring us briefly to a saner world in which cases are heard in properly constituted courts with jurymen who, if fallible, must still do their job, Angelo reveals the gaping hole in the play's presentation of judicial procedures. The choice should not have to lie between, on the one side, the repressiveness administered by Angelo at the Duke's behest, and, on the other, the lenience dispensed by the paternalistic Duke himself. What happens to the administration of the law when Vincentio is no longer available to spy, lie, manipulate, and intrigue in order to right wrongs (some of his own creation)? Will justice cease to be the plaything of the powerful?

At Winchester in the winter of 1603–4, a number of condemned conspirators against King James were taken to the scaffold but then told that they had been reprieved, James having arranged for news of the reprieve to be delayed until the last moment. Historical warrant can thus be found for part of the play's last act, the Duke's cat-and-mouse game with Angelo. But Angelo's own earlier words have reminded us that there's a better system of law and order beyond the Duke's world of cat-and-mouse games, absurd severity and absurd lenience. The Duke, however, could respond by merely pointing to the main item in the morning newspaper on my desk:

Four members of one of the IRA's most ruthless death squads laughed yesterday as they were sentenced to a total of more than 600 years in jail.

The gang, described by police as 'the most feared IRA unit the security forces ever encountered', will be eligible for release within 16 months under the terms of the Good Friday peace accord.[9]

C.W.

How many Shakespearian cannibals?

Shakespeare certainly, and Joseph Conrad probably, knew the paradoxical essay in which, speaking of cannibalism and cannibals, Montaigne says:

I am not sorie we note the barbarous horror of such an action, but grieved, that prying so narrowly into their faults we are so blinded in ours. I think there is more barbarisme in eating men alive, then to feed upon them being dead ... We may then well call them barbarous, in regard of reasons rules, but not in respect of us that exceed them in all kinde of barbarisme.[1]

In Conrad's *Heart of Darkness*, Marlow, describing his experiences in Africa, offers a deft anti-imperialistic paradox. The crew of the steamboat taking the Europeans upstream are cannibals; but, though they have been starved by their white masters, they refrain from seizing and devouring them. Marlow is puzzled by their restraint:

Why in the name of all the gnawing devils of hunger they didn't go for us—they were thirty to five—and have a good tuck in for once, amazes me when I think of it.[2]

The other half of the paradox is the possibility that the charismatic Mr Kurtz, that 'universal genius' and 'emissary of light' from Europe, may have participated in cannibalism during his time as a savage god among the Africans. He 'lacked restraint in the gratification of his various lusts'; he has a 'weirdly voracious aspect'; after 'the awakening of forgotten and brutal instincts', he has known 'abominable satisfactions'; and Marlow recoils from hearing what happened at the ceremonies which ended with heads impaled on stakes facing Kurtz's abode. In Conrad's tale 'Falk', we learn that the eponymous Scandinavian seaman, when drifting at sea on a disabled ship, felt obliged to eat the vessel's carpenter. Chips with everything. In *Lord Jim*, Marlow reports that 'Cannibal Robinson' (an Australasian of British origin) survived a shipwreck by consuming no fewer than six of his shipmates: 'it seems they did not get on very well together', remarks Marlow's tactful informant.

Conrad's large irony was anticipated by Shakespeare. In Shakespeare's works, exotic cannibalism is mentioned, but the cannibalism that is enacted is closer to home. When discussing *The Tempest*, Frank Kermode remarks that Caliban's name is

usually regarded as a development of some form of the word 'Carib', meaning a savage inhabitant of the New World; 'cannibal' derives from this, and 'Caliban' is possibly a simple anagram of that word.[3]

Well, it's a 'simple anagram' if your spelling is as erratic as Shakespeare's. Although the Caliban–Cannibal linkage is commonly mentioned by critics, it may be a libel on the unfortunate and exploited son of Sycorax. Caliban has attempted rape and is an accomplice in a murder-bid, but human flesh is not part of his diet; and, if it had been, his status as original ruler of the island might have entitled him to impose his own dietary regime. As he says:

> This island's mine . . .
> For I am all the subjects that you have,
> Which first was mine own king . . .
>
> (1.2.331, 341–2)

In *Othello*, we hear that the Moor in his travels has learnt about 'the Anthropophagi'. According to William Harrison's *Description of Britain*, this was the name given to 'a parceil of the Irish nation . . . which were given to the eating of man's flesh'; so Othello may have voyaged further than we imagine.[4] In *King Lear*, Lear himself declares that he would rather be hospitable not to Cordelia but to the barbarous Scythian—who 'makes his generation messes | To gorge his appetite' (evidently he has his children to—and for—dinner). Yes, such matters are cited; but the only act of cannibalism which is enacted on stage for us takes place, notoriously, in *Titus Andronicus*.

Titus Andronicus? Round up all the usual insults. Edward Ravenscroft in 1687 called this play 'rather a heap of Rubbish th[a]n a Structure'; Dover Wilson in 1948 likened it to 'some broken-down cart, laden with bleeding corpses from an Elizabethan scaffold, and driven by an executioner from Bedlam dressed in cap and bells'; and later Kenneth Tynan said: 'I have often heard it called the worst thing Marlowe ever wrote'.[5] To other uncharitable readers, *Titus*

Andronicus may occasionally recall the Roman Empire of Morecambe and Wise ('Have you got the scrolls?' 'No, I always walk like this'), or may seem a missed opportunity for the 'Carry On' team (*Carry On Carving; or, Bonus AppeTitus!*). Nevertheless, the Peter Brook production at Stratford-upon-Avon in 1955, with Laurence Olivier as Titus and Vivien Leigh as Lavinia, famously conferred nightmarish power and intensity on that grotesque old revenge drama. It also suggested the thematic potential of two oddly allegoric scenes within it.

In Act 4, scene 3, Titus's friends and relatives solicit the gods at his request. The manner of solicitation is bizarre: they shoot letter-bearing arrows heavenwards. They do so partly to humour a hero deranged by grief, and partly because they recognize that the arrows, falling into Saturninus' palace, will be an annoyance to that surly emperor. As far as Titus is concerned, those arrows are indeed an appeal to the heavens. '*Terras Astraea reliquit* [Justice has abandoned the earth]', he has quoted; very well, justice will be implored to return:

> sith there's no justice in earth nor hell,
> We will solicit heaven and move the gods
> To send down justice for to wreak our wrongs.[6] (4.3.50–2)

The arrows are shot into the air. The result:

> *Enter the Clown with a basket and two pigeons in it.*

'News, news from heaven', cries Titus; 'Marcus, the post is come.' He turns to the Clown: 'What says Jupiter, I ask thee?' 'Alas, sir', replies the amiably gormless Clown, 'I know not Jubiter; I never drank with him in all my life.' Instead of Justice from the heavens, a buffoon from the wings. Actually, in that 1955 production, the Clown descended from the flies, as if to emphasize the atheistic irony of the bathos. Demented by grief, a vengeful old man solicits divine justice; the bathetic answer, a mortal fool. In a stark and rudimentary manner, there seems to be an anticipation of what happens when Lear's justice-demanding tirades are counterpointed by a Fool's needling sense and nonsense.

Titus sought Astraea; he obtained revenge. Revenge of so grisly a kind, however, as to dismay those spectators who are prepared for Shakespeare to be, on occasion, snobbish, racist, sexist, and incomprehensible, but not nauseating. At that Brook production, members of the St John Ambulance Brigade were stationed at the exits in order to assist various patrons who were rendered unwell by the dénouement. Those were innocent days, before food was sophisticated by hormones, antibiotics, Creutzfeldt–Jakob particles and genetic perversions, before *Soylent Green* and *Silence of the Lambs*, before an Andean plane-crash, a Japanese *cause célèbre*, and numerous anthropophagous African atrocities. Since then, cannibal banquets have become easier to stomach.

In *Titus Andronicus*, the circumstances of the revenge are curiously ceremonious and allegorical. Tamora, the wicked empress, hopes to persuade Titus to avert the invasion of Rome. She calls at his house, accompanied by her two vicious sons who had raped and mutilated Lavinia, Titus's daughter. To humour his madness, Tamora comes disguised as the Spirit of Revenge, and agrees that the sons are Revenge's ministers, Rape and Murder. Titus recognizes them but pretends to be deceived. Tamora departs; her sons remain. He binds and ceremonially slaughters them, cutting the throats while Lavinia holds (in her wrist-stumps) a basin for the blood. In the following scene, Tamora, accompanied by the emperor, returns for a banquet. Titus, dressed as a cook, serves them hospitably, but causes some consternation when he kills his daughter. Then, when Tamora has eaten and Saturninus asks for the two sons to be fetched, Titus (anachronistically recalling the 'dainty dish' of 'Four-and-twenty blackbirds / Baked in a pie') says:

> Why there they are, both bakèd in this pie,
> Where of their mother daintily hath fed,
> Eating the flesh that she herself hath bred.   (5.3.59–61)

He then kills Tamora and is himself slain by Saturninus, who in turn dies at the hand of Lucius. Memorably gory stuff, so that around 1590 *Titus Andronicus* was ranked alongside *The Spanish Tragedy* as one of the two 'best plays yet'. (That's according to Ben Jonson, who would know.[7])

For the act of revenge which culminates in anthropophagy there were two obvious literary precedents. One was Seneca's *Thyestes*; the other was Ovid's *Metamorphoses*. In Seneca, as in *Titus Andronicus*, the avenger presides as a gloating chef while the flesh of slain sons is eaten by a parent (a nice descriptive touch is '*eructat*'—'he belches').

In Ovid, as in *Titus Andronicus*, the economical banquet is vengeance for the rape and mutilation of a young woman. Of the two sources, Ovid is the more prominent in the play. Lavinia carries a copy of *Metamorphoses* on stage, and it is the Ovidian tale of Tereus, Procne, and Philomela that inspires Titus's scheme. (The rapist Tereus unwittingly ate his son Itys, killed and cooked by the lad's mother and aunt; after eating, he asked for his son, and Philomela presented him with the head.) As Titus says to the two sons who are his victims:

> For worse than Philomel you used my daughter,
> And worse than Procne I will be revenged.
>
> (5.2.194–5)

What is striking is that neither in *Thyestes* nor in *Metamorphoses*— nor, to judge from its extant version, in a likely source tale which recounted the woes of Titus—is there any precedent for the ostentatiously allegoric heralding of this most grisly part of the plot.

When Tamora had called on Titus, she had majestically proclaimed:

> I am Revenge, sent from th'infernal kingdom
> To ease the gnawing vulture of thy mind
> By working wreakful vengeance on thy foes.   (5.2.30–2)

Titus had extended the allegory, identifying her sons as Rape and Murder. The banquet is attended by Tamora, Saturninus, Aemilius, 'Tribunes, and others'. Although in theory sufficient time elapses for most of them to make a start on the meal ('please you eat of it', says Titus, almost as soon as the food has been placed on the table), Saturninus is engaged in conversation with Titus, and the others should be waiting politely for the emperor to begin first. When Saturninus, referring to the slain Lavinia, says 'What, was she ravished? Tell who did the deed', Titus replies 'Will't please you eat? Will't please your highness feed?' At this point, evidently, Tamora starts on the loathsome repast. The scene can be so directed that while Saturninus, responding to Titus's invitation, begins to slice his plateful, she samples the pie and is the only person actually to swallow the meat. This is what Titus has been waiting and watching for; and, now that the rapists' mother 'daintily hath fed' on her sons, he can kill her. He knows that Tamora's allegory has reached its elegantly ironic and literal completion: *Revenge has engorged Rape and Murder*.

Thus, far from being evidence of an 'inferior hand', the disgusting banquet may be deeply Shakespearian.[8] In *Titus Andronicus*, his early revenge drama, we witness literal cannibalism with an allegoric gloss. In Shakespeare's mature works, cannibalism will reappear as metaphor and as mutually destructive human action. In *Troilus and Cressida*, Ulysses will speak of the 'universal wolf' of egoistic appetite, which will eventually 'eat up himself'. In *King Lear*, Albany says that if 'the heavens' do not intervene,

> It will come,
> Humanity must perforce prey on itself,
> Like monsters of the deep.[9]

The original question, 'How many Shakespearian cannibals?', has, therefore, two answers. At a literal level, there is only one canni-bal on stage in Shakespeare: the Empress Tamora, her act unwitting. At a metaphorical level, however, there are scores: we see them, for example, in the appetitive, rapacious and mutually-lethal schem-ings of *Richard III*, *Hamlet*, *Macbeth*, *King Lear*, and *Troilus and Cressida*: Shakespeare provides many examples of destructive and self-destructive voracity. So does history. Recent political events prove that humanity has not lost its readiness to 'prey on itself'.

C.W.

Notes

Cleopatra—deadbeat mum?

Anthony and Cleopatra is edited in Oxford World's Classics by Michael Neill.

1. A. C. Bradley, 'Shakepeare's *Antony and Cleopatra*', *Quarterly Review*, 204, 407 (Apr. 1906), 329–51; repr. *Shakespeare Criticism*, 6. 58. (*Shakespeare Criticism* is a multi-volume compilation of Shakespeare criticism, published by Gale Research (Detroit), currently 49 volumes and growing.)
2. Notably the social historian Lawrence Stone, in *The Family, Sex and Marriage in England, 1500–1800* (New York, 1986).
3. *Macbeth*, ed. Nicholas Brooke (Oxford World's Classics), 1.7.54–5.

The watch on the centurion's wrist

Julius Caesar is edited in Oxford World's Classics by Arthur Humphreys.

1. A good, if amused, account of the Oxfordian case is given by Jenijoy La Belle, in *Engineering and Science*, 55.1 (Fall 1991), 22–9.
2. The 'most notorious boner' description is Sigurd Burckhardt's, in 'How Not to Murder Caesar', in *Shakespearean Meanings* (Princeton, 1968); repr. *Shakespeare Criticism* 7. 331–3. Burckhardt argues that Shakespeare's 'anachronisms' in *Julius Caesar* may be dramatically calculated deliberate effects.
3. In *Complete Works*, ed. Wells and Taylor, the scenes are numbered continuously; this quotation is from scene 22, lines 1–2. Conventionally, the scene is Act 5, scene 2.
4. David S. Landes, *Revolution in Time: Clocks and the Making of the Modern World* (Cambridge, Mass.: 1983), 95.
5. Ibid. 68.

'Too much i' the sun': is it summer in Elsinore?

Hamlet is edited in Oxford World's Classics by G. R. Hibbard.

1. See J. Dover Wilson's comment on the first scene in the Cambridge edition of the play (London, 1934, repr. 1967): 'Shakespeare builds up the atmosphere of this frosty, star-lit, northern night as he proceeds,' 144.
2. Some productions and commentators conceive Ophelia's bouquet of flowers to be imaginary, see Dover Wilson, ed. cit., 225.

Where is the Ghost from? Is he stupid? and: Is Hamlet really Hamleth?

1. According to *The Times*, 25 January 1999, p. 13.
2. *Macbeth*, ed. Nicholas Brooke (Oxford World's Classics), 1.3.124–7.
3. Eleanor Prosser, *Hamlet and Revenge* (Stanford, Calif.; London, 1967). See also: G. Wilson Knight, 'The Embassy of Death: An Essay on *Hamlet*' in *The Wheel of Fire* (London 1960); Roy Battenhouse, 'The Ghost in *Hamlet*: A Catholic "Linchpin"?', *Studies in Philology*, 48 (1951), 161–92; H. D. F. Kitto, *Form and Meaning in Drama* (London, 1964), ch. 9.
4. Sir Thomas Browne: *Religio Medici*, ed. James Winny (London, 1963), 46.
5. Exodus 20: 13; Romans 12: 19; Leviticus 19: 18; Deuteronomy 32: 35; Hebrews 10: 30.
6. *Richard III*, 1.4.210–14, in *Complete Works* ed. Wells and Taylor.
7. *Johnson on Shakespeare*, ed. Walter Raleigh (London, 1908, repr. 1957), 196.
8. *The Complete Works of Samuel Taylor Coleridge*, vol. iv (New York, 1854), 156.
9. *The Complete Works of Thomas Lodge*, vol. iv (New York, 1963), 62.
10. A. J. A. Waldock, *'Hamlet': A Study in Critical Method* (Cambridge, 1931), 65–73, 97.
11. See Cedric Watts, *Hamlet* (Hemel Hempstead, 1988), ch. 1.
12. Waldock, *'Hamlet'*, 49.

Desdemona's posthumous speeches

1. *Othello* (New Variorum edition, ed. H. H. Furness, Philadelphia, 1886), 386.
2. In *Complete Works*, ed. Wells and Taylor.
3. Furness, 307.
4. Ibid. 306.
5. A. C. Bradley, *Shakespearean Tragedy* (London, 1905; repr. 1967), 438–9.

'Great thing of us forgot!' Albany's amnesia or Shakespeare's?

1. Peter Manso, *Brando* (London, 1994), 717.
2. In this discussion, quotations from *King Lear* are usually taken from *The Tragedy of King Lear* (based on the Folio text) in *Complete Works*, edited by Wells and Taylor. In the case of this particular quotation, however, I have preferred the reading of Kenneth Muir's Arden edition (London, 1964), 217. Its exclamatory intensity seems to me more appropriate to the context than is the Wells–Taylor version, which begins: 'And my poor fool is hanged. No, no, no life?' I have also retained the traditional spelling 'Edmund' instead of Wells–Taylor's 'Edmond'.

3. *Johnson on Shakespeare*, ed. Walter Raleigh (London, 1908, repr. 1957), 161, 20–1.

4. G. I. Duthie, Introduction to *King Lear* (London, 1962), p. li. Duthie's logic is self-contradictory. One premiss is that God's goodness can clearly be inferred from events on earth; the other is that it cannot. The antitheist could employ equivalent logic to opposite effect by letting the death of Cordelia be evidence of a malevolent deity and the punishment of evil-doers be evidence of his inscrutability.

5. This passage appears as 5.3. 204–21 in Muir's Arden edition and as lines 201–18 of scene 24 in the Wells–Taylor *The History of King Lear* (but it is absent from the Wells–Taylor *The Tragedy of King Lear*).

Poor Tom's a yokel?

1. A. C. Bradley, *Shakespearean Tragedy* (London, 1904; repr. 1967), 256.

2. In *Complete Works*, ed. Wells and Taylor. I quote mainly from the Folio text (*The Tragedy of King Lear*), occasionally the Quarto text (*The History of King Lear*) in their edition.

3. According to *OED* the term is used only once in recorded literature—here by Shakespeare. It is suggested that 'ballow' might be a printer's error for 'baton'. The text I quote from here is Kenneth Muir's second Arden edition (London, 1964), 173.

4. R. A. Foakes, who has prepared the third Arden edition of *King Lear* (London, 1995), thinks it is likely that Gloster, as a blind man, has a staff which Edgar seizes.

5. Arden edition (1964), p. xlv.

How ancient is Lear? How youthful is Juliet?

Quotations from *Complete Works*, ed. Wells and Taylor (Folio text).

1. The variable depictions of Lear on stage over the centuries are discussed by Alex Leggatt in *King Lear: Shakespeare in Performance* (Manchester, 1991).

2. See Leggatt, *King Lear* 127–8. In his memoir, *On Acting* (New York, 1986), 137, Olivier gave his less decorous opinion that Lear is 'just a stupid old fart'.

3. *King Lear*, ed. Kenneth Muir (Arden edition, London, 1964), p. xxvi.

4. J. Dover Wilson, in his Cambridge edition of the play (1955, repr. 1963), 136, hazards that Lady Capulet must 'inferentially' be 'about 28'.

5. Furness makes this guess in the New Variorum edition of the play (Boston, 1871), 48.

6. Coppélia Kahn discusses the observable fact that 'Verona's daughters have, in effect, no adolescence, no sanctioned period of experiment with adult identities or activities' in 'Coming of Age in Verona', *Modern Language Studies*, 8/1 (Winter 1977–8); repr. *Shakespeare Criticism* 5. 569.

7. H. Granville-Barker, *Prefaces to Shakespeare: Romeo and Juliet* (London, 1930); repr. *Shakespeare Criticism* 5. 455.
8. Norman Haire, *The Encyclopaedia of Sexual Knowledge* (London, 1934), 129–30.

What's in a name? Why does Juliet confuse 'Montague' with 'Romeo'?

Quotations are, unless otherwise indicated, from *Complete Works*, ed. Wells and Taylor.

1. Among the elaborate textual annotations in the New Variorum edition of *Romeo and Juliet* compiled by H. H. Furness and published in 1871, we find (on p. 96) a very brief entry: the ascription to 'Anon.' of a conjecture that the final '*Romeo*' in the line should be '*Montague*'. This essay may be read as a (somewhat tardy) tribute to Anon.
2. *Course in General Linguistics* (originally *Cours de linguistique générale*, ed. C. Bally and A. Sechehaye, 1916), tr. Wade Baskin (London, 1960, rev. 1974).
3. *Critical Practice* (London, 1980), 41, 43, 44.
4. *Structuralism and Semiotics* (London, 1977), 121.
5. *Écrits*, tr. Alan Sheridan (London, 1977), 65.
6. *Course in General Linguistics*, p. xxxii.
7. Cited by George Watson, *The Certainty of Literature* (Hemel Hempstead, 1989), 49.
8. Her views chime with those of Sir Thomas Overbury (1581–1613), who, in his poem 'A Wife', declares: 'Things were first made then *words*: she were the *same* | *With*, or *without*, *that title* or that name.' Samuel Johnson, in the preface to his *Dictionary*, says: 'Words are the daughters of the earth, and . . . things are the sons of heaven.'
9. Most current editions include this soliloquy in Act 4, scene 4; the Wells and Taylor *Complete Works* includes it in the appendix to the play; the Oxford World's Classics *Hamlet*, ed. G. R. Hibbard, also appends it (pp. 363–5).
10. Confirmed in 1999 by Prof. Mario Curreli of Pisa University, who remarks that, thanks to translations of Shakespeare's play, 'twenty years ago there were some 30,000 Romeos in Italy': perhaps a case of coals to Newcastle (or of Viagra to Priapus).
11. John Florio, *A Worlde of Wordes, or Most Copious, and Exact Dictionarie in Italian and English* (London, 1598), 333.
12. On the way to the ball, Mercutio says: 'Give me a case to put my visage in, | A visor for a visor'. When Capulet greets Romeo, Mercutio and Benvolio, he says:

> Welcome, gentlemen. I have seen the day
> That I have worn a visor, and could tell
> A whispering tale in a fair lady's ear . . .   (1.5.21–3)

Tybalt, initially foxed by Romeo's visor, says: 'This, by his voice, should be a Montague.' (Such an identification of clan by voice was and is entirely plausible; Shaw's Professor Higgins would relish the accents of Verona, remarks Prof. Curreli.) Tybalt draws Capulet's attention to the intruder; the host, looking at the visored person, is a little uncertain: 'Romeo, is it?' But Tybalt, who has now had time to identify Romeo or has had his memory jogged by Capulet, confirms that ''Tis he, that villain Romeo'. The stage directions in several early printed texts (Q2, Q3, Q4, and F) appropriately note that the other guests initially approach 'the Masquers', Romeo and his friends.

REAL OR PRETEND I

Lady Macbeth: feint or faint?

Macbeth is edited in Oxford World's Classics by Nicholas Brooke.

1. The Porter tells Macduff that they have been 'carousing till the second cock', that is till about three in the morning. Macbeth greets Macduff with 'Good morrow!', indicating that day has just broken.
2. Dr Johnson notes, 'It is not improbable that Shakespeare put these forced and unnatural metaphors into the mouth of Macbeth as a mark of artifice and dissimulation.' See H. H. Furness, *Macbeth* (New Variorum edition, rev. H. H. Furness Jr., Boston, 1903), 160. Macbeth is normally taciturn in his speech. See, for example, his laconic ''Twas a rough night'.
3. Others have also asked the question, see Furness, 162–5, and A. C. Bradley, *Shakespearean Tragedy* (London, 1905, repr. 1967), 484–6.

REAL OR PRETEND II

Hamlet's knock-knees

Hamlet is edited in Oxford World's Classics by G. R. Hibbard.

1. Arden edition (London, 1982), 461–2.
2. A good account of the 'Ur-Hamlet' is given by J. Dover Wilson, in the Cambridge edition of the play (Cambridge, 1934; repr. 1967), pp. xii–xv.
3. Philip Edwards, 'The Play and the Critics', in *Hamlet, Prince of Denmark* (Cambridge, 1985), 32–61.

REAL OR PRETEND III

Does Cleopatra really care about her 'petty things'?

Anthony and Cleopatra is edited in Oxford World's Classics by Michael Neill.

1. This speech, and the implications of the word 'boy' are examined in detail

by Phyllis Rackin in 'Shakespeare's Boy Cleopatra, the Decorum of Nature, and the Golden World of Poetry,' *PMLA* 87 2 (March 1972), 201–12; repr. *Shakespeare Criticism* 27. 135–44.

2. As the sources remind us, Cleopatra has four children at this point: one by Caesar (Caesarion), and three, including a pair of twins, by Mark Anthony. The awarding of these children imperial heirs' rights at the so called 'Gifts of Alexandria' ceremony (contemptuously referred to by Octavius in his speech in Act 3, scene 6) precipitated the war which eventually brings down Cleopatra.

3. As H. H. Furness notes, in his New Variorum edition of the play (Philadelphia and London, 1907), 352, the first critic to elaborate this line of analysis was the German, Adolf Stahr, for whom the treasure scene was 'a little comedy, pre-arranged and agreed upon, between [Cleopatra] and her faithful treasurer' and 'a masterstroke of the bold lady'. If this interpretation were not accepted, Stahr believed, the queen's conduct 'will severely grate every reader'. As M. R. Ridley noted, however, in his edition of the play, if it *is* a 'put-up job . . . the only trouble about the interpretation is whether it can be made plain to the audience' (Arden edn., 1965, pp. xl–xli). 'It can be done,' Ridley thinks, but it puts a heavy strain on the actress. On the question of Shakespeare never overlooking 'first-rate hints' in North, the dramatist studiously did not develop Plutarch's account of the queen being 'naked in her smocke' in this scene.

4. Dover Wilson, ed. cit., p. xxxv.

REAL OR PRETEND IV

Othello's magical handkerchief

1. Quotations from *Othello* are from *Complete Works*, ed. Wells and Taylor.

2. Thomas Rymer, *A Short View of Tragedy* (London, 1693), 89, 135 f. (the page-numbering is chaotic: the page following 135 is numbered 140).

3. In the 1990 video of the play directed by Trevor Nunn, with Willard White as Othello, the Moor brushes it aside casually. But this also makes the point. If he knows that one particular handkerchief is of such vital importance, he would be unlikely to let any be brushed aside and dropped so casually without first ensuring that it's not the vital one.

4. Umberto Eco, *A Theory of Semiotics* (London, 1977), 7.

5. Michael Riffaterre, *The Semiotics of Poetry* (Bloomington, Ind., and London, 1978), 1.

6. S. T. Coleridge, *Shakespearean Criticism*, ed. T. M. Raysor (2 vols.; London, 1960), i. 44. Other editions give 'the motive-hunting of a motive-less malignity'.

7. Rymer (pp. 91–2) provides an interesting seventeenth-century view of the matter:

With us a Black-amoor might rise to be a Trumpeter; but *Shakespear would not have him less than a Lieutenant-General. With us a Moor* might marry some little drab, or Small-coal Wench: *Shake-spear*, would provide him the Daughter and Heir of some great Lord, or Privy-Councellor: And all the Town should reckon it a very suitable match: Yet the English are not bred up with that hatred and aversion to the *Moors*, as are the Venetians, who suffer by a perpetual Hostility from them   . . .

8. In the 1990 video mentioned above, Willard White's Othello raised the weapon, pointing it away from himself, and brought it down in a semi-circular sweep until it appeared to enter his abdomen.

How much time did Richard waste?

Quotations are from *Complete Works*, ed. Wells and Taylor.

1. Nor is it long by the calendar. The historical time which passed between the trial by combat and Richard's death at Pomfret was barely two years, Jan. 1398–Feb. 1400.
2. There is an obscure comment, at 2.1.168–9, about Richard's having prevented Bolingbroke in exile from taking a noble wife.
3. Prince Henry was, historically, 12 years old at this point.
4. He was, as J. Dover Wilson elegantly puts it in the Cambridge edition of the play (1939), '"in standing water between man and boy" in his art', p. x.

Who killed Woodstock?

1. Quotations from *Richard II* are from *Complete Works*, ed. Wells and Taylor.
2. *Shakespeare's Holinshed*, ed. W. G. Boswell-Stone [1896] (New York 1966), 80.
3. Ibid. 83.
4. Michael Senior, *The Life and Times of Richard II* (London, 1981, repr. 1984), 132.
5. Anthony Steel, *Richard II* (London, 1962), 239.
6. *Shakespeare's Holinshed*, 111.
7. J. L. Kirby, *Henry IV of England* (London, 1970), 17–18 (quotation, p. 18), 25–6.
8. Steel, *Richard II*, 21.
9. A. R. Myers, *England in the Late Middle Ages* (Harmondsworth, 1952; repr. 1956), 17.
10. John Wilmot, Earl of Rochester, 'A Satire against Reason and Mankind', in *The Norton Anthology of Poetry*, 4th edn. (New York and London, 1996), 507.

Hal and Francis: what's the issue?

1. At the real Battle of Shrewsbury, Prince Henry was 15, Hotspur in his late thirties; and Hotspur was slain not by the Prince's sword but by an arrow. See M. W. Labarge's *Henry V: The Cautious Conqueror* (London, 1975), 12, 21.
2. *1 Henry IV* is edited in Oxford World's Classics by David Bevington.
3. *Sixteen Plays of Shakespeare*, ed. G. L. Kittredge (Boston, 1946), 565.
4. *The First Part of King Henry IV*, ed. A. R. Humphreys (London, 1966), 61.
5. *2 Henry IV*, 2. 4. 285, in *Complete Works*, ed. Wells and Taylor.
6. Near the end of Act 2, scene 4, we are given clear evidence of the value of a pound in this fictional world: Falstaff is charged half a crown (one eighth of one pound) for a chicken and sauce, and five shillings and eight pence (just over a quarter of one pound) for two gallons of wine.
7. Humphreys, 60.
8. Kittredge, 564.
9. See e.g. *Shakespeare's Holinshed*, ed. Richard Hosley (New York, 1968), 316.

Henry V, war criminal?

Henry V is edited in Oxford World's Classics by Gary Taylor.

1. For an analysis of Branagh's interpretation, see Robert Lane, 'When Blood is their Argument: Class, Character, and Historymaking in Branagh's *Henry V*', Shakespeare Criticism Year Book, 1994 (Detroit, 1996), 146–58.
2. This was very much a spirit-of-the-age reaction in the mid- and late 1940s. In his 1947 Cambridge edition of the play, J. Dover Wilson declares that 'Henry's words before Agincourt, and Churchill's after the Battle of Britain, come from the same national mint', p. xxi. Unsurprisingly, Dover Wilson sees Henry's slaughter of the prisoners as totally justified by military exigency. The English troops were 'enrounded' (p. xxxiii).
3. See the Riverside edition of *Shakespeare's Plays* (Boston, 1974), 932.
4. Hazlitt, *The Characters of Shakespeare's Plays* (London, 1817); repr. *Shakespeare Criticism*, 5. 194.
5. Herschel Baker gives the quotation in his Riverside edition of *Henry V*, p. 963.

Henry V's claim to France: valid or invalid?

1. Margaret Wade Labarge, *Henry V: The Cautious Conqueror* (London, 1975), 82.
2. Gary Taylor: 'Introduction' to the Oxford World's Classics *Henry V*, 35.

My quotations from *Henry V* are taken from this edition, with the exception specified in note 6.

3. The First Quarto text (1600), which bears signs of censorship, omits the opening scene.

4. John Fletcher, *The Noble Gentleman*, in *The Dramatic Works in the Beaumont and Fletcher Canon*, ed. Fredson Bowers, vol. iii (Cambridge, 1976), 167. The business of the claim occupies more than thirty lines.

5. Tom Paine, *The Rights of Man* [1791–2] (Harmondsworth, 1969), 140.

6. The Gary Taylor text (which is in both the *Complete Works*, ed. Wells and Taylor, and the Oxford World's Classics) offers the unique reading 'after ill'; but I much prefer the traditional reading 'after all', which has the authority of the First Folio; so I retain it in this speech (line 292). To say that penitence comes 'after ill' is tautological, since penitence wouldn't come after good; nor does it make sense of the previous line; whereas to say that penitence is worth nothing if it comes 'after all' (namely after Henry has accepted all the consequences of the deposition and death of Richard, helping his father to retain power and then continuing to retain it himself) makes ample sense.

7. Labarge, *Henry V*, 54–5, points out that English claims to most French territory had been rescinded by Henry III at the Treaty of Paris in 1259, and, at the Treaty of Bretigny in 1360, Edward III had relinquished his claim to the French throne. As for Henry V's case:

> [A]ll this English emphasis on the essential legitimacy of their claims and the English king's rights in France ultimately provoked the Archbishop of Bourges ... to sharp retort. He pointed out to King Henry, most undiplomatically, that not only was Charles VI the true king of France and that Henry had no right to anything in France, but that he even had no right to the kingdom of England and that the king of France should rather treat with the true heirs of the late King Richard. Henry's anger at the ambassador's presumption was unbridled.

8. *Hamlet*, ed. G. R. Hibbard (Oxford World's Classics), 3.3.51–5.

9. To put matters politely: *foot* sounds to her like *foutre*, 'to have sexual intercourse with', *cown* like *con*, 'vagina'.

10. Niccolò Machiavelli, *Il principe* [1513] (Florence, 1951), 149 (my translation).

11. *2 Henry IV*, ed. René Weis (Oxford World's Classics), 3.1.44–8, 52–5.

What happens to Viola's 'eunuch' plan?

Twelfth Night is edited in Oxford World's Classics by Roger Warren and Stanley Wells.

1. Quoted in the New Variorum edition of *Twelfth Night*, ed. H. H. Furness (Philadelphia, 1901), 29.

2. The entry on 'Castrati' in Vol. 3 of *The New Grove Dictionary of*

Music and Musicians, ed. Stanley Sadie (London, 1980), 875, is relevant. Castrati were reported as having been recruited for musical purposes in Spain as early as the mid-sixteenth century and there are references to them in the Sistine Choir in Italy from about 1565. Castrati featured centrally in Italian opera from its beginnings in 1600. They were mostly selected from among boy singers. Their parents gave consent for the operation 'in return for payment', or other reward.

3. Op. cit.

4. Anne Barton, in the Riverside edition of *Twelfth Night* (Boston, 1974), 404.

5. Since Viola does not sing and Feste does, it has been suggested that there was a hasty change of boy actors, necessitating a change of the plan by which the 'eunuch' Viola would sing. See Arthur Quiller Couch and J. Dover Wilson's Cambridge edition of *Twelfth Night* (Cambridge, 1930; repr. 1958), 91–4. The point is also taken up by John Astington in 'Malvolio and the Eunuchs: Texts and Revelations in *Twelfth Night*', *Shakespearean Criticism Yearbook, 1994* (Detroit, 1996), 1–8.

Malvolio: vengeful or reconciled?

1. This is the version in the Oxford World's Classics' *Twelfth Night*, ed. Roger Warren and Stanley Wells. Other editions punctuate less lightly and give: 'Dost thou think, because thou art virtuous, there shall be no more cakes and ale?', which suits a boozily pompous delivery.

2. Quoted by Warren and Wells in the introduction to their Oxford World's Classics edition, p. 59.

3. Ibid. 43.

4. The ambiguity is heralded by editorial variations in the punctuation of this line. In the First Folio, the line ends in a question-mark, which sometimes (as, I'm sure, in this case) served as an exclamation-mark. Some editors (e.g. Warren and Wells) substitute a full stop; others (e.g. J. M. Lothian and T. W. Craik, Arden 1975) maintain the intended exclamation-mark. In this essay, my quotations from *Twelfth Night* are usually from the Oxford text, but for this line I prefer the exclamatory version, which seems to me more appropriate to the context: it's the parting shot of a man who has reason for vehemence.

5. Warren and Wells, p. 68.

6. Ibid. 219. They refer to Fabian's speech at lines 346–59 (in which Fabian displayed notable diplomatic skills).

Does Bottom cuckold Oberon?

A Midsummer Night's Dream is edited in Oxford World's Classics by Peter Holland.

1. Harold Brooks, Introduction to *A Midsummer Night's Dream* (London, 1979), p. cxv. Peter Holland, on p. 73 of his Oxford World's Classics

edition, says: 'What is so remarkable about Titania's night with Bottom is . . . the innocence'; it is 'touchingly naïve'; 'sexuality is diminished rather than intensified'.

2. *The Winter's Tale*, ed. Stephen Orgel (Oxford World's Classics), 4.4.24–9.

3. The orgiastic tradition continued. In *The Times* (29 March 1999, p. 18), Benedict Nightingale, reviewing a new production at Stratford-upon-Avon, reported:

> When Titania begins her amour with furry-eared Bottom, the effect is usually a little less erotic than the teddy bear's picnic. Not in Michael Boyd's bold and brilliant revival at the Royal Shakespeare Theatre. Multiple orgasms are clearly occurring in the bed hovering above the stage; and the excitement does not end with the feverish moaning. When Josette Simon's squirming, leggy fairy queen tells Daniel Ryan's post-coital Bottom that one of her ogling attendants will 'fetch thee new nuts', her hand is on a part of his body that suggests she does not just mean tasty acorns.

4. Rottingdean Drama Society: *A Midsummer Night's Dream*, directed by Ronald Taylor and Frances Acton, June 1989.

5. In the passage quoted here, 'enforcèd chastity' could mean 'person forced to remain a virgin' or 'chastity violated by force'. Either way, sexuality is made an issue; but the latter reading seems to me more likely. In Act 3, scene 1, of Beaumont and Fletcher's *The Faithful Shepherdess*, Satyre (a counterpart to Puck) says:

> Then must I watch if any be
> Forcing of a chastity,
> If I finde it, then in haste,
> Give my wreathed horn a blast,
> And the faeries all will run,
> Wildely dauncing by the moone,
> And will pinch him to the bone,
> Till his lustfull thoughts be gone.

(*The Dramatic Works in the Beaumont and Fletcher Canon*, ed. Fredson Bowers, vol. iii (Cambridge, 1976), 537).

6. *Paradise Lost*, viii. 615–29, in *The Poetical Works of John Milton*, ed. Helen Darbishire (London, 1958), 180–1.

7. The Geneva Bible (1560) ends this passage with the phrase 'the deepe things of God'. I quote William Tyndale's translation (1525–6): *Tyndale's New Testament*, modern-spelling edition by David Daniell (New Haven and London, 1989).

8. It obviously suggests 'buttocks' to modern audiences. Holland, p. 147, says that there is no proof that 'bottom' had that meaning when Shakespeare was writing. I think it would be unwise to underestimate Shakespeare's associative talents, particularly where the human body is concerned. 'Bottom', at that time, could certainly refer to the base of anything and to

the capacious curvature of a ship, so an association with 'buttocks' seems natural enough; and the word had long been synonymous with 'fundament'.

Never act with dogs and babies

1. This chapter is inspired, to an almost plagiaristic degree, by Stephen Fender's monograph, *Shakespeare's* A Midsummer Night's Dream (London, 1968); extracts repr. *Shakespeare Criticism*, 3.459–66.
2. Quoted in the New Variorum edition of *A Midsummer Night's Dream*, ed. H. H. Furness (Philadelphia, 1895), 187.
3. As Furness's New Variorum edition points out, Spartan hounds were 'celebrated for their swiftness', p. 186.

Why is Shylock unmusical?

1. Brian Pullan, *Rich and Poor in Renaissance Venice* (Oxford, 1971), 539–40, 543.
2. Ibid. 571.
3. Ibid. 555.
4. Samuel Schoenbaum, *William Shakespeare: A Compact Documentary Life* (Oxford, 1977; repr. 1987), 322. In 1570, John was fined forty shillings. In later decades his son, William, seems to have been vigilantly litigious in recovering debts and claiming damages.
5. Pullan, *Rich and Poor*, 551–2.
6. Quotations from the Oxford World's Classics text of *The Merchant of Venice*, ed. Jay L. Halio. *Complete Works*, ed. Wells and Taylor, has small differences in punctuation here.
7. Pullan, *Rich and Poor*, 553. The adjective *premeditada* should be *premeditata*.
8. Ibid. 557.
9. Ibid. 562–3.
10. Schoenbaum, *William Shakespeare*, 169–70.
11. Ibid. 170. Schoenbaum points out that in the source-tale the character's name is not Bassanio but Gianetto.
12. The commentators include J. Weiss in 1876 and R. Noble in 1923. J. Russell Brown, in his Arden edition of the play (London, 1964; repr. 1975), 80, gives reasons for doubt: notably that Bassanio's long speech of cogitation 'would be an odd elaboration if he believed that the song had given him the secret'. As so often in Shakespeare, though, much depends on the staging. An actor might register immediate recognition of the clue before embarking on the lengthy rationalization of the choice.
13. When Thomas Platter visited a production of *Julius Caesar* (probably Shakespeare's play) in 1599, he noted that 'at the end of the play they [the actors] danced together admirably and exceedingly gracefully, according to their custom, two in each group dressed in men's and two in women's apparel' (Schoenbaum, *William Shakespeare*, 209).

14. If we look at two other Puritanical characters, we see that even Malvolio, in his downfall, is given just a hint of tragic pathos and passion ('you have done me wrong, | Notorious wrong . . . | I'll be revenged on the whole pack of you'); and there is pathos if not passion when the disgraced Angelo says 'Immediate sentence, then, and sequent death | Is all the grace I beg'.

15. See 'The *Othello* Music' in G. Wilson Knight, *The Wheel of Fire* [1930] (revised edn.: London, 1949).

16. Ben Jonson, *Every Man in His Humour*, ed. J. W. Lever (London, 1972), 171. The reference is found not in the first (1598) version of the play but in the revised version (1605), and thus post-dates *The Merchant of Venice*.

Is Portia a virgin at the end of the play— and will she stay one?

1. According to H. H. Furness, in the New Variorum edition of *The Merchant of Venice* (Philadelphia, 1888), 167, 60,000 ducats is 'equal to at least one million of dollars now' ('now' being the late nineteenth century).

2. Quotations are from the Oxford World's Classics edition of *The Merchant of Venice*, ed. Jay L. Halio.

3. The New Variorum edition has a long appendix (pp. 403–20) discussing the legal niceties of the trial scene. The consensus is that Shylock was unfairly dealt with. That Portia is acting on the learned advice of Bellario is suggested by her mention of certain 'notes' which she has had from him, together with her court apparel.

4. In his Cambridge edition of the play (1926; repr. 1968), 167, J. Dover Wilson suggests that we should imagine the moon shining 'fitfully' at night, rather than fading at dawn.

5. The speculation was sanctioned by W. H. Auden's persuasive essay in his collection *The Dyer's Hand* (London, 1962). The subject is authoritatively reviewed by Alan Sinfield, in 'How to Read the *Merchant of Venice* without being Heterosexist', *Shakespeare Criticism Year Book, 1996* (Detroit, 1998), 86–93.

6. Alan Bray, *Homosexuality in Renaissance England* (London, 1982; repr. 1988), 75. 'Bugger' derives originally from 'Bulgar', or Bulgarian.

Muddle or method?

1. G. B. Shaw, Preface to *Plays: Pleasant and Unpleasant*, vol. i (London, 1898), p. xxi.

2. *The Riverside Shakespeare*, ed. G. Blakemore Evans (Boston, 1974), 443. A more recent confirmation of Shaw's wisdom was provided in a review by Benedict Nightingale of a National Theatre production (*The Times*, 17 March 1999, p. 34):

> [T]he play has been revived twice by the RSC in the past three years, is now in the Olivier rep, and may get yet another showing in the West

End this autumn. Is there a piece that better embodies the disillusioned soul of the departing century? 'Nothing but wars and lechery,' repeats the arch-cynic Thersites, and, yes, that is what our era's dictators and scientists have left us feeling about honour, chivalry and love.

3. John Dryden, Preface to *Troilus and Cressida, or, Truth Found too Late; A Tragedy* (London, 1679), unnumbered page [viii].
4. Quotations are from the Oxford World's Classics edition of *Troilus and Cressida* by Kenneth Muir.
5. E. M. W. Tillyard: *The Elizabethan World Picture* (1943; repr. Harmondsworth, 1963), 21, 22. In 1983 a Conservative Chancellor of the Exchequer said that Ulysses' speech proved Shakespeare to be 'a Tory, without any doubt'.
6. Caroline Spurgeon: *Shakespeare's Imagery and What It Tells Us* (1935; repr. Cambridge, 1965), 321–4 and chart VII.

The mystery of the putrifièd corpse

1. In Edgar Allan Poe, *Tales of Mystery and Imagination* (London, 1993), 312.
2. Quotations from the play are from the Oxford World's Classics edition of *Troilus and Cressida* by Kenneth Muir.
3. In Act 2, scene 1, Thersites (imagining an Agamemnon converted to a mass of boils) says: 'Were not that a botchy core?' Kenneth Muir (p. 84) annotates this as follows: '*botchy* ulcerous | *core* centre of a boil (with a possible quibble on *corps*, body).' OED confirms the 'core / corps' reading. 'Putrifièd' (gone rotten, turned putrid) seems unambiguous. In *1 Henry VI*, Act 4, scene 7, Joan la Pucelle says that if the British corpses on the battlefield were left unburied, 'They would but stink and putrefy the air'.
4. I have modernized Caxton's English here. Geoffrey Bullough's *Narrative and Dramatic Sources of Shakespeare*, vol. vi (London, 1966), 206, reports thus Caxton's translation of Raoul Lefevre's account:

   Amonge all these thynges Hector had taken a moche noble baron of Grece moche queyntly and rychely armed, and for to lede hym oute of the ooste at his ease had caste his shelde behynde hym at his backe and had lefte his breste discoverte. And as he was in thys poynte and toke none hede of Achylles that cam pryvely unto hym and putte thys spere wyth in his body. And Hector fyll doun dede to the ground. [Bullough here makes small emendations to Caxton but preserves the sense.]

5. Bullough (pp. 177–9) quotes the account of the death of Hector in Lydgate's *The Hystorye Sege and Dystruccyon of Troye*. This stresses that the rich armour is encrusted with jewels, and that Hector, moved by 'false covetyse', carried the dead knight away on his horse, and, having put his own shield behind him, was mortally vulnerable to Achilles' spear.

6. I find that this notion was offered in S. L. Bethell's *Shakespeare and the Popular Dramatic Tradition* (London, 1944), 104. He says that the scene is 'a symbol of all the play presents to us'. Nothing new under the sun, in Shakespearian studies. Except Shakespeare.

7. Here and in *Troilus and Cressida*, Shakespeare was doubtless recalling Matthew 23: 27, on hypocrites: '[Ye] are like unto whited tombes, which appeare beautiful outwarde, but are within ful of dead men's bones, and of all filthines' (Geneva Bible).

Shakespeare's feminist play?

1. The First Quarto has the puzzlingly corrupt line, 'With men like men of inconstancie.'; the Folio has 'With men, like men of inconstancie.' Some editors, including G. R. Hibbard in the Oxford World's Classics text (1998, p.169), give: 'With men like you, men of inconstancy.' Others, including Richard David's Arden text (1956, p. 104) and John Dover Wilson's New Cambridge (1962, p.52), give: 'With moon-like men, men of inconstancy.' The last reading seems to me far the most Shakespearian, given Shakespeare's recurrent association of the moon with inconstancy, as in *Love's Labour's Lost*, Act 5, scene 2: 'Thus change I like the moon.'

2. For clarity in summarizing, I refer to her consistently as 'the Princess'. After Marcadé's announcement, some editors refer to her as 'the Queen'. (Ferdinand promptly addresses her as 'your majesty'.)

3. Like other commentators, I have modernized Meres's '*Loue labours wonne*' and the bookseller's 'loves labor won' as *Love's Labour's Won*, for that makes a symmetrical counterpart to the title *Love's Labour's Lost*. It does not, however, make very satisfactory sense (for the intended meaning cannot be that *labour* is 'won', gained). If *Love's Labour's Lost* means 'the labour of love is wasted' (because no nuptials result), then a more appropriate modernization of *Loue labours wonne* would have no apostrophe in *Labours* and would be *Love's Labours Won:* in other words, the labours of love did (on this occasion) win the prize of matrimony. Indeed, for full harmony between the titles, *Love's Labours Won* should follow *Love's Labours Lost* (without an apostrophe in '*Labours*', and thus meaning 'the labours of love have been wasted').

4. Meres did not mention *The Taming of the Shrew*: hence that speculation. Later suggestions were that *Love's Labour's Won* was another title of *Much Ado About Nothing* (so Robert F. Fleissner in *Shakespeare Survey*, 27 (1974), 105–10); of *All's Well That Ends Well* (T. W. Baldwin, *Shakspere's 'Love's Labour's Won'* (Carbondale, Ill., 1957), 15); and of *Troilus and Cressida* (Leslie Hotson, *Shakespeare's Sonnets Dated and Other Essays* (London, 1949), 37–56).

5. A. R. Hibbard, Introduction to the Oxford World's Classics edition of *Love's Labour's Lost*, 83. Unless otherwise indicated, quotations from the play are taken from this edition.

6. John Dover Wilson, cited by Richard David in *Love's Labour's Lost* (London, 1956; repr. 1965), 196.

7. *Love's Labour's Lost*, ed. Hibbard, 235; *Love's Labour's Lost*, ed. John Kerrigan (Harmondsworth, 1982), 239.

8. *Love's Labour's Lost*, ed. Richard David, 196.

9. In this production at the Old Vic Theatre, Armado was played by Ronald Pickup.

10. F. E. Halliday, *A Shakespeare Companion* (Harmondsworth, 1964), 288.

11. In the eavesdropping scene (Act 4, scene 3), Biron remarks: 'Like a demigod here sit I in the sky.' He could be speaking from a gallery or from a stage tree of the kind specified in Marston's *The Fawn*.

12. Dover Wilson, Introduction to *Love's Labour's Lost*, p. liii. Halliday, *Shakespeare Companion*, 288. Hibbard, ed. cit., 2. The Second Quarto (1631) title-page says it was 'acted by his Maiesties Seruants at the Blacke-Friers and the Globe'.

13. All the action from Act 1 to Act 5 could possibly be accommodated within a (very crowded) fictional day. In Act 2, scene 1, however, we are told that settlement of the legal dispute will depend on documents to be produced 'tomorrow', and, in the final scene, the dispute is settled; but perhaps the love-smitten King did not bother to wait for the evidence. Costard had been apprehended with Jaquenetta on the evening preceding the events of Act 1, scene 1. It's in Act 3, scene 1 (lines 40–3 in Hibbard) that Armado makes clear that he has not yet enjoyed Jaquenetta.

14. Hibbard adds some stage business (Biron '*whispers to Costard*', p. 223) to support this idea of his.

Why does the Duke leave town?

Measure for Measure is edited in Oxford World's Classics by N. W. Bawcutt.

1. Critics have traditionally seen these lines as alluding to the furtive practices of King James. See Josephine Waters Bennett, *Measure for Measure as Royal Entertainment* (New York, 1966), 78–104.

2. Expressions of bewilderment and disgust at the Duke's behaviour range from Charlotte Lennox's robust eighteenth-century opinion that 'The character of the Duke is absurd and ridiculous' (*Shakespeare Criticism*, 2. 389) to Arthur Quiller Couch, in his CUP edition of *Measure for Measure* (Cambridge, 1922): 'From the first no one quite knows why he has chosen to absent himself ostentatiously and to come back pretending to be somebody else. His game puzzles Lucio only less than it puzzles us' (*Shakespeare Criticism*, 2. 421).

3. Rosalind Miles, in *The Problem of Measure for Measure* (New York, 1976), reviews various opinions on the impossibility of explaining the Duke's behaviour in any rational way and concludes that he cannot be regarded as a 'real person' (p. 34).

4. See Bernard J. Paris, 'The Inner Conflict of *Measure for Measure*: A Psychoanalytic Approach', *Centennial Review*, 25/3 (Summer 1981), 266–76; repr. *Shakespeare Criticism*, 44. 89: 'It seems then, that a major concern of the Duke and a major theme of the play, is the corruption

which is fostered when the laws are not enforced, when the person in authority is too permissive. The major thrust of the play, however, is to present a case against the strict enforcement of the law; and when the Duke reassumes his authority at the end, he gives no indication that he will behave in such a way as to curb the license in Vienna.'

5. *Measure for Measure*, Riverside edition (Boston, 1974), 547.
6. Ibid. 546.

Why Barnardine? and: Angelo: guide to sanity?

1. A similar bed-trick works for Helena with Bertram in *All's Well That Ends Well*; but that one takes place in a chamber. Angelo and Mariana copulate in a garden. Can the night be so moonless? (Such devices are gloriously parodied in the three-in-a-bed scene in Rossini's *Le Comte Ory*.) The bed-trick was an essential but implausible plot-device in the film *Consenting Adults* (1992), a thriller directed by Alan J. Pakula.
2. Quotations from the play are from the Oxford World's Classics edition of *Measure for Measure*, by N. W. Bawcutt.
3. An authoritative guide to traditional Roman Catholic doctrine, Archbishop Sheehan's *Apologetics and Catholic Doctrine* (Dublin: Gill, 1952), says: 'The Subject of Extreme Unction is any one of the faithful who having attained the use of reason is in danger of death from some bodily infirmity ... Hence ... prisoners about to suffer the extreme penalty of the law, cannot be anointed' (Part II, p. 233). Barnardine, it therefore seems, is not entitled to Extreme Unction; but he would, of course, be entitled to the Sacrament of Penance—administered by a genuine priest. Incidentally, several plays of Shakespeare's period express the belief that a person killed while drunk goes straight to Hell: these include George Peele's *David and Bethsabe*; The Revenger's Tragedy, by Cyril Tourneur or Thomas Middleton; and John Fletcher's *The Triumph of Death*.
4. *James I by His Contemporaries*, ed. Robert Ashton (London, 1969), 65–6. See also John Nichols, *The Progresses, etc., of King James the First*, vol. i (New York, n.d.), 89.
5. A. D. Nuttall, 'Measure for Measure: Quid Pro Quo?': *Shakespeare Studies*, 4 (1968), 231–51, quotation, p. 239.
6. Bawcutt, ed. cit., 39–41, gives a good summary of the theatrical options.
7. In *The Wheel of Fire* (1930; repr. London, 1960).
8. Nuttall, 'Measure for Measure', 240, 241, and 242.
9. *The Times*, 20 March 1999, p. 1.

How many Shakespearian cannibals?

1. 'Of the Canniballes' in *The Essayes of Michael Lord of Montaigne*, tr. John Florio (1603; repr. London, n.d.), 96. That essay was the source of Gonzalo's speech beginning 'I'th' commonwealth I would by contraries | Execute all things' in Act 2, scene 1, of *The Tempest*.

2. Joseph Conrad, *'Heart of Darkness' and Other Tales*, ed. Cedric Watts (Oxford World's Classics; Oxford, 1990), 194.

3. Frank Kermode, Introduction to *The Tempest* (London, 1964), xxxviii.

4. William Harrison, *Description of Britain*, iv, quoted in *King Lear*, ed. Kenneth Muir (London, 1964), 11.

5. Edward Ravenscroft: cited by J. C. Maxwell, Introduction to *Titus Andronicus* (London, 1961), p. xxxviii. J. Dover Wilson, Introduction to *Titus Andronicus* (Cambridge, 1948), p. xii. Kenneth Tynan, *Curtains* (New York, 1961), 103. Tynan adds: 'To lose one son may be accounted a misfortune; to lose twenty-four, as Titus does, looks like carelessness.'

6. Quotations from *Titus Andronicus* are from the Oxford World's Classics edition by Eugene M. Waith.

7. Ben Jonson, Induction to *Bartholomew Fair*, in *Ben Jonson's Plays*, vol. ii (London, 1910), 181–2.

8. J. C. Maxwell notes: 'In the palmy days of disintegration of the Shakespeare canon, almost all practising dramatists of 1585–95 were called in to take a hand in *Titus*, but at present the only serious candidate for a share in the play is George Peele.' (Introduction, p. xxxvi.) Peele is thought to have contributed to Act 1 rather than the later parts.

9. *King Lear*, ed. K. Muir (Arden; London, 1964), 4.2.48–50.

The Oxford World's Classics Website

www.worldsclassics.co.uk

- Information about new titles
- Explore the full range of Oxford World's Classics
- Links to other literary sites and the main OUP webpage
- Imaginative competitions, with bookish prizes
- Peruse *Compass*, the Oxford World's Classics magazine
- Articles by editors
- Extracts from Introductions
- A forum for discussion and feedback on the series
- Special information for teachers and lecturers

www.worldsclassics.co.uk

American Literature

British and Irish Literature

Children's Literature

Classics and Ancient Literature

Colonial Literature

Eastern Literature

European Literature

History

Medieval Literature

Oxford English Drama

Poetry

Philosophy

Politics

Religion

The Oxford Shakespeare

A complete list of Oxford Paperbacks, including Oxford World's Classics, OPUS, Past Masters, Oxford Authors, Oxford Shakespeare, Oxford Drama, and Oxford Paperback Reference, is available in the UK from the Academic Division Publicity Department, Oxford University Press, Great Clarendon Street, Oxford OX2 6DP.

In the USA, complete lists are available from the Paperbacks Marketing Manager, Oxford University Press, 198 Madison Avenue, New York, NY 10016.

Oxford Paperbacks are available from all good bookshops. In case of difficulty, customers in the UK can order direct from Oxford University Press Bookshop, Freepost, 116 High Street, Oxford OX1 4BR, enclosing full payment. Please add 10 per cent of published price for postage and packing.